Mister Hastings

John Collier 1685–1760
His life, his town and his country

A biography and history

by

Kent Barker

Published by KBP with The Hastings Local History Group

ISBN
978-0-9568421-4-5

Ah my poor son! Ah my Tender child
My unblown flower and new appearing
sweets!
If yet your gentle soul flies in the air
And is not fixed in doom perpetual –
Hover about me with your airy wings,
An hear your Father's lamentation!

Lines written by John Collier on the death of his 12-year-old son.

For Suzie

whose enthusiasm and love for Hastings past and
present has been an inspiration

Upfront

This is a biography of a remarkable man from Hastings who lived both there and in London in the early Georgian period - the first half of the 18th Century. He was a lawyer, mayor, town clerk, customs official, political fixer and agent to two prime ministers.

The book is also a history of Hastings and of England during that period, usually seen through the eyes and letters of John Collier and his family. Historians or experts on that age may already know much of what is recounted, but it is primarily designed for the rest of us – we who vaguely knew about the Hannoverian kings and the Jacobite rebellions, as well as the London coffee houses and pleasure gardens and Hogarthian scenes in the capital - without perhaps being able to recall many of the details.

Somewhat unusually for a biography the narrative is not chronological. It observes different areas of Collier's life and interests without much regard to precise period. There is, however, a chronology of his life at the end.

There are a lot of characters involved, both on the local and the national stage, and so each chapter ends with a brief who's who – which is collated in a full appendix. While there is a detailed list of sources and a full bibliography, this is not intended as an academic work so there are no footnotes or lists of references by chapter. The story is largely drawn from a single prime source – the voluminous letters from and to John Collier – of which more than 2000 have been preserved in the National Archive. I have endeavoured to make it clear, and give credit, whenever I have drawn on the work of others.

Spelling and capitalization in the 18th century were extremely idiosyncratic. I have retained a number of examples to give a flavour of the letters as written, but where I feel it impedes understanding or the flow of the text I have tended to modernise them.

Before 1752 the new year started on March 25th. To avoid confusion I have standardised it to begin on January 1st throughout.   KB 2021

CHAPTERS

Appendices

Chapter 1.

The Opening View.

Come and walk with me on a Hastings evening, up the footpath behind Tackleway. It's a fairly steep climb to the East Hill, but the view is always worth it. Let's sit at the top, perhaps on a fallen tree rather than one of those memorial benches, and look out across the Bourne valley to the West Hill, the Castle, and beyond, towards Eastbourne and Beachy Head.

Below us is the town of Hastings we are so familiar with today. The little houses, many half-timbered, nestling in the valley along All Saints Street and the High Street. There are the two imposing medieval churches, St Clements and All Saints, the latter with its grey painted parsonage next door. Opposite it is the elegant early Georgian 'Old Hastings House'. Down to our left are the fishing boats drawn up on the Stade.

The setting sun is shining in our eyes, making us squint. Some of the newer buildings appear indistinct. We can't see the funfair or seafront attractions at all and the heat shimmering on the tarmac of the Old London Road makes it look more like a small stream flowing down the valley.

A man appears and sits on the log next to us. He's wearing a wig and a strange costume, but that's hardly unusual in Hastings. He introduces himself as John, John Collier. Lately arrived in the town from Eastbourne. He's a young man, no more than 20, and he tells us he's here to take up his first job. He's just qualified as a lawyer and says he has been appointed Town Clerk. We congratulate him and gaze into the setting sun at the vista before us. It must be a trick of the light but there seem to be rather fewer buildings than we're used to. We can no longer see Pelham Crescent and St Mary in the Castle. The pier has disappeared and where the White Rock Hotel and Theatre should be ... a large imposing white rock juts out from the land into the sea making travel along the coast towards St Leonards clearly quite impossible.

Yes, says our companion, this is a good year for me. A new job and a new bride, Elizabeth Elphick , and her father has been much accommodating. Indeed sufficient that I've been enabled to buy that new house down there – and he points to Old Hastings House which, in the curious light looks, shed of its ivy and patina of age, to be newly constructed of raw red brick. "Of course I shall have to increase the stables in time," he says, pointing to where we had thought the theatre stood, but now seems to be occupied by a ramshackle collection of sheds. Behind them Torfield Close has gone, and in place of the local authority houses is an extensive orchard and garden. "I have in mind to extend my stake in this town," John tells us in his funny accent and quaint syntax. "Meet me back here in say forty years and I'll show you what I've achieved – that's if I make it to 60 and the smallpox doesn't get me first."

We look away for a moment and when we turn back he's gone. There's just the empty log. But gazing down in the valley, we seem to be stuck in the early years of the 18th century. So why don't we come down off the East Hill and explore the town as it was around 1706.

§§§

Our ancient path leads down to what is now the southern end of Tackleway and thence to All Saints'

Street. There are virtually no maps of Hastings before Samuel Cant, local schoolmaster and friend of John Collier, produced a detailed drawing in 1746. But even though that's forty years in the future it's likely very little had changed. So Tackleway was just a footpath with no buildings evident, while All Saints' street was heavily built up on both sides. These were the homes of the fishing community – indeed it was known as Fisher or Fish Street. This was by far the largest industry in the town, providing the main income for around 200 households either directly or via ancillary jobs such as chandlers, sail makers, net spinners and barrel makers. During the mackerel and herring runs, hundreds of townsfolk would help crew the boats – rather as, inland, almost everyone would be expected to turn out to help with the harvest.

On the eastern side of the street the houses all have long gardens rising up the hill. On the western side there's little room for gardens as they back on to a small and often muddy stream called the Bourne. This river is, today, completely covered and flows under the A259 Old London Road before disgorging into the sea via a large cast iron pipe on Rock-a-Nore beach. In 1706 it was the lifeblood of the town, providing many with their drinking water, as well as supplying a number of breweries. It also offered a water supply to assorted wildfowl and livestock that occasionally trespassed down to its banks.

If you drive through nearby Sedlescombe today you'll likely have to negotiate the large gaggle of white geese that wander at will over the street and village green. The scene before us in Hastings is not dissimilar. Interestingly the populations of Sedlecombe now and Hastings then are almost identical at around 1,600 people. The 21st century town we know, stretching from

Ore to Rock-a-Nore, across to St Leonards and Bulverhythe, and up to Hollington and Baldslow contains 86,000 people. Three hundred years ago Hastings was equivalent to just a tiny village, sandwiched in the Bourne valley and consisting largely of just two streets - All Saints' where we're now standing, and Market Street (now the High Street) where we're heading.

We can't get down to the Bourne here so let's turn right up All Saints' Street and then left down Courthouse Street. This road is also lined with houses until we get down to the stream. There, on the bridge surveying the water, we find an official looking man. He holds the ancient office of Bailiff of the Bourne or Water Bayley. He's elected annually at the Hundred Court and, on taking office, he swears an oath, promising not to "suffer any disorder with horse, pigge, geese, ducke, or hogges sullage." Nonetheless, court records show numerous fines are levied on townsfolk for 'annoying the Bourne' by allowing animals to foul it.

Keeping the water clean was clearly important not just for the people who used it for drinking and cooking but also for brewing. Most large houses had their own microbrewery on the premises – the Colliers certainly did. But additionally at least half a dozen commercial brewers had been operating in the town for a century or more. They included the renowned John Brett whose beer went to Yarmouth each year when Hastings' fishermen, along with others from the Cinque Ports, attended the great Herring Fair. But Brett himself was not immune from the problems of the Bourne and was injuncted by the town's authorities not to use its water from its lower reaches before it joined the sea, on pain of a 100 shilling fine.

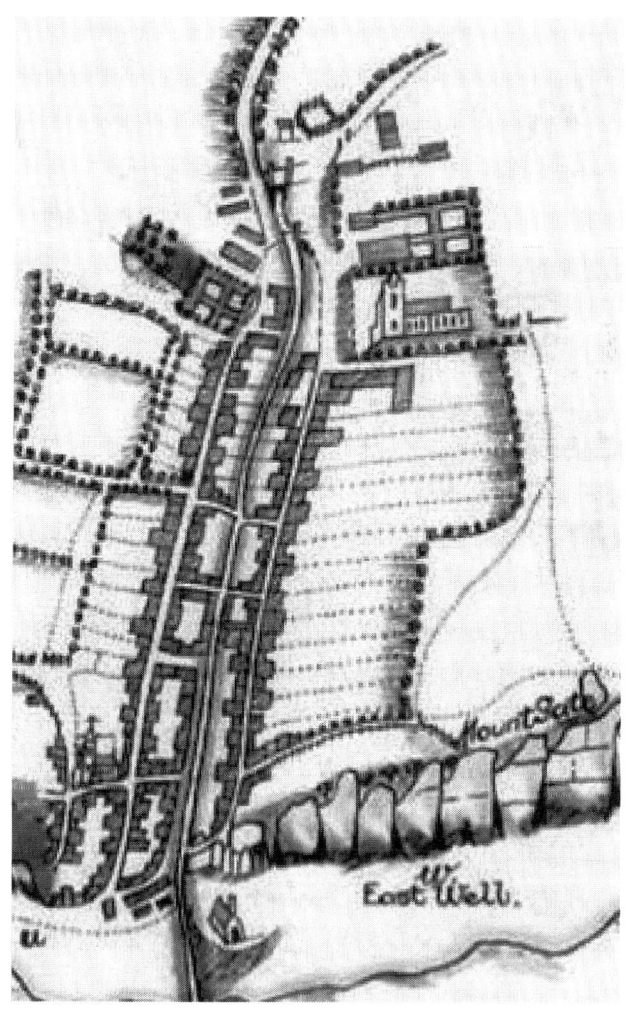

Detail from the 18th Century map by Samuel Cant. All Saints Church is top right, the East Cliffs bottom right. Running north to south, Market Street (now High Street) is on the left, All Saints' Street on the right, and between them is the River Bourne.

13

Standing, as we are, on Courthouse bridge over the Bourne, there's a surprising bustle all around. Hastings in 1706 may be a small municipality in population terms, but it's busy with commerce. Just nine years from now the Chamberlains' records will show that there are seven carpenters and seven masons plying their trade along with three coopers, two glaziers, five smiths, three weavers, two periwig makers and assorted chandlers, cheesemongers, maltsters, millers and mealmen, rippiers, ropemakers and saddlers. There are eleven shoemakers, five barbers, and a full ten butchers. The latter are concentrated in the 'Shambles' on Butcher's Row which is situated on the hill leading past the front of St Clement's church just up from the High street. Since the sixteenth century they have been a source of annoyance to churchgoers and other townsfolk for their propensity to slaughter their animals on public roads, to ignore the Sabbath, and to hang the meat "at their doors in such a way as to annoy passers-by." The Shambles we see in 1706 is relatively new, the old buildings having been demolished in 1692 and rebuilt at the turn of the century.

But we are getting ahead of ourselves. We have wandered off the bridge and are walking up Courthouse Street – so named because of Court Hall part of which we can see before us. This has, for centuries, been the seat of the Hastings Corporation - the municipal authority that runs the town. This complex of buildings also houses the local prison. One part actually overhung the stream – particularly convenient for punishing female offenders by ducking. But no longer. In 1702 the Assembly orders that particular wing to be pulled down. Part of the reason is that a new Town Hall has been built just a few hundred yards away in Market Street. People walking along the High Street in the early 21st century will remember the

Artist's impression of a house in Bourne Street in the 1700s

Old Town Hall Museum next to the Jenny Lind pub. This building was erected in 1823 on the site of the one which replaced Court Hall.

As we walk past it now we might well see the young John Collier leaving at the end of another day's labours as Town Clerk. He will, likely as not, be walking home up Market Street, to his new house. Today it's called Old Hastings House and earlier was known as the Mansion. But when the Colliers lived there, in common with most properties, it had no name. Letters were simply addressed to Mr John Collier at his home in Hasting (the 's' wasn't added until midway through the 18th Century). And what a lot of letters there were. Throughout his life he was an extraordinarily prolific writer and more than two thousand letters from him, or addressed to him, have survived down the centuries. They give us an unparalleled knowledge of his life – and that of the town he ran, both as clerk, Mayor, Customs Surveyor and 'fixer' for Members of Parliament and Prime Ministers. In short they will help us tell the life of "Mister" Hastings.

§§§

Chapter 2.

The Colliers at Home

The entrance to John Collier's home hasn't changed much in the 250 years since his death. You walk up the short path from the top of the High Street, venture under the Doric-columned portico and enter through the partly glazed front door. Sloping straight up in front of you is the elegant early Georgian staircase with its slender banisters, rising up two floors and illuminated from the top by an ornate roof light.

You don't realise it at first but the house is built into the side of a hill so the main reception rooms are on the first floor. However the door on the left at the bottom of the stairs leads to Collier's study. It's not a large room, but the southern light streams in through the windows, and you can almost feel him sitting at his desk there, quill pen in hand, writing yet another letter or worrying at another legal argument.

The room is filled with books. Collier had an extraordinarily extensive library. On his death his executors catalogued 800 or more volumes – ranging from history and travel to religion and biography. Many are in Latin. Some are simple 'pot boilers': *Gentlemen's Recreation* and *English Worthies,* others are weightier tomes – several histories of the Reformation along with two and three volume works on theology and philosophy. Whatever else, this innkeeper's son was an avid reader on a widely eclectic range of subjects.

Up one flight of stairs on the same side of the house, almost directly above his study is the drawing room. It's a large and elegant room with three big, floor-to-ceiling, sash windows. They give a panoramic view out over almost the whole of 18th century Hastings and down to the sea. This would have been his wife's domain. One can see her sitting by the fireplace as she approached another of her confinements, or mourned the loss of another of the children who died in infancy.

One can also feel John Collier in this room. Probably standing at the windows surveying his town. He would, with some justification, have been proud of his house. It was far grander than almost anything else in Hastings at the time and marked the conspicuous rise of the *middling sort* – what we today would call the middle classes. Few outside the land-owing classes or the aristocracy would have had such an extensive establishment. For centuries English society had been divided between the rich landed gentry and the poor peasant or labouring class. There had been the more prosperous traders, but professional men, doctors or lawyers or some members of the clergy were much more of a rarity.

The tantalising question is just how did Collier achieve such visible trappings of wealth and respectability so early in his life? He was, as we recall, only 20 when he arrived in Hastings in 1706 and bought this house. We know his Town Clerk's salary was just £10 a year. He had been through a legal apprenticeship which would have carried no remuneration – indeed he, or his family would almost certainly have had to pay for it. There is no evidence that his father, Peter Collier was particularly wealthy. His grandfather, Richard Collier, had been a thatcher and his will from 1690 suggests, according to Heather Warne, that 'the family's means were then quite small'. Peter acquired sufficient property to be able to vote as a 'forty-shilling freeholder', but although his will of 1717 showed enough money to support his wife, again according to Ms Warne, he possessed 'no great fortune'.

The history of The Mansion or Old Hastings House is an interesting if somewhat complicated one and can be gleaned from the deeds that have survived and by records uncovered by Hastings historian J Manwaring Baines.

In 1686 one Charles Buck of London, a framework knitter and Martha his wife "releases" (sells) to Marmaduke Dickenson, citizen and Draper of London, among other properties the messuage (dwelling house) with barns and stables, edifices, yards and gardens and orchards situate in the town and port of Hastings, for £100.

Later that year Dickenson sells the property to Edward Bromfield who, the following year, 1687, marries Timothea Dyne. She's the daughter of Thomas Dyne, a mercer (cloth trader) and former mayor of Hastings (1681). But tragically Timothea dies in childbirth and within a year Edward too is dead.

Thomas Dyne becomes the house's owner, possibly inheriting it from his son-in-law and he then sells it to Edward's brother Thomas Bromfield.

On his death, Thomas leaves it to his widow Anne Bromfield who lived on there for a number of years before bequeathing it to her son Thomas Bromfield (jnr). He was apparently living in Lewes and didn't want the house so, in 1696, sold it to Charles Harris for £107.10.

Ten years later, on 6 November 1706 it is 'released' by Charles Harris of Greenwich gent to John Collierd (Collier), Hastings Gent, for £300.

But just what did Collier buy? Was it the Georgian mansion we see today or some earlier, perhaps half-timbered building in the local vernacular, that Collier later rebuilt? There's no evidence from his letters or

19

John Collier's home - Old Hastings House - today

accounts that he ever embarked on a major rebuilding programme – though in 1732 he mentions some repairs:

> *Pray speak to Mr Mead when he alters the Windows in the little parlour and other rooms on that front, that he takes all the care he can to prevent breaking through in the Winter.*

The architectural style of the house also provides a clue. It is clearly not Jacobean or Palladian – the predominant styles of the 17th century. Even by 1686 when we have the first deeds, it's unlikely that the emerging classic Georgian style would have been prevalent, especially outside London or the bigger cities. And then there's the dramatic increase in value between 1687 and 1706 - up from £107.10 to £300. The Hastings historian J Manwaring Baines concludes: *'This very marked increase in the value of the property strongly suggests that Harris demolished the old house and, on its site, built the house we see today. Its architecture supports this view."*

In which case John Collier was buying a brand new mansion in the latest 'a la mode' style for £300 – thirty times his annual salary. Where on earth did he get the money?

The answer, sadly, is that we just don't know. Though we can, I believe, take a fairly good guess. Just a couple of months before he acquired the house, Collier married Elizabeth Elphick on 28th May 1706 in Eastbourne. Little is known about her, her family and her father Edmund, save that they came from Willingdon which is a small village just outside Eastbourne – the latter being the town where Collier grew up. So we could perhaps surmise that Edmund Elphick was sufficiently well off to be able to give his new son-in-law the house – or at least enough money to buy it - as a dowry on the marriage of his daughter. Since married women couldn't hold property in their own right at the time, vesting the money in the young ambitious lawyer and town clerk would have been the best way for her father to ensure she started out married life with some degree of comfort and social standing. However there is another possible explanation.

It would seem that their first child, Elizabeth, was born before the Colliers were actually married. The dates are recorded as 14th of March 1706 for her baptism, but the 28th May 1706 for their marriage. This could, of course have been the result of an 'accident' common enough in the days before reliable contraception, but if a family legend is correct, then it would seem just possible that Elizabeth was carrying another man's child and that John Collier married her anyway. Is it stretching credulity too far to wonder if Elizabeth's father might have offered him the money for the house as a 'sweetener' to marry his pregnant daughter who would otherwise face disgrace?

There are few records of John and Elizabeth's life together in Hastings. We know they had five more children over the next 8 years. Elizabeth was the oldest and later married a lawyer in Battle called George Worge. Their names appear in a number of the Collier letters, and they seem to have remained in close contact with Collier after his second marriage, as well as with the later Collier children.

Elizabeth, her mother, gave birth to a second daughter, Mary, in 1709 and we must assume she died in infancy for, the following year, their third daughter was born and also christened Mary. She died the same year. The couple's fourth child Sarah arrived in 1711 and, as

and the elegant drawing room

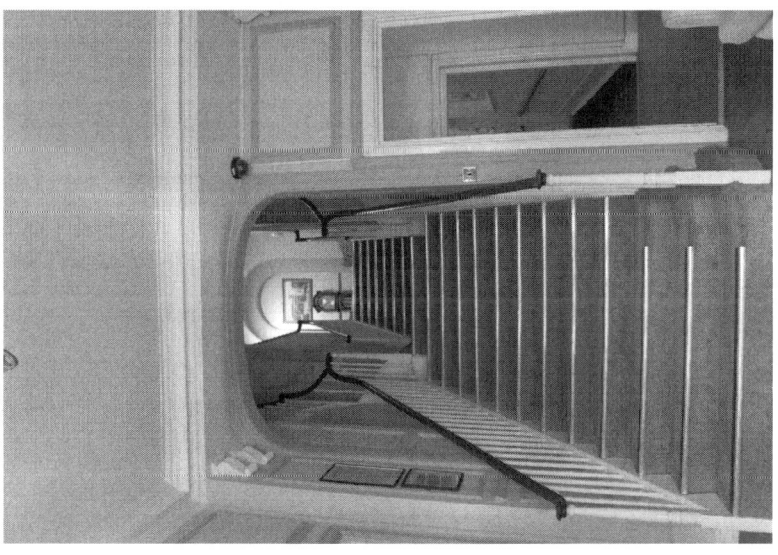

Old Hasting's House, The Georg an staircase ...

records show, survived into adulthood and married a Roger Mortimer. A fifth daughter was born in 1713 but we know neither her name nor any details of her life. It seems probable that she also died young as there are no references to her in any of Collier's correspondence. Finally a son, John, was born 1714 but died the same year. The loss of at least three of their children in infancy must have profoundly affected the couple. Charles Lane Sayer, in the introduction to his 1907 transcription of the Collier letters, refers to family papers: *"According to my late aunt Mary Sayer's family memoranda, Mr Collier's first marriage was an unhappy one,"* he says without elaborating. The loss of three or possibly four children would certainly be sufficient cause for unhappiness, but the suggestion seems to be that personal relations between John and Elizabeth were not good. In the event, Elisabeth died in 1714 – though whether in connection with her confinement with baby John is unknown. It left Collier a widower at the age of 29, with two daughters aged 7 and 3 to look after, plus, possibly, a one-year old infant.

§§§

It's May 1716, two years after Elizabeth's death, and John Collier is writing from Hastings:

> *Dearest Madam, Tho I had not your permission to write it would almost be a crime in you (if 'twas possible you could be guilty of any), not to pardon me, when I solemnly assure you its doeing what is or can be the most pleasing and agreeable in your absence ... I take this, as all other opportunities to express my Inviolable*

esteem and affection...I hope, Madam, you are satisfied of my sincerity, and with what true passion I adore ... a devotion so grounded on merit can never be thought counterfeit.
I am, Madam, your faithful and constant Slave.

The recipient of this rather flowery love letter is Mary Cranston from Hastings who at the time is staying in London. Her father is rector of both All Saint's Church across the Bourne from Collier's house, as well as St Clement's Church off the High Street, at which Collier worships. In all likelihood both John and Elizabeth when she was alive would have known the Cranston family well. In the two years since he was widowed, John's relationship with the vicar's eldest daughter has clearly blossomed. When the letter is written she is 20 and Collier 31, and he's clearly trying for the good opinion of her father. The Rev Cranston writes to her in London at the same date:

We were all very merry on Wednesday at Mr Collier's ... I fancy we take as much pleasure in our Country visits as you have in your City diversions. Mr Collier is busy repairing his house ... you have so contrived matters as to keep me sober by taking away the keys to my cellars and if you send them not by the carrier next Saturday I must break open the doors ...

By the following month Mary has returned to Hastings and Collier is in London, writing to her about politics and current affairs but concluding: "*I am, Dearest*

Madam, with all possible affection, Your faithful and most Constant admirer." Another letter begins with him quoting poetry from Ovid: *"With Such delight I read your letter o're / Your presence only could have given me more."* And ends: *"Dearest Charmer, your constant Lover J. Collier."* It seems that in the interim they had become formally engaged, for he is soon writing:

> *I am now, dear charmer, to acquaint you how much (if 'twas possible) I want to see you and that I hope before two revolving moones to bee Joyn'd in a more stricter Union, not that I think it possible ye Respect and value I have for you can ever be elevated to a greater height - and I verily believe the materiall assurances we have given each other of Love and friendship are genuine and as such believed.*

Then shortly afterwards:

> *Till this morning it did not lie in my power to proceed on the Nuptiuall affair ... but I have now given ye necessary directions to have those preliminaries settled.*

Some of these preliminaries involved buying the material for her bridal dress for which no effort was spared. Collier personally viewing the 'choicest silks':

> *I can now acquaint you of my having bought your clothes & flatter myself Dear Misse will not think I have a Dull fancy, for without vanity I think it very rich and*

*handsom, there's 27 yards at 11 shillings a
yard – the lining is not so light a blew as
you directed but I was advised to have it
somewhat stronger colour as being much
more fashionable.*

The letter could almost be written by a lovelorn
teenager rather than a man in his 30s, so brimming is it
with excitement and enthusiasm, not to mention
boasting at the amount expended, and ignoring her
wishes as to the colour of the lining! It shows Collier in a
very different light from most of his other
correspondence which is of a much more sober nature.

The couple were married on 13 August 1717 at St
Clements Church in Hastings, quite possibly with her
father, the Rev James Cranston officiating. Mary then
moved into the Collier house, within sight of, and less
than 50 yards from, the vicarage where she'd grown up.
It seems likely that her new household included Collier's
two daughters from his first marriage as, in February the
following year, he writes to Mary sending greetings to
'the Girles'.

So for the moment let's leave Mary, the new bride,
in her elegant drawing room looking out from the huge
sash windows over the town. For the next forty years
this will be her domain and she'll be parted from her
husband for extended periods three or four times a year
while he's living and working in London. For us, of
course, the advantage of this arrangement is that he
writes copious letters to her. A considerable number
express his oft-repeated desire to be back with her in
Hastings, but others are more informative, charting both
national and family events as they unfold. Young Mary
will have a constant and, in all probability, entirely
faithful husband. Her eighteen pregnancies bear

testimony to the fact that there was little lacking in his physical attentions when he was at home. She would have wanted for little as Collier became ever more prosperous. And the social standing of the vicar's daughter was enhanced as he worked for, and moved among, some of the leading aristocrats and politicians of the age. Was she happy? It's not entirely clear from the correspondence. Certainly there are some expressions of a desire to be in a more exciting place than Hastings, but if she resented his life in the city, then she gave little sign of it. The life and letters of this early 'commuter' does, however, enable us to see and understand the mechanics of how life was lived in early Georgian England.

§§§

WHO'S WHO Chapter 2 – The Colliers at Home

Peter Collier. John Collier's Father. An innkeeper of Eastbourne

Richard Collier. John Collier's Grandfather. A thatcher of Eastbourne.

Heather Warne – *catalogued the Collier papers for a thesis in 1966 and wrote a detailed biographical introduction.*

J Manwaring Baines - *Hastings Historian. Author of Hastings Tapestry of Life*

Elizabeth Collier, nee Elphick. Collier's first wife. Died 1714

Edmund Elphick of Willingdon. Her father.

Elizabeth Collier. b 1707. Eldest daughter of John Collier and Elizabeth Elphick.

Mary Collier. b 1710. Second daughter of John Collier and Elizabeth Elphick

George Worge. Husband of Elizabeth Collier. Solicitor in Battle.

Charles Lane Sayer – *descendent of John Collier, transcriber and editor of The Correspondence of John Collier and his Family pub. 1907*

Mary Cranston. Second wife to John Collier.

Rev James. Cranston. Mary's father. Hastings vicar.

Chapter 3

Life and Death

On 9 December 1735 John Collier wrote to his wife Mary from London:

"I thank God my cold is almost over but have a very troublesome cough and a good mind to be bloodied this morning but would avoid it if I can."

More than the lack of electricity, railways, motorcars or digital technology - if there's one thing that sets the 1700s apart from our age, it is medical knowledge and practice. If the people of early Georgian Hastings were ill, there was little difference in the treatment they could expect from that of their counterparts in ancient Greece more than two thousand years before.

One of the central principles in Western medicine since the time of Hippocrates around 460–370 BCE, was Humoral theory. This held that the human body contained a mix of the four humors or fluids: black bile (also known as melancholy), yellow or red bile, blood, and phlegm. Each individual had a particular humoral makeup, or "constitution," and health was defined as the proper humoral balance for that individual. An imbalance of the humors resulted in disease.

John Collier's letters vividly describe different remedies for correcting imbalances in the humors, including the most common one, bloodletting. He wrote to Mary in 1729:

My cold, tho not near soe bad as it was, is very much, & I cough'd the whole night. I am very sorry I was not bloodied for it, being what the doctors advise immediately on being seized.

The standard way to be 'bloodied' was by *phlebotomy*, or *venesection* in which a surgeon barber cut into in one or more of the larger external veins, such as those in the forearm or neck, and allowed the blood to flow into a receptacle. More affluent patients might employ leeches usually supplied by a physician.

This exemplified the early split in the medical profession between surgeons and physicians and, interestingly, provided the prototype of the red and white (surgeon) barber's pole which signified the colours of blood and bandage. It was only somewhat later – towards the end of the 19th century - that it was realised that removing quantities of blood from an ill person was going to make them weaker rather than stronger. Leeches, however, are still used today in some forms of surgery and secretions from their 400 teeth have actually been shown to be an antiseptic and a coagulant. This rudimentary knowledge of medicine coupled to basic and generally unsanitary living conditions meant that death was commonplace. As we know John Collier's first wife Elizabeth died in 1714 when he was around 29 - we don't know her date of birth for certain though an Elizabeth Elphick is recorded as being baptized in Willington in 1681, so she may have been around 33 at her death. Of the five children she is believed to have borne him, probably only two outlived her. John's second wife Mary had eighteen children by him. Only five outlived her. Eleven died either in infancy (before the age of one) or in childhood.

Early 18th Century French print of a doctor about to perform an enema

Statistically the Colliers were unlucky. Infant mortality was then around 140 out of every 1000 births. Today, on average, 3.6 children in a thousand don't survive their first year. In the 1700s unidentifiable fevers, and a lengthy list of diseases, killed an estimated 30% of England's children before the age of 15 - among them the bloody flux (dysentery), scarlatina (scarlet fever), whooping cough, influenza, and pneumonia.

The high early-Georgian infant mortality rate had a depressing effect on life expectancy statistics suggesting that the *average* age of death was under 40 years old. Today it's about 70 worldwide.

So it is unsurprising that health is such an important topic in Collier's letters. In 1735 when he's writing home about his own very troublesome cough, he notes that colds or influenza had reached almost epidemic proportions in London:

> *There's hardly anyone Escap'd it & a distemper of this kind was never known so universal; 10 of the 12 Judges have had it, & 7 of them don't stir out, The Master of the Rolls could not set, nor in the King's Bench the famous business of Dr Bently could not go on, most of the Councell being ill with this cold. It has not been very mortal, Tho' 2 or 3 of my acquaintance have been conquered by it.*

Colds or flue, however mortal, were far from the biggest health fear of the time. Without any doubt at all, that was Smallpox. Eight years after the last letter he tells Mary:

Little Jackie has been ill with a little sort of
fever two or three days and was yesterday
let blood. I had not a little apprehension of
the smallpox ...

'Little Jackie' was the son of his London legal
partner William Cranston who happened also to be
Mary's younger brother, making Jackie the Colliers'
nephew.

And it's especially relevant because a few years
earlier, in 1732, Cranston had nursed their son (and
therefore *his* nephew) John when he contracted the
disease. Collier was in Hastings and his son at school in
London. So it fell to 'uncle' William Cranston to look
after him. The ensuing letters from Cranston to Collier
are among the most poignant in the entire collection that
was saved for posterity by the Sayer family – the Colliers'
descendants through the female line.

Collier's rising prosperity in the early 1730s
enabled him to send his two sons to Westminster school
where they enrolled in 1732 when John (Jacky) was 12
and James (Jemmy) 11. It was clearly a wrench for their
parents even though Collier was a regular visitor to
London to attend to his legal work. On 16 November he
arrived at his chambers (and the Cranston's home) in
Johnson Court off Fleet Street where the boys visited him
on an exeat from school. He wrote to Mary:

We expected them every moment till 3, when
they jumped in very brisk and lively, and I
think both grown, but I was amazed to see
them without a shoe to their feet, especially
Jacky. I sent for a shoemaker and equiopped
them each with a new pair ... They seem very
brisk and like the school and their master

Hogarth's view of the medical profession - two doctors argue over treatment for a dying woman (from the 5th painting of a Harlot's Progress 1731)

(Rev George Carleton). *I intend to go tomorrow to Mr Carleton's . I think it is odd they would let them bee without shoes ...*

Five days later Collier writes to Mary in Hastings:

I received your letter by last post and had your little boys along with me who are very well and this day Jemmy has his new warm clothes ... It's a great pleasure that the dear boys go through their hardship with courage and cheerfulness and seem very well pleased with the school.

Having settled their school fees, bought them new clothes and shoes and attended to his legal work, Collier returned to Hastings in the first week of December. Mary was pregnant again and gave birth to a boy, Thomas, just before Christmas. The older boys in London went to stay with their aunt and uncle for the festivities, but on Boxing Day William Cranston wrote to the Colliers:

I am sorry likewise to tell you that Jacky was yesterday, about noon, taken with a violent pain to his head which continuing till night I sent for Dr Tilden. Upon enquiry finding that Jacky and Jemmy were tumbling over each other's heads in the morning, upon the carpet in the parlour thought it might proceed from thence.

Jacky was given hartshorn – a concoction of burned or shaved hart's antler with white wine. The following day the headache was better but he had a 'pain cross his stomach'. That evening, on the doctor's orders, he was given a 'gentle vomit' which seems to have worked well and brought away 'vast quantities of filth' but he continued to be sick and restless. Cranston concludes his letter: "by next post you shall know how he goes on but that hope in God I shall give you an account of his perfect recovery.

Sadly it was not to be. Writing to the Colliers on 28th December 1732 he detailed the boy's worsening condition:

> *About 10 the pain came again much more violent than before and twas to such a degree I thought he could not long hold it. Upon that I immediately left him and with Jemmy took a coach to Mr Tilden. Met with him at home and went to Dr Barrowby and after some time found him and he soon came after us hither. He viewed Jacky and made enquiries as to what he had eat drank etc., and viewing him with a candle narrowly, he thought he saw something over his left eye like the small pox; and being told of his headack the Monday, his sickness a Tuesday, and by what he then saw as to his pains, he was verily perswaded twas it.*

It can only be imagined what the effect this news would have had on the Colliers when they received it. Smallpox was, in most cases, fatal. Although only 60 miles away, travel from Hastings to London was a full two days journey in good conditions, necessitating a horse ride to Tonbridge or more usually Sevenoaks and then a stagecoach from there to Southwark. But conditions were generally far from good especially in midwinter. It would have been quite impossible for Mary Collier, having just given birth, to have made the journey. And John, having only a few weeks earlier taken the arduous trip down from London, would have been understandably reluctant to rush back. Instead they could do nothing by wait for letters from Cranston to bring the latest news.

His next was dated the 28th and detailed the further treatment that Jacky was receiving, including a 'glister'. This was a liquid enema designed to purge the intestines of ill humors. Contemporary prints show it being administered into the rectum by an extremely large wooden syringe-type device. Cranston felt that it had worked well, bringing away "a great deal of excrement most of it so hard 'twas like sheep's turds".

But the Cranstons now had a problem. Smallpox was known to be readily transmitted to those around a patient, or from their clothes or bed linen. Only people who had previously contracted and survived the disease had any immunity. Mary Cranston had not had it. So it was extremely dangerous for Jacky to remain in their house. William urgently looked round about for lodgings that would be prepared to accept someone in the throes of the dreaded disease. He rejected a place at the lower end of Fleet Street as being too noisy before finally persuading a Mrs Canan in another part of Johnson's Court to take him in. Jacky was carried in a hackney chair with all his blankets and sheets around him to a warm and 'wainscotted roome' two flights of stairs up. A nurse was hired to care for him.

By the 30th of December Jacky's condition had worsened still further. Cranston now felt unable or unwilling to write directly to the Colliers with the news, but instead sent a letter via the family doctor in Hastings, Dr Henry Carleton. He begged him, as a friend, to give the news in person that the London doctors attending Jackie had pronounced *"the most unhappy sentence that ere yet pierced my ears that they were both of the opinion that he would not survive this night'.* The news spurred John Collier into action and he immediately left on the unwelcome trip back to London.

On the second of January Cranston again wrote to Dr Carleton:

After what you received from me last post, little hopes could remain of Jacky's living. And accordingly, as the doctors but too truly foretold, he died Sunday morning at six. Mr. Collier came at ten and my grief was then too fresh to be unable to conceal the unhappy news a moment.

Collier clearly took the news of the death of his son very hard:

The suddenness had just the effect I dreaded, but, thank god, with all proper care being taken of him he is now very well and only stays to see him decently interred which will be on Thursday, and he then proposes to sett out a Fryday .... Thank God Jemmy continues very well, which pray also to mention to my sister.

They were words that William Cranston would almost immediately have cause to rue. He accompanied John Collier on the first part of his journey home, leaving him to proceed alone from Tonbridge. By Wednesday 7th January Collier was back in Hastings. Cranston clearly stayed in Kent an extra day or so because on Friday 9th he wrote to his father, the Revd. James Cranston in Hastings with the worst possible news:

> *As one misfortune seldom comes alone, so neither has it in our case for I received a letter from my wife Sunday morning at Sennocke* [Sevenoaks] *with an account of Jemmy's having the Friday and Saturday before some symptoms like the forerunner of the smallpox.   You may be certain this hastened me from hence immediately.*

So William Cranston mounts his horse and rides as fast as he possibly can to get back to Fleet Street. But, as we shall see, in the early years of the 18th Century, 'fast' is a relative term when applied to travel.

§§§

Who's Who. Chapter 3 Life and Death.

William Cranston. Mary Collier's younger brother. John Collier's legal partner based in London. John Collier always refers to William as his 'brother' rather than brother-in-law.
Mary Cranston. William's wife, nee Swaysland.
John Cranston. (Nicknamed Jackie). William's son – thus John and Mary's nephew.
John Collier (jnr). John and Mary's eldest son. Confusingly also nicknamed Jacky.
James Collier. John and Mary's second son. Nicknamed Jemmy.
Rev George Carleton. Jacky and Jemmy's Schoolmaster at Westminster
Dr Henry Carleton. The Collier's friend and physician in Hastings. A former Mayor and deputy Mayor.
Doctors Tilden and Barrowby. London physicians.

Chapter 4.

Free Movement

If you leave Battle today at, say, 8.00 am, you can, with some confidence, expect to join the A22 at Maresfield some 30 minutes later. It's a drive of just 20 miles.

In November 1755 William Cranston wrote to John Collier telling him in some detail about the difficulties making the same journey in a post chaise – a four-wheel carriage. It took nine hours after leaving Battle at 8.00 that morning:

> *Taking our route through grounds by Beech furnace till we came to Netherfield Down, but in the intermediate Space met with many a dolorous Hole* [in the road]. *From Netherfeld Down we took ye High Road about half a mile – confounded bad – down to Brightling Down – very indifferent – through Dollington fforest - very bad indeed – Heathfield Down to Cross at Hand intolerable. Here we arrived soon after one – being 5 hours comeing 12 miles, notwithstanding our postilion performed wonders and drove excessive hard   ... between Buxted and Maresfiled we met some road as bad if not worse than any before & so bad that the horses could not draw us through – so forced to get out in ye middle of it & scramble through it as well as we could – but it did not last far for getting leave to go through two fields of private property (the owners of which saw our*

distress and generously offered it) – we got
to Maresfield just before 5.

Here Cranston's party stayed the night and next morning joined the Turnpike road – what is now the A22. He describes this, by comparison, as a 'bowling green', enabling them to arrive in Croydon - a journey of around 40 miles – at about 5.00 pm.

The first part of this journey was far from untypical. In his letters Collier is forever complaining about the state of the roads from Hastings: '*I thank God I got safe to town today ... had yesterday exceeding bad roads and hardly the patience to ride them.*'

As his legal practice took off from the 1720s he was having to spend increasing amounts of time in London. His visits to the capital generally coincided with the four law terms when the Westminster courts were sitting – Hilary Term (around 23 January to 12 February), Easter (a moveable feast, but always three weeks from as early as 11th April, ending as late as 7th June), Trinity (mid to late June or early July), and Michaelmas Term (23rd October to 28th or 29th November). Certainly by 1832 when he became Usher and Cryer of the Court of the King's Bench, Collier was traveling to and from London at least four times each year Pretty much every journey was made on horseback to Tonbridge or, more usually, Sevenoaks from where he could pick up a stagecoach which travelled – in relative speed and comfort – along a turnpike into London.

Latterly it became, theoretically, possible to take a carriage all the way from Hastings. In 1745 a stage coach called the Regulator was advertised thus:

This fast coach will leave the Swann Inn,
Hastings at four o' clock on Monday

Dover Stagecoach from an early 19th century engraving by R G Reeve after G S Treguar

*mornings, arriving at Robertsbridge the
same day, Sevenoaks the next, and
London on the third.*

However the idea of three days spent entombed in
a small coach, without any suspension on the sort of
roads described by Cranston, clearly had limited appeal.

The ride on horseback out of Hastings to join a
turnpike was not without its problems either. In
February 1733, just a month after the death of Jacky, on
his way back up to London, Collier wrote to Mary from
Sevenoaks:

*The roads are extream bad, and though we
have had a great deal of rain I was much
surprized to see the waters up to a great
degree. That at Robertsbridge I could not ride
over; soe got a man to lead my horse, and the
clappers at the end of the cloak bags were wet
by the height of the water... I rode about an
hour in the rain which is come on very smart.*

The vicissitudes of the swollen river Rother at
Robertsbridge were not confined to horsemen.
Stagecoaches were recorded as having actually floated
while trying to cross it.

As he got older John Collier found riding on
horseback increasingly difficult and, in 1745 when aged
60, he decided to invest in his own coach. The ever
obliging William Cranston was left to make the practical
arrangements and provided progress reports from
London while Collier was at home in Hastings:

The coachmaker called here on Friday ... we firnished him with your crest ... I was yesterday with your equipage which I like very well, tis strong and will be heavy, but Sussex roads might shake a lighter one too much ... Mr Gower called yesterday and told me that on his way to town he had bought a pair of horses [for the Coach] *at Reading for which I paid him £31 ... I went to your coach which I found quite finished and the setting out tomorrow quite fixed. Your first letter on this occasion mentioned £45, but Gower told me on Friday several additional articles have since been thought of etc etc and that the money must be £50 neat.*

Even after he'd acquired his coach with the pricy 'extras' Collier's problems were by no means over. As we've seen the route to the turnpike at Maresfield was extremely slow, not to say treacherous. There was, effectively, no route suitable for coaches out of Hastings directly to the north (today's A21) so the only alternative was to go via Canterbury where the carriage could join the Old Dover Road running along the route of the Roman Watling Street to London. This had been 'turnpiked' at different times; the Rochester to London section in 1712, and Canterbury to Chatham in 1730. The problem was getting to Canterbury from Hastings across the Romney Marsh.

After suffering what appears to have been a stroke John Collier began visiting Bath to take the waters. But in February 1756 he wrote to his son-in-law Captain James Murray saying he had hoped to set out for the west country, but had to abandon the trip:

I believe Bath journeys have been of service to me but as the roads are Extremely bad, in my helpless condition for travelling and my wife in so great a terror in Regard to Dymchurch Wall in the road to Canterbury, and which I think is the only road could be taken with safety, its present Impracticable.

It's not recorded why Mary was so terrified of the Dymchurch Wall which had, for centuries, been a defence against the sea encroaching on Romney marsh. Perhaps it was the fact that it was more than 20 feet high, and the road along the top only 20 feet broad, that disquieted her. In any event the route to Canterbury had other hazards. In a note to his 1907 publication of the Collier Correspondence, Charles Lane Sayer remarks that his late Aunt Mary Sayer, in her family memoranda says of one of Mr. Collier's journey's to Bath:

At that time the ways being so bad, that though they went round by Canterbury, as being a rather better road to London, they were obliged to take 20 men with them to lift the carriage over the ruts and other obstructions and help up the hills.

One apparently popular method of avoiding the ruts and potholes was to eschew the roads altogether when travelling along the coast. Journeys were carefully timed to take place at low tide so as to be able to gallop unobstructed across the sand:

I and my family went to E. Bourn last Wednesday morning, and set out by six for the advantage of the sand, and returned yesterday by the road. . . [Edward Milward, from Hastings, to Collier at Bath 31 May 1755].

From the middle 1500s a series of statutes had made it the responsibility of individual parishes to maintain the roads that traversed them. However, since they were given no money to appoint surveyors, and any repairs had to be carried out using unpaid labour, generally little or no maintenance was actually done. This was clearly the case around Hastings. Teams of packhorses or ponies carrying goods churned up the Sussex clay while wagon or carriage wheels made deep ruts. In many places the lanes were too narrow for wheeled vehicles to pass each other and reversing a horse or ox-drawn vehicle was no mean feat. Wagons often had bells to warn of their approach, and as late as 1794 a Hastings guidebook advised
private coaches to have a man on horseback ride well in advance to warn of oncoming traffic.

The state of England's roads was a well-known national disgrace – and a diplomatic embarrassment. In 1702 King Charles III of Spain arrived with his entourage in Portsmouth and journeyed to Petworth in Sussex. There the Queen's husband, Prince George of Denmark, was to meet them and escort them to Windsor. This journey of forty miles from Portsmouth, which took fourteen hours, was described by one of the attendants:

> *We set out at six in the morning by torchlight to go to Petworth and did not get out of our coaches (save only when we were overturned or stuck fast in the mire) till we arrived at our journey's end. 'Twas hard service for the Prince to sit fourteen hours in a coach that day without eating anything and passing through the worst ways I ever*

saw in my life. The nearer we approached the Duke of Somerset's house the more inaccessible it seemed to be. The last nine miles of the way cost us six hours to conquer them.

The roads even forced King George I to hole up in Rye for a full four days in January 1726 after a violent storm had driven the royal yacht into the harbour there. The route up to London was impassable following a fall of snow and so the royal party stayed with the Mayor, James Lamb at his home, The Lamb House. The honour of having the monarch to stay may have been slightly diminished by the fact that the Mayor's heavily pregnant wife had to give up her bed for her King and that Hanoverian George spoke no English and Mayor Lamb no German, leading, it is reported, to lengthy gaps in the conversation.

It was clear that something had to be done. And that something was nothing less than the effective privatisation of many of the country's roads.

The first route on which travellers paid a toll to travel was a section of the Great North Road in Hertfordshire - authorised in 1663. It was dubbed a turnpike after the military practice of placing a pikestaff across a road to block or control passage.

An act of Parliament in 1707 established the first turnpike trust, enabling a section of the Chester to London road to be managed and maintained by trustees who were allowed to levy charges on users. This formed a model that spread rapidly across the country, each trust being set up by private Parliamentary legislation. Trustees could not be paid directly for their administrative work, but as local landowners they often

Country Toll Gate by Samuel Williams
Turnpikes were not always heavily used in the 18th and
19th centuries

benefited from an increase in trade and rising property prices. They were also able to lend trusts money for the capital works at enhanced interest rates. Just over a hundred years after the opening of the first turnpike road there were more than 1,000 trusts, administering some 30,000 miles of toll roads in England and Wales, collecting money from almost 8,000 gates. Only farm traffic and pedestrians were exempt. Thus huge swathes of public roads were effectively taken into the ownership of private individuals. Which was by no means universally popular with many resenting the necessity to pay for passage.

In some parts of England people demonstrated and even rioted, smashing toll gates and assaulting the keepers or pikemen.

And it's far from certain that all turnpike roads were maintained much better than their predecessors. One anonymous traveller in Sussex wrote:

> *I arrived at the Turnpike Gate where the toll was being paid and then proceeded upon a firm road full wide enough for a single cart but by no means wide enough for two and one must drive down and into the mud at the side of the road bank and as there were no ditches nor any drains to carry off the standing waters from these flats they must soon be worse than the old clay deep roads.*

It took a while for the concept to be adopted in Hastings. However in 1753 a number of prominent citizens including John Collier along with his future son-in-law Edward Milward, obtained an act of Parliament to establish The Flimwell and Hastings Turnpike Trust.

Within three years this trust was running the *'road from Flimwell Vent* [cross-roads] *to the town and port of Hastings, by way of Robertsbridge, Battle and Ore.'* It had a total of nine toll-gates, the first being at the top of Hastings Hill (Old London Road) where it meets the Ridge.

This turnpike act was renewed in 1779, 1801, 1821 and 1849 but by the final date it had a formidable rival. James Burton's St Leonards to Sedlescombe Turnpike had been created by an act of Parliament in 1836. This became the route of today's A 21, by-passing Battle and cutting about three-and-a-half miles off the previous journey. By the early 1850s three railway lines were serving Hastings and the Flimwell and Hastings Trust went bust.

At the end of the last chapter we left poor William Cranston rushing back to London from Sevenoaks having received the news that the Collier's younger son James (Jemmy) was ill with symptoms of the Smallpox.

> *You may be sure this hasened me from thence immediately. I lost no time in rideing for I got from the Crown at Sennocke to my Inn in Southwarke in two hours and 40 minutes.*

That's a distance of around 23 miles so he was averaging just under 8.5 miles an hour along the turnpike road. Rather faster than the 2.2 MPH he managed on the cross-country route from Battle to Maresfield. And the good news was that although Jemmy had contracted Smallpox, it was a variety much less severe than the one that had just killed his brother. In fact within a few weeks he was writing to his parents in Hastings telling them he felt much better.

George Worge – Collier's son-in-law, married to Elizabeth his daughter from his first marriage (to Elizabeth Elphick). Worge was an attorney in Battle.

William Cranston – Mary Collier's younger brother. John Collier's legal partner based in London.

Charles Lane Sayer – *descendent of John Collier, transcriber and editor of The Correspondence of John Collier and his Family pub. 1907.* **Mary Sayer**, *his aunt.*

Prince George of Denmark (1653-1708), Husband to Queen Anne of England

King George I of England (1660-1727). Born Hanover. Great grandson James I. Succeeded Queen Anne in 1714

James Lamb Mayor of Rye

Edward Milward. Collier's son-in-law. 26 times Mayor of Hastings. Married Mary Collier in 1754.

Colonel James Murray – Collier's Son-in-Law, married to Cordelia.

Chapter 5

Mayor Making

Come on. Hurry up or we'll miss the start. You know what today is don't you? It's April 9th - which is the third Sunday after Easter – the one after Hock Day. That's when Hastings' mayor has always been chosen. And this year, 1719, our town clerk, John Collier is standing.

From early this morning the 'Serjeants at Mace' have been touring the town sounding the brazen horn in order to summon and prepare the assembly for the election. In the old days – before 1603 – elections were held outside at the 'Hundred Place', but in that year a decree was made:

> *'That to avoid the great inconvenience which by common experience are found to be by reason of the election of the mayor of this town ... in the public view of the whole multitude ... whereby all matters of council is disclosed and may not be kept secret, that from henceforth all elections of mayors of this town shall be solemnized, made done and performed in the Court Hall ... any old custom usage or decree to the contrary not withstanding.'*

So ever since then the meeting has been called in the Hundred Place - in Windings Lane - and immediately adjourned to the Court Hall or, since 1702, to the new Town Hall in Market Street. But today's ceremony is probably pretty much identical to the ones held before 1603.

So here we are gathered in the town hall. The outgoing mayor, the jurats, the clerk and all other officers of the court are assembling. It's traditionally been the task of the Bailiff of the Bourne to decorate the place 'gaily'. Now, if we listen carefully we can hear the Town Serjeant proclaiming:

> *'All manner of persons that have to do with the election of the King's Majesty's head officer of this town and port of Hastings, for this year to come, now give your attendance, upon pain and penalty that may fall thereon...'*

The freemen of the town who are actually going to elect the new Mayor are coming in now and lining up with the dozen Jurats. Now the Serjeant is addressing them:

> *You good men, free of this town and port of Hastings that are assembled to the election of his Majesty's head officer of the said town and port for the year to come, answer to your names every man as you are called over, upon the pain to lose your voices at the said election.*

Now we'll have to wait a few moments while the clerk calls out the names from a list he prepared earlier and one by one each freeman answers to his name. Once that's done the clerk addresses them again;

> *All you that have made your appearance draw near and receive your charge. It is not*

unknown to you that of long time and custom used upon this day the King's Majesty's head officer of this town and port of Hastings hath been elected and chosen successively to continue the weal public and good government of this town and corporation, which head officer you the freemen of this town, by accustomed continuance, have used and now in like intent are appointed to choose and elect. And therefore Mr Mayor in his Majesty's name chargeth you and every one of you, by virtue of then oath that you and everyone of you have taken at the several admittances to the liberties of this town that you get together by yourself to elect, name and chose one Jurat of this town which shall be an inhabitant and one of the brethren and associate with him at the bench one whole week before the present day and such one as you shall think most meet and able to exercise the office within this town, the liberties and franchises thereof as his Majesty's lieutenant for the year following and such a one will tender then glory of Almighty God, the good service of his sacred Majesty, and the public weal of this corporation and the private peace of us, the inhabitants thereof, which God grant!'

Come on, stop yawning. This is an important ceremony. All he's saying is the freemen are going to elect the mayor and that any candidate must already be a Jurat. John Collier was made one last year so he's alright. In a few moments the freemen will withdraw and you're not to go anywhere near them or you'll be in serious trouble. Just listen to what the Serjeant is about to say to everyone about trying to influence the voters. This should wake you up!

> *Oyez! Oyez! Oyez! Mr Mayor and his brethren strictly charge and command, in his Majesty's name, that none of you be so hardy as to approach the said electors by one hundred foot, upon pain of losing his upper garment: and that every man lay from his person all weapons, upon pain of losing the same; and that every man keep his Majesty's peace, and that no man disturb this election nor give his voice in choosing his majesty's head officer, but such one be thereunto assigned, upon pain of imprisonment and to be fined at the will and pleasure of Mr Mayor and his brethren.*

Look, there's Robert Bartholomew. He's the current Mayor. What's he doing? It seems as if he's handing over his mace, the symbol of his office and his authority, to the oldest Freeman in the hall. And see, he's also giving him a list of the Jurats who are eligible to be elected. Now the Freemen are all trooping out to the next room. I suspect that they've already decided who they want so it probably won't take very long. But if there was a disagreement, or more than one Jurat really wanted to be Mayor, the elections could take some time. No, it's OK. Here they are coming back. Shush... The elder Freeman is about to read out the name. And .... yes ,as we expected, it is John Collier. Look, there he is, looking really smart in his Whig and robes.

Late 18th Century View of Hastings Beach by Samuel Grimm

Now the Freeman is handing him the mace and telling him to take the oath of office. Listen carefully, for these words have been spoken by the new mayor every year for many centuries. Collier draws a big breath and says:

> *'I will bear faith to our sovereign the King of England and the commonalty of Hasting, and the franchise and the usages of the same rightfully will maintain and the common profit will keep, and to rich and poor will do right so far as I can, so help me God and the Saints'*

So John Collier is now Mayor of Hastings, aged just thirty-three. It's an important position. He's not only head of the council, but he's also the first citizen of the town, the King's representative, the chief magistrate, the coroner, collector of national taxes, and has to conduct civil marriages if called to do so. His first duties now that he's taken office will be oversee the election of the clerk, the chamberlain and all other civic employees. Then to the important part of the mayor-making ritual – the civic dinner. Forty or more people will gather in the banqueting room at the Swan, including all the Jurats and Freemen and many of their sons. A typical feast of this period included 14 lbs of pork, 12 stone of Beef, 80 lbs of veal, 7 stone of mutton and a whole lamb of 27 lbs. [One stone is 6.3 kilos, one pound is just under half a kilo]. There were also shrimps, bread, and vegetables, and to wash it down, beer, brandy and punch. The total cost was £11 12s 6d. And this at a time when the entire annual salary of the clerk was around £10.

One must not think either the ceremony or the mayoral responsibilities typical of all English town councils in the 18th century. Hastings was special because of its role as a Cinque Port. It meant that its civic authority was not a mere Council but a Corporation.

The Cinque (five) Ports were originally Hastings, Romney, Hythe, Dover and Sandwich and it's believed the confederation preceded the Norman invasion of 1066. It was said to be the annual landing of the autumn herring catch at Great Yarmouth that first brought them together and, from the time of Henry II, they obtained rights over these landings in exchange for providing the King with ships should he require them. The five ports had to make available 57 ships, each manned by 21 men and a boy, for 15 days each year. Hastings and Dover were the biggest ports and by 1229 they were providing 21 ships each. Hastings originally encompassed Rye and Winchelsea but they subsequently became part of the confederacy in their own right from the 1400s.

As far as the civic administration was concerned, the unusual rights and privileges pertaining to a Cinque Port were handed down in what was known as a 'custumal'. The Hastings custumal established there would be twelve 'Jurats' the 'most wise of the same town', chosen and sworn on the same day as the Bailiff (after 1588 known as Mayor). It also established how a Freeman was to be chosen which, as we shall see, later became a vital issue for John Collier in his efforts to control the Hastings electorate for the Whig cause. Only Freemen could become Jurats and only Jurats could be elected to Mayor. Curiously, both putative Jurats and Mayors could receive a hefty fine if they refused to take up the office when nominated.

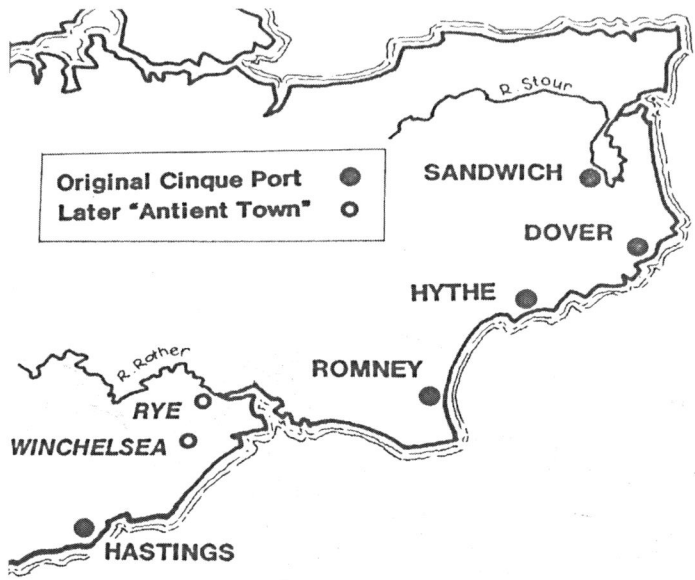

The Cinque Ports

13th Century Cinque Ports Ship by Candy Sencicle

Map and drawing courtesy of Sencicle family collection

To give some idea of the power of a Mayor it's worth looking at events in neighbouring Rye a few years later. Here a local oligarchy has been running the town council for a decade or more. In 1743 it's headed by the Mayor, James Lamb, and his brother-in-law Alan Grebell – a former Mayor - both of whom have made a number of enemies among the town's tradesmen. One in particular is a butcher and inn-keeper called John Breads who had been fined by Lamb a few years before for using short weights.

On the night of 16 March, Grebell is returning home from a dinner on board the Rye customs sloop. Lamb should have attended but was not feeling well and it's possible he may have loaned his cloak to his brother-in-law. In any event as Alan Grebell walks home through the churchyard, Breads attacks him with a knife from which he suffers fatal wounds. It seems possible or even likely that this was a case of mistaken identity and there is evidence to suggest that Breads is mentally unstable or ill.

There is no doubt that, as chief law officer, Lamb was entitled to imprison the suspect in the local jail rather than in the county prison, even if the cost of the three months incarceration fell upon the town of Rye rather than the county. As chief coroner, Lamb was entitled to conduct the inquest and to bring in a verdict of wilful murder. Even so some questioned whether, as a relative and close friend of the deceased – and possibly the intended target, he should not have recused himself. But the Mayor went much further, insisting that the trial itself was held in the town and that he himself would be the judge. This was extremely unusual in such serious cases which would normally have been heard at the Sussex Assizes. There the jury would be unlikely to know the accused personally. In Rye at least one juror was a fellow Jurat along with Lamb and, before he died, Grebell.

The result was that Lamb conducted the trial himself in a building he owned. Breads was found guilty and Lamb sentenced him to death, ordering that he should be hanged locally and his body placed on display in an iron gibbet.

Questions were raised about the entire procedure, and curiously, news of the case was relayed to John Collier by his son, James from London where it has clearly caused a stir:

> *Yesterday being the day appointed for Breades' execution I suppose he suffered. I heard on Monday he was to be hanged in chains* [gibbeted]; *Mr Moneypenny* [legal counsel for Rye and Dover] *informed me before the trial that Mr Gybbon had made use of his utmost endeavors to persuade Mr Lamb to send the prisoner to the county goal and have him tried at the Assizes and that the Lord Chancellor had told young Lamb that considering the circumstances he would not have his father try the affair at Rye.*

The fact that James Lamb was able to resist such pressure from government law officers does give a very real indication of the power of a mayor in a Cinque Port at this time. Fortunately it seems John Collier never had to, or indeed sought to, use his power in a similar manner. But as we shall see, he certainly went to considerable lengths to manipulate the electorate in Hastings.

§§§

Who's Who. Chapter 5, Mayor Making.

Robert Bartholomew. Mayor Hastings 1718

James Lamb. 20 Times Mayor of Rye

Alan Grebell. Mayor Rye brother in law of James Lamb. Murdered 16 March 1743

John Breads. Rye Butcher. Convicted of killing Alan Grebell. Executed by hanging 1743

James Collier. (Jemmy) John and Mary's second son. b 1721, d 1747 aged 26. Lawyer. Hastings Mayor, 1745

Chapter 6

End of a Catholic Age – Politics and Religion

As we know, John Collier was born in 1685. It was a year that marked an important transition in English history, as the ostensibly Protestant King Charles II died and his brother, the Catholic James II, ascended the throne. The game of religious ping-pong, in which the English citizen had been batted backwards and forwards between the two competing strands of Christianity, had been going on for a hundred and fifty years - ever since Henry VIII's Act of Supremacy. But it remained an important backdrop throughout most of Colliers life.

The restoration of the monarchy after Cromwell's Commonwealth, seemed to have created a consensus that the majority of English men and women preferred Protestantism and looked to the monarch rather than the pope to head their church. But then, between 1679 and 1689, a huge row erupted in parliament over various bills designed to prevent Charles' Catholic brother James from the taking the throne.

This reopened old wounds and gave rise to two competing political parties – Whigs and Tories. The latter, believing in the divine right of kings and hereditary succession, prevented the bills from becoming law. Thus on Charles' death James did indeed take over. The new monarch's espousal of Rome at first appeared tolerable to England. However, with the birth of a son, the likelihood of a new Catholic dynasty so unsettled the English hierarchy that many coalesced around the Whig party. Before long they'd invited William of Orange and his wife Mary - James II's protestant daughter - to take the crown.

Collier was only three in 1688 when this 'Glorious Revolution' occurred, so he would have had little idea of the significance of events. But as the son of an innkeeper in Eastbourne he must have overheard the talk in the bar, and may well have been aware of events as James and his French-backed army landed in Ireland the following year. Their eventual defeat by King "Billy" at the Battle of the Boyne in July 1690 would also have been vitally important news. As an adult in 1708 and again in 1715 he would certainly have followed the invasion plans of the 'Old' Pretender, James Francis Edward Stuart, (James II's son and Queen Mary's half-brother). The second of these uprisings was a momentous event for England as the French backed Jacobite army landed in Scotland and marched south before finally being confronted at Preston in Lancashire. The ensuing battle could have gone either way as could an equally important confrontation at Sheriffmuir in Scotland, and for a while it was touch and go as to whether the Hanoverian George I might be deposed by James Stuart, and Britain once again returned to Catholicism.

So the Jacobites and Jacobitism – the movement to restore a Catholic king to the throne – were to permeate more than half-century of Britain's history and politics, and are interwoven throughout almost all of John Collier's life. His dislike, or fear of, or even prejudice against Catholics will cause him considerable heart-searching in later life when his daughter decides to marry into the family of one. On the other hand his

William of Orange "King Billy" and his wife Queen Mary
accept the crown.

career was founded on, and prospered because of, his espousal of the Whig cause.

The Tory party, with its support for James, had lost much of its influence following the Glorious Revolution. Many of the county gentry within the party evolved and ended up supporting the protestant William and Mary, Queen Anne and the Hanoverian George I. The Tories tended to a strict Anglicism - as opposed to the Whig toleration of religious dissent. A further difference was that the Whigs favoured the extension of Britain's influence overseas while the Tories remained more insular, opposing foreign involvement.

The importance and influence of Whig-ism throughout Collier's adult lifetime cannot be understated. Politically, the period from 1715 to 1760 became known as the Whig Supremacy, headed by leaders such as Robert Walpole and by John Collier's direct benefactors, Henry Pelham and his brother the Duke of Newcastle.

We have no way of knowing why Collier decided from an early age to support the Whig cause. However it would have been by no means an automatic choice. Tory roots ran deep in Sussex and included wealthy landowners such as the Ashburnhams, the Fullers and the Frewins. The battle for political control of Hastings' close neighbour, Rye has been well documented by Paul Monod in his book 'The Murder of Mr Grebell' which is a comprehensive portrait of the town at this period. There the Tories only slowly lost their ascendancy around the end of the 17th century.

The Royalist Ashburnham Family had dominated Hastings politics since the mid 1600s, supplying MPs on several occasions. In 1710 John Ashburnham was elected as Tory member for the constituency – even though he had to stand down within a few months after inheriting his brother's baronetcy. So there seems little to suggest that Hastings was a Whig stronghold when Collier arrived in the town in 1706 to take up his position as Clerk to the Corporation. Indeed it's a reasonable supposition that the Tory influence could have been as strong there as it clearly was in Rye.

Nonetheless our young lawyer rapidly hitched his wagon to Whiggery - eventually going to the extraordinary lengths to 'fix' the town for the great Whig magnate, the Duke of Newcastle.

Newcastle was to be a defining patron in Collier's career and so a short diversion to look at his background and early career will aid our understanding of later events.

Thomas Pelham had been born in 1693, eldest son of Lord Pelham and Grace Holles – she was the younger sister of John Holles, then Duke of Newcastle. Holles' estate (though not his title) went to his nephew, Pelham, in 1711. And the following year Pelham succeeded to his father's estate. Now calling himself Pelham-Holles, this left him one of the richest men in England with enormous land holdings and patronage in Sussex. His support for the Hanoverian Succession in 1714 and his vigorous action against the Jacobite rebellion the following year earned him the titles Earl of Clare and Duke of Newcastle. So by the time he enters John Collier's life, this enormously wealthy and incredibly influential young man is a doyen of the Whig party.

By 1715 John Collier has been Hastings town clerk for nine years. He's 30 years old. It hasn't taken him long to acquire other work and responsibilities. Following the 1708 Commission of Sewers Act he was chosen to be Clerk and Sole Collector of Hooe, Barnhorne, Cowding and East Levels, at an annual salary of £12 0s 0d. This made him responsible for the 'maintenance of sea banks and other defences, which protected low-lying areas from inundation by the sea and the removal of obstructions in streams and rivers caused by mills, weirs and gates'. This appointment alone provided rather more than his remuneration as town clerk. But he was also building up other sources of income and influence. In 1714 he'd been appointed as Joint Solicitor of the Cinque Ports at the Coronation of George I and there's evidence that he was already practising as an independent solicitor in Hastings and had, or was in the process of, expanding his practice to London.

Possibly as a result of John Collier's suggestion, in 1715 the Hastings Corporation invited the Duke of Newcastle to 'recommend' a candidate to stand for the town in the impending General election. Newcastle did better than that. He descended on Hastings where he was treated to a civic reception and in return offered lavish entertainment. Most such events were held in the Swann Inn, and one can just visualize the anticipation and excitement of entertaining such a scion of the nobility. We can also imagine the meeting between Collier and Newcastle. The Duke is only 22 years old but owns much of the port including the castle and the administrative district known as the 'Rape' of Hastings which included the town as well as Battle.

So was it at the banqueting room at the Swann in the midst of the civic reception in his honour that Newcastle first spotted the town clerk and young lawyer and thought he might be useful to him in later years?

In the event, Newcastle recommended his cousin Henry Pelham of Stanmer for the parliamentary seat. He was duly elected in the subsequent poll, along with the sitting MP, Archibald Hutcheson, then an independent

Thomas Pelham-Holles, Duke of Newcastle

Whig. But Hutcheson proved 'unreliable' and, the following year, voted with the Tory opposition against the Septennial Bill to increase the length of Parliaments from 3 to 7 years. The Hastings Corporation also opposed the bill and lobbied their other MP, Pelham, who ignored the pressure and voted with the government.

Thus by the following election in 1722, Hastings has become an uncomfortably unknown quantity for Newcastle and the Whig party. One MP has joined the opposition and the other has angered the town's electorate. Now Hutcheson is standing against two Whig nominees - Sir William Ashburnham (not directly related to previous Hastings MP John Ashburnham) and John Pulteney both of whom had previously served as MPs for the town.

In this period the electorate is incredibly narrow. Only Jurats (modern day Aldermen) and Freemen can vote - a total of about 65 people. Those with government jobs were always likely to support the government candidate. And, mysteriously, government appointments often seemed to be made just as elections were approaching! As Newcastle subsequently wrote:

> 'I did him [Pulteney] whatever service I could, but the disposition of the town is such that I could publicly recommend but one, which was Sir William Ashburnham'.

In fact Newcastle and his brother Henry Pelham had come down to Hastings in order to go from house to house 'canvassing' for Ashburnham and Pulteney. One former Customs employee, Richard Carswell, was suddenly awarded a government pension of £20 a year and decided to vote for them. Indeed 11 of the 32 people who voted for Pulteney just happened to be employees of the Customs. But would that be enough to get him elected?

Three Jurats and 28 Freemen voted for the independently minded Hutcheson. So with 31 votes, he is just two short of a majority. But the votes of two people have not yet been included – those of John Collier and fellow civic dignitary, the Mayor, Edward Milward. Both cast their votes for Hutcheson.

On the face of it this is a considerable rebuff for Newcastle. And it might have been seen as a high-risk strategy for Collier were he hoping to gain the Duke's patronage. In fact it worked to his advantage. Newcastle realised that he couldn't take Hastings or Collier for granted.

At the general election of 1727 Newcastle's two candidates, Ashburnham and Thomas Townshend were unopposed. But Collier's influence was clearly increasing because in 1731 Newcastle was promising him a job as agent for his estate and another as election manager in East Sussex. However a much more lucrative sinecure was also in the offing – as Collier wrote to Mary on 24 February 1732:

> *I had orders from the D of N* [Newcastle] *to Tarry 3 or 4 days. Tho' perhaps it may and will be only a Wildgoose chase, there is a little place dropped in the Law that I would gladly accept of and did make some application for at my first coming to Town, but now gave it over. He told me last night he thinks I shall have it. The place is to be executed by a Clerk &* [is] *Easy & Creditable. & I believe about £80 a year – a*

Sergeant at Law had it before ... I shall be confoundedly vex'd if I miss it ..."

It turned out Collier didn't miss it, and that it was well worth tarrying in London an extra few days. Not only did the position that Newcastle provided him pay upwards of £80 a year, but apparently didn't involve Collier in actually doing anything – all duties were carried out by a deputy. And it lasted well beyond his lifetime. Collier was able to pass it on to Cranston's second son John and two further generations beyond.

So by the early 1730s Collier had achieved greater financial security and had come to the attention of the great Whig politicians of the day. Newcastle's younger brother Henry Pelham was then a senior minister in Walpole's Government. In 1733, just a year before the next general election, Pelham wrote to Newcastle:

> *As to Collier, you can't do too much, for, if I can judge, that town absolutely depends upon him, and perhaps, if he were cool, would leave you. I desire therefore you will from me tell Sir Robert Walpole, if he has a mind to have two Whigs chosen at Hastings, he must provide handsomely for Collier.*

It was to lead to an even greater change of fortune for John Collier both in prestige and income. But nothing comes without a price and, as we shall see in chapter 9, he soon found himself embroiled a seemingly intractable legal dispute that split the corporation of Hastings down the centre.

Who's Who Chapter 6 - End of a Catholic Age

Charles Stuart – King Charles II 1660 –1685. A Protestant.

James Stuart – King James II 1685 – 1689. A Catholic.

James Francis Edward Stuart. The 'Old Pretender'. Catholic. Son of James Stuart. Half brother of Mary.

Mary Stuart (Queen Mary II) 1662-1694 – Protestant, daughter of James II. Reigned (with husband William) from 1689 until her death from Smallpox in 1694.

William of Orange. King William III 1689 -1702 (ruled jointly with wife Mary until her death in 1694). aka King 'Billy'. His mother was daughter of Charles I.

John Ashburnham. Hastings MP 1710. Resigned after inheriting brother's Baronetcy.

Robert Walpole. Leader of Whig administration 1727– 1740. Considered first British 'Prime Minister'.

Henry Pelham. Whig Prime Minster 1743- 1754

Duke of Newcastle. Whig. Elder brother of Henry Pelham. Statesman. Secretary of State. Prime Minister 1754-1756

Henry Pelham of Stanmer. Cousin to Newcastle and Prime Minister Pelham. Hastings MP 1715 – 1722

John Pulteney Whig. Hastings MP 1695-1710. Unsuccessful candidate 1722

Sir William Ashburnham. Hastings MP 1710-1713 and 1722-1741

Edward Milward (1682-1749). Hastings Freeman, Jurat and Mayor 1721. His son, also Edward, married Collier's

Daughter Mary in 1754. His grandson, also Edward (1765–1833), was 20 times Mayor of Hastings.

John Cranston. Second son of Collier's London Partner William Cranston, and Collier's nephew via Mary. John Cranston seems later to have taken over his father's legal practice in London, and was an executor of Collier's will.

Chapter 7

Communication – Horses, Carts and Boats.

In our current era of instant communication, with mobile phones, emails, tweets and texts, it's hard to comprehend the importance of letter writing to previous generations. Clearly for John Collier it was vital to his work and business interests but also to keep in touch with his family during the regular and prolonged separations. Letter writing at this period was, however, the exception rather than the rule. General literacy in England was only around 40% in 1640, rising to 60% in the mid 18th Century. So throughout much of his lifetime, fewer than half the population of a town like Hastings would have been able to write at all, let alone have considered communicating by letter.

As is apparent from the Collier letters, there is little or no standardisation of spelling at this period, but grammar and syntax are also markedly poorer among those unused to writing regularly. For the educated classes, on the other hand, the ability to write a good letter was both demanded and prized by parents. Indeed John Collier insisted that both his sons wrote regularly. Jemmy was only 11 and had just started at Westminster school when he received this admonishment from his father via a letter to his brother Jacky:

> *We both very much wonder that Jemmy has not once wrote and think him very naughty in not doing it, and shall not excuse him without his writing next Saturday.*

Jacky himself was not immune to his father's censure and wrote to him on 19 December 1732:

> *Honoured sir, I hope you will pardon my false writing in my last letter, and to be sure I will take care for the future not to write any false concords, as we was or to spell anything wrong.*

Jemmy also apologised to his father in a letter written the same day:

> *I am very sorry that in my last letter I made so many mistakes in my spelling but promise to be more careful for the future.*

As we will see, Jemmy later turned out to be an excellent correspondent while he was studying for the law in his 20s and reporting to his parents on many of the great parliamentary debates of the day.

There would, of course, have been little point in writing so often or with such style if the letters were not to be delivered. And this is a remarkable feature of the 18th Century. Given how appalling was the state of the roads at this time it seems extraordinary that mail got though at all. Today we expect to be able to post a letter in one part of the country and have it delivered to another within 48 hours. Amazingly, this was pretty much the expectation 300 years ago! It was not at all unusual for William Cranston to write a letter in London, and for Collier to receive it on the south coast the following day. And this was long before a unified mail service, before stamps, or even before post boxes.

Given the importance of letters throughout Collier's life, it may be worth a short diversion to look at the development of the Royal Mail. To begin with it was 'Royal' because of the need for the monarch to receive and send messages through the kingdom. In the late 1200s, Edward I established a series of fixed 'posts' where fresh couriers and horses were stationed. By 1517 a Master of the King's Post – or Postmaster General – had been appointed, and traders and merchants were increasingly using the 'Royal' service. In 1635 one Thomas Witterings introduced a fixed scale of charges based on the number of pages and the distance they were carried. He reorganised the 'posts' and established five lines out of London along which letters would travel to a series of Post Towns on the routes.

Throughout the Commonwealth, and after the Restoration, the Royal Mail was something of a political football. Day to day management was 'farmed' out – or effectively privatised. Anyone who could afford to buy a franchise stood to make a great deal of money. John Manley was appointed 'Farmer of the Posts' having agreed to pay a 'rent' of £10,000 a year in the 1650s – a very considerable sum indeed and he must have been confident it would show a handsome profit. Soon parliament was legislating for unified charges, and for all official letters and those to and from Members of Parliament to be carried free. By the end of the 17th century there was a general post office headquarters in London's Lombard Street as well as posting and receiving stations at Westminster, Charing Cross, Pall Mall, Covent Garden and, most usefully for William Cranston and John Collier, at the Inns of Court. Thirty-two carriers were employed to collect letters from these stations and to take them to Lombard street. From

The Dover Mail Coach.
The print probably dates from the late 18th or early 19th century

there they would be dispatched to all parts of the country on Tuesdays, Thursdays and Saturdays. This was overseen by eight Clerks of the Road who monitored outgoing and incoming mail along the six 'great' roads, to Holyhead, Bristol, Plymouth, Edinburgh, Yarmouth and Dover. Subsequently a daily post was established to 'Kent and the Downs', branching off to Rye on two days of the week.

But if we know how letters left London for Canterbury and Dover or even for Rye, we have much less idea of just how they got from there to Hastings before 1717. Generally the mail was carried on horseback by post boys, but they were often unreliable and were sometimes robbed - it wasn't until 1784 that Mail Coaches were introduced. Up until then it's possible that, as a Cinque Port, Hastings may have established its own mail courier system between the town and Rye or even Canterbury. It certainly seems that the service was more frequent than twice a week.

In 1711 another Act of Parliament effectively re-nationalized much of the post office, cancelling the leases which the 'farmers' had held and bringing the 'private' country post offices back under the direct oversight of the Postmaster-General. A number of 'post towns' had been established along the six great roads generally in market towns – though there is no evidence the Hastings was one such. It seems possible, though, that Collier's town was actually awarded a 'farmed lease' for a branch in the town. Local Historian J Manwaring Baines provides a tantalizing note for what happened after 1711: "managers of the nine branches (of which Hastings was one) found they were losing money. In 1716 seven of these leases were cancelled, but the Hastings Branch survived until 1768/9." But *what* nine branches is he referring to – he simply doesn't say. And was Hastings a 'branch' before 1711 or was it established as one thereafter?

To add to the mystery, it seems Hastings had a Postmaster in 1677 – a Mr Stephens – but the next one, according to Manwaring Baines was Thomas in 1742 who it seems was 'Manager of the Hastings Branch'. There are, however, references to John Geery who was a Freeman, and Jurat of Hastings and appears to have been the town's postmaster up until his death in 1733.

What we do know is that Hastings had a regular postal service at least from 1711 and probably before. The Colliers and Cranstons could expect letters travelling between the coast and London to arrive within 48 hours of posting – with a similar timescale in the other direction. Letters were just one sheet of paper folded into quarters and sealed with wax. They did not use envelopes. A precise address was not required in Hastings - generally 'Mr Collier's house' would suffice. Payment was made on receipt of the letter, not when it was posted – the first pre-payment stamp the Penny Black wasn't introduced until the following century in 1840. From 1677 a single letter of one sheet could be sent up to 80 miles for two pence and above 80 miles for three pence. However in a letter from William Cranston to his sister Mary Collier in 1730, it appears that the cost of a letter from London to Hastings at that time was three pence.

A curious side note appears the following month when Collier asks Mary to send him some banknotes from Hastings to London:

I find I am kept in suspense about some money & that I may be prolonged in town about that; desire next post you will send me the 3 bank notes in the book I showed you. If my Brother Cranston is in Town. I desire he will take copies of them for fear of miscarriage and show them to Mr Halsted – if not send for Halsted & shew them to him and make the letter safe. [21 November 1730]

Halsted seems to have worked in the Hastings post office and it is interesting to see that banknotes sent through the post had some sort of guarantee if their dispatch had been witnessed by a post office official.

Curiously, Collier didn't have much regard for Halsted, and seems actively to have campaigned against his succeeding John Geery after the latter's death. Collier wrote to Mary on 15 November 1733:

...on receiving the letter I find it was an account of the death of poor Mr Geery which I am heartily concerned for and think there's a great family left in a poor situation. I reckon we shall have plague enough about the post office ... Halsted sent the messenger to have the place but I see noe reason. I need not caution you not to take any notice of what I write about Halsted. I have not seen any of the Newcastle family. But shall tomorrow, but I have sent a letter to postpone any disposal of it.

The letter is interesting for a number of reasons. First it is clear that the position of Hastings Postmaster is in the gift of Newcastle, and second that Collier held sufficient sway with him to be able to get him at least to postpone a decision on a new appointment. Pending, presumably, consideration of Collier's preferred candidate. Just what he had against Halsted is not clear, but it's possible that within the Hastings corporation, he was no supporter of Newcastle and the Whig faction.

There is one specific reference in the Collier letters to an 'express' postal delivery. It was on 28th June 1735 at a moment when Collier was involved in a legal dispute over who was entitled to be created Freemen of Hastings and thus be eligible to vote in elections. Collier and fellow jurats were awaiting a court hearing but, as he wrote to Mary, the action was withdrawn at the last minute:

> At eleaven a clock at night notice of tryall was countermanded. My Brother [Cranston] and I got a coach and drove to the post office to send an express to stop our witnesses if possible. If they had given notice 2 hours before, 30 guineas could have been saved to councell.

The following day – 29th June - the Mayor of Hastings, William Coppard wrote to Collier:

> We adjourned till 2 in the afternoon, and while we was in the Swan Mr Godley received your express ...

So from this it seems clear that it was possible to send an express letter from the Post Office in London at nearly midnight, and for it to be delivered in Hastings before 2.00pm the following day - less than 14 hours later. Sadly there are no details as to how this was achieved or how much it cost. Presumably an individual messenger carried it by hand through the night, which would not have been cheap. Indeed the cost of sending letters generally was relatively high. In 1733 the wage of "the best carpenter, rough hewer, rough mason, joiner, shingler, (shingle roofer) gardener, bricklayer, glazier, brickmaker, tilemaker, lime burner, slate, tile layer and thatcher" was a maximum of 1 shilling and five pence a day. So sending a 'threepenny' letter would cost 17% of a day's earnings for most manual workers.

Even for professional people such as Collier and Cranston postal charges would have mounted up, especially given the volume of mail they generated, and so it seems to have been common to try to get your mail sent free under the "franks" system. The 1660 Post Office reforms had established that all letters from the 'great officers of state' should be carried free, as should mail to and from members of parliament. This was achieved by 'franking' the letter with an authorised stamp and a signature.

Collier's correspondence records a number of what would certainly appear to be abuses of the system. Writing to his two young sons away at school in 1732, he tells them he has *"enclosed a Frank (so) you may both write and both put letters in it"* which would seem to have little to do with government business! Eleven years later James Collier writes to his father about an initially fruitless attempt to get more than two dozen 'covers' franked :

> *I sent my man in the afternoon ... to ask the clerk with whom I left the covers, if they were delivered to Mr Stone [Hastings's MP]... I did not call again until Tuesday when I was informed the clerk with whom I left the covers had been ill since the delivery and that he had made an enquiry of the other clerks ... but*

could gain no intelligence but acquainted me at the same time, that he had frequent opportunities of seeing Mr Stone's gentleman ...and would ask him if the covers were received.... I took some covers to Mr Stone's house and had delivered to me the covers franked.... I have only two dozen franked now but if insufficient will wait on Col Pelham [also Hastings MP] *with the like number. Six I shall give to my uncle, two keep for myself, three send now, and the remaining (at) the first opportunity.*

Whether or not all these franks were to be used on official government business, it is instructive to see just what lengths the Colliers went to in order to get free postage.

Even if it was possible to convey letters relatively quickly in early Georgian England there was one major constraint – weight. Since the mail was generally carried by messenger on horseback, only light letters – usually one page folded into quarters – were accepted. Other items had to be sent by carrier:

I desire you will look in the upper great draw of my escritoire in my study and take out the fine red box that has my patent in it as crier and usher of the King's bench and send it by Nich to the carrier Munday for I want it. Send all the papers in the box with it and put in officer's journals that lie in the corner next to the fire place to fill the box quite full or the seal will be in danger of breaking. Then wrap him up in two or three sheets of brown paper and I will send a Wednesday to the carrier for it.

Thus Collier beseeched Mary in November 1734. A considerable number of the letters between them refer to a carrier, and it seems that there was a weekly service between Hastings and London with a cart or carriage carrying boxes of a pre-determined size. It's worth quoting extracts from a number of the letters from Collier to Mary to give an idea of the sort of things that they were transporting back and forth:

I have sent a box this week by the carrier in which is your gown... There's only a greatcoat of mine and my intended servant's clothes and your gloves and the girls stockings beside two or three other little things to fill up, but at the top there is a small parcel for Mr Woirge from Mr Isted which I believe are the whiggs he left.
[3 March 1737]

I have spoke to my sister about Dely's shoos and gloves ... but hope they will be all compleat and go by the next carrier. The weather is now very hot in town and I begin to be very weary of it.
[29 June 1738]

Though I think I take all precautions to put everything I want when I go for London, yet very often I leave some papers etc., I want; now I have left a memorandum paper of business and things to buy and a book with green vellum cover which I have in London to write everything in. They are together in one of the partitions over the place I write upon ... the book to be tied up in paper and sent by the carrier a Saturday. [June 1740]

The hats went yesterday by the carrier – they are tip top of the mode.
[12 May 1743]

While the carrier's service generally seems to have been weekly, it appears there was some flexibility. In December 1744, three days before Christmas, William Cranston in London writes in a semi stream-of-consciousness style to Collier in Hastings, detailing a conversation his son James Cranston has had with the carrier Guy:

When I sent the Brawn to the carrier Wednesday I bid James ask Guy whether he came up again on that day sennight [seven-night ie a week hence]. *He at first said not until Thursday, but upon his asking James the reason of the enquiry and James telling him it was because I should send a lamb by him to use as usual he then said he would be up on Wednesday and I shall accordingly be ready with it for that day but yours of today makes me doubt lest James should be mistaken but upon calling him this instant he preserves that Guy promised to be up on Wednesday.*

Cranston details a number of other consignments of food sent by carrier from London to Hastings.

> *Having a present made me last week of a pott of charr* [small freshwater fish] *which is esteemed a great rarity in this part of the world, it being the produce of Westmorland only, I yesterday sent it by the carrier to the port, having never seen or tasted any of it before myself. Tis at last agreed on all hands that Sir Robert* [Walpole, Prime Minister] *resigns this day.* [6 February 1742]
> *I yesterday sent by the carrier your tea, coffee, chocolate, sturgeon, brawn for a share of which I return thanks, and a lamb all which I hope will arrive safe.* [23 December 1742]

Brawn was the flesh of a pig's or boar's head that had been boiled and then pickled or potted in its own jelly. Collier also sends food to Mary in Hastings by the carrier:

> *I had last Thursday a present of a large pot of pickled oysters which is sent by Guy though opened and I think pretty good but I forgot to tell Patrick to put carriage and porterage paid but that you'll supply* [1 May 1742].

Interestingly, one of the local carriers was a woman – Dame Palmer - who operated between Hastings and Battle as well as elsewhere in Sussex. In 1731 she was carrying shoes from John Collier in Hastings to Jacky who was at prep-school in Battle: "*I desire him to send us some shoes which he promised to do by Dame Palmer"*, wrote Jacky.

Ten years later when the Collier daughters were in their late teens and early 20s, they spent a good deal of time in Battle staying with friends or their relatives, the Worges. The local social life seems to have been rather better than in Hastings. This Dame Palmer was still working, and was pressed into service, carrying gowns backwards and forwards, as Cordelia records writing to her Mother in January 1741:

> *Next Wednesday is fixed for Mrs Tilden's Ball, so hope you will send my white clothes by Pallmer; my purple hand-kerchief is here and my sister is to lend me a short apron...*

There was another method of transporting goods, and sometimes people, between the south coast and the capital, and that was by boat. The main 'coaster' plying between Hastings and London was a sloop called the Cordelia whose master was James Bossom. Bossom appears to have been a personal friend of the Colliers. He was certainly a leading man in the town, a freeman, jurat, and chamberlain. In 1737 Collier records that:

> *James Bossom and his wife dined with my brother* [Cranston] *a Thursday.*

One of Collier's schemes to improve the facilities in Hastings involved piping water from the upper reaches of the Bourne directly to people's homes. As we shall see in chapter 14 it was not uncontroversial, and eventually involved Collier in a protracted lawsuit.

A Carrier's Waggon by Thomas Rowlandson (detail) around 1785. Courtesy YCBA

It was Bossom who transported the pipes down from London:

> *Master Bossom designs to sail tomorrow. I hope he will bring down some pipes for the water ... there's a box of china and glasses a small box of candles, two close stools and a few other things aboard Bossom.* [26 June 1740]

Later the same year Collier is telling Mary of another Consignment coming to her from London:

> *I presume master Bossom will be at Hastings before me. There is on board him currants and spices (there are no raisins this year, being the growth of Spain and therefore a prohibition) a Cheshire cheese, candles, a flitch of bacon, a small box of china. A box of stationary, paper etc., a table a little chest of drawers and a screen... I begin to be very weary of this hurly burly uncomfortable place and wish myself at home with you.* [25 Nov 1740]

The lack of Spanish raisins was due to the fact that, in 1740, England was involved in two conflicts with Spain, one as part of the 'War of Jenkins' Ear' and the other being the War of the Austrian Succession.

Given the state of the roads it might have been thought that travelling by sea would be preferable to the overland route to or from London. In fact there are few references to sea journeys – and then generally only for servants and children:

It's at present settled that my sister's maid is to goe down with Master Bossom the next time he comes up. [Collier to Mary - 29 June 1738].

Then in May 1740 William Cranston writes to Collier referring to advice from his sister Mary about his son Jemmy who is to make the sea trip:

I think my sister's thoughts of tyeing Jemmy to some part of the vessel will be right and hope twill be put into execution, for twill be terribly melancholy for him to sit all the while in the cabbin as well as very unsafe to be lose on deck. Therefore this middle way will be right to steer and he must be told that upon these terms and no other he may see the open air, of which you'll be so good as to acquaint master Bossom and I hope he'll observe them.

James Cranston would have been about seven years old at the time, and there's a delightful irony to the story. A few years later Collier helped him obtain a commission in the Royal Navy and the boy who'd been roped to the Cordelia on its way to Hastings from London later rose to become a distinguished naval Captain.

Bossom's name appears frequently in the Collier correspondence and eventually it seems that the two families were involved in a business deal that turned sour. James Bossom, his brother Nicholas and John Collier were co-owners of a vessel – possibly a fishing boat – named the Charming Molly apparently after Collier's daughter Mary.

James Bossom wrote to Collier in February 1757 about his brother's failure to honour his part of the business deal. It's interesting to note how different is the spelling and the style of writing from Collier's epistles.

> *I am sorry that I am a blige to a Quaint you that my Brother Nicholas and I have met and I Desired him to Settell a Count for the Charming Molly, which he refuses to do. On that denial I have taken the vesell into my Custerday, which I a Quaint you of the same and desire you and the rrest of the Howners what is best to be done with her.*

Collier rarely loses his temper or his cool in his correspondence, but in his reply to Bossom, he fairly lets rip about Nicholas and his character:

> *It's to no purpose to write anything about the wretch you know how he has served me and how many letters I have sent to so worthless a creature ... the first costs and earnings of my part must be at least £100, and by fair account I'll spend such another sum to make him an example ... & if he is falsified in any one instance he shall be transported as a felon for 7 years – his usage has been so base that nothing shall stop my resentment till I receive full satisfaction or rid the country of a very great Rascal.*

There was a postscript to James Bossom's letter to Collier. It concerned the youngster he'd had to tie to the deck of his sloop seventeen years earlier:

> *I have ad ye pleasure of seeing Mr Cranston often ... I don't know a man better respected in ye Navey, and if please god will make a fine officer.*

§§§

**Who's Who: Chapter 7   Communication –
Horses, Carts and Boats.**

Jacky (John) Collier, eldest son, died 1732 aged 12
Jemmy (James) Collier, second son, died 1747 aged 26
Dely - Cordelia Collier, eldest daughter 1722-1779
Mary Collier, their mother.
William Cranston, Mary Collier's brother and John's London partner
James Cranston, his eldest son. Later Captain, Royal Navy
Thomas Godley, Manager and postmaster Hastings Post Office 1742
John Geery. Hastings Postmaster until 1733
Mr Halsted, employee of Hastings Post Office applied to succeed John Geery
Duke of Newcastle, Sussex Landowner, Whig Politician and benefactor of Collier
William Coppard, Hastings Mayor 1727, 1735, 1742, 1746, 1751
George Worge, Battle Solicitor. Collier's son-in-law from first marriage
James Bossom, 1688-1764. Boat owner and carrier between Hastings and London. Freeman and Jurat of Hastings. Sometime friend of Collier's.
Nicholas Bossom. His ne'er-do-well brother co-owner of boat with Collier

Chapter 8

Life in London

On 25th February 1740 John Collier in London wrote to Mary in Hastings:

> *I begin to be very weary of this hurly burly uncomfortable place & wish myself at home with you ...*

For the past decade Collier had spent nearly four months of each year in London, his sojourns coinciding with the Westminster law terms, Hilary, Easter, Trinity and Michaelmas.

So what was his life like in the capital? Indeed what was the city like in the early to mid 18th century? Let's walk with him down Fleet Street as he makes his way home from the Court of the King's Bench which has been sitting, as usual, in Westminster Hall

His lodgings are in the City of London, and he crosses the boundary from the City of Westminster at Temple Bar. This is a Baroque ornamental arched gateway designed by Christopher Wren and erected in 1672, six years after the great fire. It's situated just beyond St Clement Danes church where the Strand meets Fleet Street, immediately to the south of the modern Royal Courts of Justice. However architecturally attractive, the Bar is just that - a physical restriction to entering the City. It has one wide central arch – though not sufficiently wide to allow two carriages to pass at the same time – and, on either side, smaller arches for pedestrians. Thus there is, inevitably, a queue of carriages, carts, horses and sedan chairs waiting to pass and a crowd of people pushing and shoving their way through the narrow side openings.

The great fire didn't reach up as far as here so, as we wait our turn, we can examine the buildings through the arch. Many are old and half-timbered, with upper stories jettying out over the street and with gable-ends adorned with quaint carvings and ornately patterned plaster. On our right is The Devil Tavern, a large and rambling building reputed to have nineteen fireplaces. Here you might find – at different dates of course, the literati of the day, including John Evelyn, Ben Jonson, John Aubery, Jonathan Swift, Oliver Goldsmith, James Boswell and Dr Johnson. We'll pass under the inn sign which depicts the devil's nose being tweaked by pincers wielded by St Dunstan

We find the street has no pavement, and only rough stone as a road surface, so we jostle with riders and horse-drawn transport. We want to avoid being splashed because it's not just mud in the puddles and the channel that flows down the centre of the road, but effluent too. There are no sewers at this time and waste is generally thrown straight onto the street from chamber pots. In summer the stench is appalling. In winter the air is thick with smoke and soot. Coal fires are the only form of heating. In 1727, more than 700,000 pounds of coal was burned in London.

On either side, the street is busy with commerce. And most enterprises advertise themselves with a large hanging board outside – like the Devil inn sign. These are not always stable and in high winds come can crashing down, sometimes with catastrophic consequences for those beneath.

On the 2nd of December, 1718, a signboard opposite Bride Lane, Fleet Street, having

Temple Bar Gate from a mid-18th century print

loosened the brickwork by its weight and movement, suddenly gave way, fell, and brought the house down with it, killing four persons, one of whom was the queen's jeweller. (Old and New London Volume 1)

We're going to join John for a dish of coffee in his favourite haunt, the Sussex Coffee house just off the main thoroughfare. But if we didn't like this establishment there are plenty of alternatives. Coffee has become the drink of the age since its introduction by a young Greek, Pasqua Rosee, in 1652. By the 1730s, there were more than 550 coffee houses in London - 132 of them here in Fleet Street – indeed early eighteenth-century London is reputed to have more coffee houses than any other city in the western world, save Constantinople. According to an article in the *National Review*, you generally choose yours by its clientele:

Every profession, trade, class, party, had its favourite Coffee-house. The lawyers discussed law or literature, criticized the last new play at Nando's or the Grecian, both close on the purlieus of the Temple. Here the young bloods of the Inns-of-Court paraded their Indian gowns and lace caps of a morning, and swaggered in their lace coats and Mechlin ruffles at night, after the theatre. The Cits met to discuss the rise and fall of stocks, and to settle the rate of insurance at Garraway's or Jonathan's; the parsons exchanged university gossip, or commented on Dr. Sacheverell's last sermon at Truby's or at Child's in St. Paul's Churchyard; the St. James's and the

Smyrna were the head-quarters of the Whig politicians, while the Tories frequented the Cocoa-tree or Ozinda's, all in St. James's-street; and the leading wits gathered at Will's, Button's, or Tom's, in Great Russell-street, where after the theatre was playing at piquet and the best of conversation till midnight. At all these places... smoking was allowed. A penny was laid down at the bar on entering, and the price of a dish of tea or coffee seems to have been two-pence: this charge covered newspapers and lights. The established frequenters of the house had their regular seats, and special attention from the fair lady at the bar, and the tea or coffee boys.

So we are now heading for the coffee house where those with Sussex connections tend to gather. Conveniently it's just across the road from Collier's lodgings and finds its way into many of his letters. Most poignant perhaps is from his letter to Mary on 17th February 1733:

The poor woman that kept the Sussex coffee house dyed last Sunday morning and has left 4 young children in a miserable condition everything being seized. It has been a little talked about to make a collection for to put out one of them which I shall readily come into.

William Cranston refers to it as 'our' coffee house, and Collier held birthday parties for his son Jemmy at the

Sussex and seems to have used it as a sort of home from home, as he wrote to Mary in 1743:

> *I have just been at the Coffee house and intend on finishing this letter to be there again.*

Along with many others Collier had his mail delivered there, and The Sussex was a centre of news from, and gossip about, friends, colleagues and acquaintances from the south coast:

> *I heard yesterday that Mr Wardroper* [former Town Clerk and future Mayor of Winchelsea] *who has been in town almost as long as I, brought up with him Holt's wife of Peasmarsh and took lodgings in Hatton Garden. It seems it's an old intrigue. I see him every day at the Coffee house and he has dined here 2 or 3 times but nothing has been hinted ... this must be condemned by all.*

Coffee houses are also the news outlets of the day. It was usual for patrons to be seated round a communal table, expected to converse with each other, exchanging news, opinions and political argument. As newspapers grew in popularity they became a key attraction of the coffee houses. In 1702 Britain's first daily newspaper, the Daily Courant, was published from premises on the Eastern bank of the River Fleet. By the mid 1730s, 31 titles ranging from dailies to weeklies are being sold on the streets of London. They had a combined weekly circulation of around 100,000 – making an astounding estimated readership of some 2 million.

A letter from young James Collier to his mother in Hastings in January 1741 gives a real sense of the political discourse in the coffee houses and the importance of newspapers therein:

> *As the opposition in the House of Commons is at present very strong on those days in which the votes are expected down, the coffee houses are crowded, and happy is the man who can seize on them first, tho' sometimes he is forced to read out to a gaping attentive audience, to prevent their being snatched out of his hands before he has completely finished.*

We need to be careful after we leave The Sussex and cross Fleet Street. The crime rate is high in early Georgian London. There's a marked division between rich and poor and the latter are not averse to robbing the former on the street. William Cranston records in January 1733 that his wife Mary's watch was *'stole from her side this morning in Fleet Street'*. However we successfully negotiate our way across the road, avoiding pick-pockets, carts and carriages as well as the open sewer running down to the Fleet 'river'. We turn left once on the north side of Fleet Street and after a few dozen yards take a little alley on our right. This is Johnson's Court, opening out on a paved space with tall Jacobean houses on all sides. Although the famous lexicographer Samuel Johnson did live here, that was not until 1765, so the courtyard was not named after him but rather Thomas Johnson, a City tailor, whose residence was here during the reign of Elizabeth I.

Collier has lodgings at the home of his brother-in-law William Cranston who it seems he had helped into a career in the law, subsequently making him his defacto legal partner in London. William Cranston chose to live full-time in town and, after he'd completed his apprenticeship in 1726, moved into rooms in Johnson's Court where Collier was already renting chambers or office space while he was in London. There Cranston brought his first wife Mary Swaysland after their marriage in 1732, and together they raised their children James and John. Whenever John Collier was in town he lived with them at number 4, and almost all of his letters from London are written from that address.

It's hard to work out the precise domestic arrangements - there are few clues in the letters. A sense of the scale of the houses in the court can be gleaned from James Boswell's description of Dr Johnson's lodgings at number 9 a few years later:

> *I returned to London in Februray (1766) and Found Dr Johnson in a good house in Johnson's Court, Fleet Styreet, in which he had accomodated Miss Williams with an apartment on the ground floor while Mr Levett occupied his post in the garett.*

It seems that, before Cranston's marriage, Collier recommended some alterations to the apartments which the former failed to commission. Indeed it appears he was reluctant to discuss his forthcoming nuptials or to organise the domestic staff, as Collier told Mary in November 1731 upon his arrival in London:

> *I found my brother very well and Johnson's court just the same viz noe alterations in the house and noe manner of notice has*

Dr Johnson's House.
Cranston's and Collier's dwelling at number 4 - since
demolished - was just around the corner to the left of
the picture

been taken to me of the match. There is noe
servant in the room of Nicholas so that Mrs
Alice and her helper are all in all.

Two days later he adds that they are expecting a visit from the mother of Cranston's intended:

Yesterday I dined at home with my brother
[Cranston] and the match came on the
carpet and we had it thoroughly over. I find
it goes forward, and Mrs Swayland is to be
in town next week to settle the affairs, but
I believe noe time is as yet fixed for the
marriage, nor nothing done to the house,
etc, which really wants.

However some alterations at number 4 were subsequently commissioned, as Collier records in a letter to Mary the following June:

I find the workmen have almost finished
and I think great alterations for the best.

Since we know he addressed both his domestic and professional letters from Johnson's Court and there is no mention of Collier having any other office or business premises in London, it would seem probable that Cranston's house served as both a domestic lodging and office. Perhaps Collier occupied the apartment on the ground floor that Boswell described at Dr Johnson's house just round the corner. In any event this was his base in London from the late 1720s until he effectively gave up his London practice and retired to Hastings at the end of the 1740s or beginning of the 1750s. It's also where his sons John and James spent their school holidays under the care of the Cranstons. Indeed it's where both boys went down with the Smallpox at Christmas 1732 (See chapter 3).

It seems the Cranstons occasionally used John Collier's own rooms in Johnston's court when he was in Hastings, or in the event of some domestic problem or other:

> The bugs have been very strong in my
> sister's bedchamber, so they have layn in
> my room this month.

Although Collier hankered after Hastings – as he professed to Mary in countless letters – he clearly did enjoy some of the entertainments that London had to offer. As a young man even while he was wooing Mary he was telling her about his visits to the theatre in a decidedly jocular fashion:

> I was in Lincolns Inn Playhouse a friday
> night to see the Plain Dealer [by
> Wycherley] acted. I did not intend to goe
> but was prevailed on by the Intreaties of
> the person whose benefit it was for who
> was formerly a goldsmith of our Trade. I
> found Trumble in the pit with three young
> ladies none of which I knew, but I have
> assured him that, unless a large Bribe, I
> will acquaint cousin Mercy. [26 June 1716]

The theatre was a few minutes' walk to the north-west of Fleet Street in Lincoln's Inn Fields, a fashionable and agreeable open space. This had been laid out in the 1630s by a speculator, William Newton, from original plans by Inigo Jones. Theatrical performances had been banned during the sixteen years of Cromwell's Commonwealth, but upon the restoration of Charles II, theatre flourished and there was a rush for new venues. A tennis court on Portugal Street to the south of the Fields was hastily converted and opened as the first Duke's Theatre in 1662. However it soon moved to purpose-built premises In Dorset Gardens by the Thames. But in 1714 the Theatre Royal, also known as the Lincoln's Inn Fields Theatre, opened on the same spot. It seems to have become a favourite of Collier's from when he first arrived in London:

> *I was last night at the playhouse in Lincoln's inn to see the dramatic Opera called the Island Princess orb the Generous Portuguese. We had interludes of musick singing and dancing, very fine, but was surprised at the performance of a little boy and girle not above 5 or 6 years old in Dancing which at present carries the applause of the Towne and is very uncommon.* [29 November 1716]

Were we to travel back in time to early Georgian London and visit a play with Collier we would hardly recognize the experience. Alcohol and food were consumed throughout the performance and people came and went at will. It was not unknown for actors to be pelted with food. Audiences were noisy and had little or no respect for what was happening on stage, as James Boswell recalled in his Hebridean Journal:

> *...in the pit of Drury-lane play-house, in a wild freak of youthful extravagance, I entertained the audience PRODIGIOUSLY,*

by imitating the lowing of a cow. I was so successful in this boyish frolick, that the universal cry of the galleries was, 'Encore the cow! Encore the cow!'

A German writer, Sophie la Roche, visiting London around the same time recalled a visit to Sadler's Wells:

The scenes in the pit and boxes we found as strange as the ten-fold comedy itself. In the pit there is a shelf running along the back of the seats on which the occupants order bottles of wine, glasses, ham, cold chops and pasties to be placed, which they consume with their wives and children, partaking while they watch the same play. The front seats of the boxes are just the same. In three hours we witnessed nine kinds of stage craft. First, a comedy, then a ballet, followed by a rope-walker, after this a pantomime, next some balancing tricks, an operette, and the most miraculous feats by a strong man; another comedy, and finally a second operette. All the decorations were exceedingly well painted, the dresses very fine and the music good.

Detail from The Laughing Audience.
William Hogarth's view of the Drury Lane Theatre
1733

Despite its rowdy – and sometimes bawdy – reputation, the theatre was a place to see, and be seen by, the nobility - both British and foreign. In November 1731 Francis Stephen, the Duke of Lorraine, later to be the Holy Roman Emperor visited London and his host, King George II, took him to the Lincoln's Inn theatre to see Thomas Betterton's restoration comedy the Amorous Widow. Among the audience that night was John Collier:

> *By the last post I wrote you word of going to the play to see the Duke of Lorrain. We were in 5 minutes after 4 and if we had been 5 minutes later could not have got a place. The King and Queen and 5 princesses were there and numerous audience and it was past 11 before the play and entertainment was over, so that I was heartily Tired and got a little cold. The Duke of Lorrain is a young good-looking man, dressed very plain, and not at all like the Modern Butterfly.*

The London theatre scene during Collier's period was certainly vibrant and undoubtedly popular. The impresario John Rich had taken over the Lincoln's Inn Theatre from his father. One of his greatest managerial coups was to premiere the Beggar's opera at the Fields in 1728, where it ran for an almost unprecedented 62 consecutive performances. Rich subsequently moved to the Theatre Royal, Covent Garden and so began a famous rivalry with the other Theatre Royal at Drury Lane. Collier records how his son James attended a performance at Covent Garden in November 1740:

He is gone to the play tonight. The King is to be there and the countess Yarmouth is also expected and that the house will be full by four. I think he mentioned our being to see the new actress and the fine dancer Signora Barberini.

At one point John Rich hired, for a few performances, an up-and-coming young actor named David Garrick. It is a pity he wasn't able to put him under contract because Garrick rapidly became a huge star on the stage, and a noted theatrical producer off it. Indeed he became a co-manager of the Drury Lane Theatre Royal in 1747, and rapidly turned it into the leading playhouse in town.

However, five years earlier, Garrick had been invited to act at Drury Lane for a one-off Royal Command performance. And John Collier had the good fortune to be there on that historic night – even if he had to fight for seats that footmen were reserving for their employers, and his daughters, who were staying with him in London at the time, missed out altogether:

T. [Thomas] *Green and I went to the play to see Mr Garrick it was debated whether to fetch Molly and Jenny but the company considering the warm weather were against it and if had been done it was impossible to have got them in, for I never saw a more crowded audience of good company. The Duke* [of Cumberland] [Princess] *Amelia and* [Princess] *Caroline were there and we*

David Garrick playing Richard III
Detail from a 1745 painting by William Hogarth

in the little gallery over the stage box on the opposite side tho' that was taken up & Footmen in possession but by good words and promise to resign when the ladys came we kept possession the front seat the first act and then only 2 ladys, that we had the second the whole play and Mr Webster came in in the second act and we had a good deal of discourse between the acts. The play was Richard the Third - King Richard by Garrick. The Justest Actor I ever saw the House Extremely hot I was at home before half an hour after nine.

Outside the theatres, the main entertainment of early Georgian London was undoubtedly to be found within the pleasure gardens. Here, in little oases of verdant calm, rich and poor, nobility and tradespeople, could walk and talk in peace and listen to music, watch entertainers of all sorts and, occasionally, be thrilled by fireworks.

Although a few had existed earlier, pleasure gardens began to proliferate following the restoration in 1660. Initially they were simply formal gardens serving refreshments which were open to the public – for a price. A number were attached to taverns, tea rooms and spas. As time went on they became larger and more sophisticated. In 1691 Boydell Cuper opened an altogether more ambitious affair on Bankside. Dozens of others followed suit and by the 1750 there were thirty or more such gardens dotted round the edges of the conurbation. Two, however, stood out for their magnificence and – possibly as a result – for their elevated clientele: Vauxhall and Ranelagh.

Vauxhall Spring Gardens were undergoing a facelift in the early 1730s - apparently at the suggestion of William Hogarth - with the introduction of *Ridottos al Fresco* – an outdoors ball or dance often in masquerade.

It seems that John Collier was at the first, or one of the first, to be held at Vauxhall in June 1732. He was clearly not unduly impressed:

> *The Ridotto at Spring Gardens is a little talked of, but I find did not extremely take (to it). There were ten men to a woman, and thought none of the last but prostitutes, the P of Wales was there but went away in two hours. There is to be another next week but it is not thought that any good company will be increased.*

Either this put him off the whole experience, or he was insufficiently impressed to write about further visits until five years later. But in May 1737 an impromptu family outing was organised – though it didn't include a somewhat reluctant Mary Cranston who, nonetheless, seems to have resented being left behind:

> *I have been at Vauxhall where there is great improvements of the musick. The Prince of Wales was there with a party that night but not the princess. It was last Saturday night being a sudden motion. Mr Fuller, Coppinger, Brother Cranston and myself and Jemmy. My sister not a little affronted, I believe about it – with my brother at her not going tho she had complained the whole day - & I don't know whether she yet knows the prince was*

*there. We accidentally went with them on
the Water from about Westminster and
there was a music boat with trumpets and
French horns that made it very agreeable.*

The last sentence is interesting in that, before the
opening of Westminster Bridge in 1750, the main –
indeed almost the only - method of approaching the
South Bank pleasure gardens was by boat, and the craft
containing the Collier party had clearly shadowed that of
the Prince of Wales as they rowed down the river.
Certainly the presence of royalty, or indeed, nobility,
increased the attraction of the Pleasure Gardens and
helped justify the fairly hefty cost of admission - around
one guinea for the Ridottos. We find Collier grumbling
that some visits were deficient on this score.

*I was last night at Vauxhall with my bro &
sister & Mr Nouns. There were an
abundance of people but not many of the
Tip Top company.* [1 July 1738.]

Perhaps because of the cost, visits to the Pleasure
Gardens seem to have been infrequent. But as Collier's
children got older and began to visit him in London they
wrote to their mother in Hastings about their
experiences.

*I write with great pleasure to let you know
that we with Mr Coles, family etc eleven in
number, were last night at Vauxhall where
we were most agreeably entertained and
supped very elegantly. I believe there were
more lamps since you saw it and the
pavilions one of which is exceeding grand
and altogether I think it far preferable to*

116

Ranelagh especially in hot weather. I went in my pink gown, but it really was hardly good enough for it is not almost white as I have been forced to wear it constant. [17 June 1742 Molly Collier to Mary in Hastings]

The drawback, of course to *al fresco* entertainment was the British weather. Vauxhall, it seemed, only opened its doors from the beginning of May each year. However an enterprising theatrical impresario James Lacy hit upon the idea of having an indoor arena and so raised £36,000 by public subscription to build a huge rotunda at Ranelagh, just south of the Royal Hospital in Chelsea. It was modelled on the Pantheon in Rome, but was larger, built of wood and decorated with burnished gold and fake marble. It had a massive fireplace in the centre to warm winter visitors. Horace Walpole attended the opening in April 1742, remarking that it totally beat Vauxhall and *"you can't set your foot without treading on a Prince or Duke of Cumberland. Nobody goes anywhere else."*

Walpole's sentiment was not entirely shared by the Colliers. Molly, as we've seen, found the rotunda too hot in summer. And a month after it opened, John wrote to Mary:

There was a ridotto last night at Ranelaugh Gardens but I have heard there was indifferent company there, and great numbers at Vauxhall

1737 Print from a music sheet of a song titled
The Adieu to the Spring-Gardens

George Bickham the Younger, after Gravelot

And the following month William Cranston wrote to Collier in Hastings that Vauxhall was *"exceedingly pleasant – the water still as a pond - & it vastly exceeds Ranelagh"*. But James Collier seems to have disagreed, even if he personally remained loyal to his old stomping ground.

> *On Saturday next [a large party] is to go to Vauxhall. At present Raneleagh is the politest place, all the great people going there, and since the late robbery near Newington turnpike, nobody has ventured in a coach to the former place.* [31 May 1744]

Even though Collier was arranging a different outing the following month, he seems to have agreed that Ranelagh was winning the competition for attracting the 'best' people.

> *I treated Jemmy and Jacky at Cuper's gardens who were both extremely pleased at the fireworks and indeed the taste in which they are done is so curious and uncommon that the gravest man in the temple need not be ashamed to cross the water and see them. I have not lately been at Ranelagh but am informed that the amphitheater is crowded every night with the best of company.* [16 June 1744]

So with his 'home from home' at the Sussex coffee house, and with visits to the theatre and, occasionally, to the various pleasure gardens, Collier seems to have led a reasonably active life during his quarterly sojourns in

London. Throughout his life he was a keen churchgoer and appears regularly to have attended services at St Bride's in Fleet Street and occasionally at St Paul's just a short walk up Ludgate Hill. But in his letters he seems always to be hankering after Hastings. There are dozens of references to being weary of life in the city, and impatient to return to Mary on the south coast. At the end of each law term he's busy planning his return journey and arranging for his groom to bring his horse up to Sevenoaks so he can meet it from the coach and ride the remainder of the way home along the atrocious roads. As we shall see life in London becomes more attractive once his children are either at school there or, in Jacky's case, embarking on a career in the law. But from all the hints in his letters Collier seems much to have preferred the undoubtedly quieter life in Sussex with Mary to the 'hurly burly' of the city.

§§§

Who's Who Chapter 8, Life in London

William Cranston – Mary Collier's younger brother. John Collier's legal partner based in London. John Collier always refers to William as 'my brother' rather than brother-in-law.

Mary Cranston nee Swaysland. William's first wife

Jemmy (James) Cranston **Jacky** (John) **Cranston**, their sons – not to be confused with Jackie (John) and Jemmy (James) Collier – John's sons

Anthony Trumble, solicitor and friend of Collier's

Mr Green(e) Senior and Junior. A Mr Green is mentioned frequently in the letters, particularly in those from Cranston and James Collier. But it's not always clear which Green is being referred to. Thomas or Tommy seems to have been 'the young Mr Green' who it seems was a contemporary of James Collier and clearly a close family friend as he regularly accompanies them on outings. Mr Green senior, his father, was a friend of John Collier who, in November 1734 invited him, his wife and his son to dinner at Johnson's court. Green seems to have had land in Norfolk, and it looks as if Collier was an executor of his will and loaned his estate a considerable sum of money.

Edwin Wardroper town clerk and later mayor of Winchelsea, dubbed a '*Rye Beau,*' by Cranston and was, by all accounts, a bit of a rake. Supported by Newcastle he opposed James Lamb's mayoral hold on Rye and, despite his morals, was a friend and colleague of Collier's. He held offices in the Customs as Collier's deputy, acting as sub agent for the eastern part of Sussex. He died Boulogne 1771.

Dr Samuel Johnson 1709–1784 poet, playwright, essayist, moralist, literary critic, biographer, editor and lexicographer made famous by Boswell.

James Boswell 1740 – 1795, Scottish biographer and diarist. Best known for the biography of his friend and contemporary Samuel Johnson,

James Collier. John and Mary's second son. Nicknamed Jemmy.

Francis Stephen, the Duke of Lorraine 1708 –1765. Holy Roman Emperor and Grand Duke of Tuscany. Founder of the Habsburg-Lorraine dynasty. In 1737 he traded the duchy of Lorraine to the former king of Poland in exchange for the Grand Duchy of Tuscany .

David Garrick 1717–1779 popular actor, playwright, theatre manager and producer, immensely influential on 18th Century theatre. A pupil and friend of Dr Samuel Johnson.

Chapter 9

Patronage of the Pelhams

John Collier's considerable rise in status and wealth was, as we saw in Chapter 6, largely due to the patronage of the Pelhams and in particular the great Whig 'fixer' Thomas Pelham-Holles, Duke of Newcastle. His brother, Henry Pelham, a government minister, had told the Duke in September 1733 that if Prime Minister Sir Robert Walpole had a mind to have two Whigs chosen at Hastings, Newcastle *'must provide handsomely for Collier'*. This was duly done. The previous winter, February 1732, the Duke had told Collier he should have the *'little place dropped in the law that I would gladly accept'* which was that of Cryer and Usher of the King's Bench – effectively a sinecure often worth some £100 a year. Additionally, Newcastle made Collier land agent for all the Pelham family estates in Sussex as well as his election agent. Then, in November, the Duke obtained for Collier the lucrative post Surveyor General of Riding Officers for Kent. This was worth some between £200 and £400 a year and came with an office and staff in Hastings. Taken together these posts were both for services rendered and to keep Collier completely 'on side' for the future.

To our modern way of thinking payments on this scale might be thought extremely questionable – if not overtly corrupt. In the mid 18th century however it was pretty much standard practice. As we shall see the tiny number of people eligible to vote could be – and often were - easily manipulated or bribed by the offer of lucrative government jobs.

Having accepted Newcastle's sinecures and positions, Collier was left with a problem - how to ensure that the marginal seat of Hastings remained firmly for the Whigs in the forthcoming 1734 election. The first thing was to know who was on which side and, if necessary, provide some 'incentives' - as Collier outlined in his letter to Newcastle in the late summer of 1733:

> *I had the honor to receive your grace's commands of the 14th and have, in obedience, thereto made out and inclosed a list and present situation of this town, and have no reason to doubt that I have given the opponents all their votes and the five mentioned as dubious think shall not fayle of three or four of them and more especially Fellowes firmly fixed if he is to be appointed mate of the Rye Customs sloop. Your grace may depend that though there is such a majority, I shall not be too sanguine and behave to all as if the numbers were a greater equaling.* [16 August 1733]

There was a second problem: the county elections. Although the 203 English boroughs returned 405 members of Parliament, each of the 40 English counties also returned two members, generally at an election held a little later.

The franchise was somewhat different, encompassing '40 shilling' freeholders plus lease-holders for life. As far as Hastings was concerned, being a relatively poor fishing and trading town, this property qualification meant there were actually fewer electors locally for the county seats than for the town ones.

Overall, though, the country electors were much more widely dispersed, making them a more difficult group to 'fix'. As a result Newcastle went to extraordinary lengths - and extraordinary expense - to ensure that his brother Henry Pelham and James Butler were elected in Sussex. Initially, however, there had been some doubts about their popularity. In his letter to Newcastle, Collier sought to offer reassurances:

The country hereabouts stands very well. There is some discourse that Rye will be much against your grace's interest, but I have not yet been there ... I will soon send you grace a list of our freeholders and how it's believed they will stand.

Two days later Collier was as good as his word, sending Newcastle a list of those whom he believed would vote the Whig way. 96 were 'actually promised' he told the Duke, while he had an 'absolute denial' from only about 20. Newcastle asked him to shore up the votes and Collier told him he had paid two visits to the 'houses where your friends met' and laid out an 'extravagant sum' in expenses totalling just over £119. But Collier noted that the other side was busy trying secure support for the ultimately unsuccessful Whistler Webster

Last Wednesday an invitation was given to the wives of the mayor, jurats and freemen to breakfast at Mr Broadway's and proceed to dine with Lady Webster that day at Fairlight. There were about 16 went. Thursday last there was an entertainment to the freeholders of some

neighbouring parishes at a little alehouse in Fairlight Down ... Tarried till about 3 or 4 o'clock in the morning. But I don't hear or believe a convert was made. [10 November 1733]

So it would seem even lavish entertainment was not always successful in turning voters' heads. But the Tories hit on another way to try to combat the Whig supremacy which was to have far reaching ramifications for Hastings, its Corporation and its citizens.

Under the arcane rules of the day in most boroughs, and certainly in the Cinque Ports, only freemen were enfranchised to vote for the town's MPs. The question in Hastings was, who were entitled to have the 'freedom of the town' and how were they chosen? If the Tories could increase the number of voters and ensure the newcomers supported them, then there was a chance that Hastings would cease to be a 'treasury' borough in the pocket of the Duke of Newcastle. It was, therefore, Collier's job as the Duke's agent, to oppose any such moves and ensure the electoral role remained as low as possible.

Now into our story comes the enigmatic figure of Sir Thomas Webster. Born just a few years before Collier, Webster was the son of a London clothier so wealthy that, aged only 21, he was able to buy the estate of Copped Hall in Essex for £20,000. He was determined to get into Parliament and after a few unsuccessful elections he finally won the seat of Colchester in 1705 under the Whig banner. However the poll was challenged by his Tory opponents, claiming he'd falsified the number of freemen entitled to vote for him and he was expelled from parliament in 1711. He stood again two years later, was re-elected and again challenged, and again expelled.

William Hogarth's view of a pre-election dinner
Detail from 'The Humours of an Election' 1755

With this background you might have thought that Sir Thomas would have grounds heartily to dislike all Tories. But after he purchased Battle Abbey in 1721 and Bodiam Castle the following year, he seems to have fallen in with local Sussex gentry including John Fuller and Sir Cecil Bishop, and to have switched political sympathies. In the 1730s his son, Whistler Webster, stood as the Tory candidate in Hastings. It is a moot point whether Sir Thomas genuinely believed in extending the franchise by creating more freemen. He could have been motivated by his resentment of the Whigs in parliament for failing to support him in his time of trouble or it may just have been to support his son. In any event Sir Thomas took up the Tory cause locally by supporting and funding a lawsuit on behalf of a Hastings man who had been denied the freedom of the town. This was by way of a 'mandamus' - a judicial writ issued as a command to an inferior court or ordering a person to perform a public or statutory duty. In the words of the writ:

> *Whereas one John Sargent is of the age of one and twenty years and upwards and is the son of John Sargent deceased, late one of the freemen of the said town and port and was born after the admission and swearing of his said father into the place and office of one of the freemen of the said town and port. And whereas the said John Sargent by virtue thereof and according to the said custom ought by you to be admitted and sworn into the said place and office of one of the freemen.*

In Hastings this was not well received. The corporation regarded it as gross interference of their prerogative to choose their own freemen, while the Whig faction worried it could dilute their pool of supporters. The town's MP Sir William Ashburnham asked Collier and Cranston to intervene. Cranston replied to Sir William on 29 January 1734:

> *Immediately upon receipt of yours I went to Mr (Henry) Masterman who as you imagined is concerned for the other side ... I went also last night to the Attorney (General, Sir John Willes) and Solicitor (General, Sir Dudley Ryder) and saw both of em, the first would not take a retainer not knowing whether he could attend ... as to the other he would on no terms attend ... as he was very little conversant with the court of the King's Bench I don't apprehend he could do you much good.... Masterman tells me Sir T (Thomas Webster) is very hot and believes he will push it to the utmost.*

As it happened, consulting the leading solicitor for the other side – Henry Masterman – and even lobbying the most senior government law officers did little good. But the judge sitting in the case gave greater cause for hope. Phillip Yorke's career in the legal profession had been nothing less than meteoric. He was called to the bar aged 25, appointed Solicitor General at 30, and made Lord Chief Justice of the King's Bench (taking the title Lord Hardwicke) thirteen years later in 1733. But more importantly he had been elected the Whig MP for Lewes in 1719 and was a close confidant of the Duke of Newcastle. However, according to Richard

Saville in his admirably detailed introduction to the *Letters of John Collier of Hastings*, the judge found for Sargent and ordered the Hastings Corporation immediately to admit him to the freedom 'according to the custom.' But even worse, Hardwicke also ruled in favour of one John Shorter who had claimed his freedom it on the grounds that he was married to the daughter of a freeman, Benjamin Meadow.

Saville observes that neither the Duke of Newcastle nor Sir William Ashburnham were prepared to let this pass. And so the stage was set for a major battle between Sir Thomas Webster and the Tories on the one hand and Newcastle and the Whigs on the other. Thomas Pelham, the other Hastings MP, wrote to John Collier at the end of January 1734:

> *My Lord Duke (of Newcastle) desires me to acquaint you that his Grace hopes you will take the effectual methods for preventing admission of any freemen by virtue of such mandamus's (sic) as you mention are already served on the mayor and jurats in favour or John Sargent and John Shorter.*

Collier and Cranston embarked on a lengthy discussion as to how they might achieve this. Writing home to Mary in February 1734, John seemed confident of the outcome:

> *Sir Thomas Webster has given himself very great airs about the mandamus's in Westminster Hall, but I believe there will be a disappointment to him and his party in that matter.*

However this view was misguided and the corporation failed to overturn the Hardwicke judgment. And worse was to come. Another man, Henry Moore also had his freedom request rejected and also received the backing of the Websters in taking the corporation to court. This case was to drag on for more than three years and had disastrous consequences for the town.

Before considering the Moore case, it's worth taking a pause and looking at the results of the 1734 election in Hastings and Sussex. On 29th April Hastings returned the two Whigs, Sir William Ashburnham and Thomas Pelham who got 50 votes apiece. Whistler Webster came third with 29 votes. In the Sussex County election Henry Pelham and James Butler were returned for the Whigs with 2,271 and 2,046 votes respectively, beating the Tories, John Fuller and Sir Cecil Bishop who polled 1,581 and 1,704 votes. So this was an undoubted triumph for the Newcastle faction. His brother retained his county seat and his cousin Thomas Pelham of Stanmer held on to Hastings. Of course this did no harm to John Collier as Newcastle's election agent and local fixer. A fascinating study of the 1734 elections in Sussex was conducted by Basil Williams in the English Historical Review of 1897, based on the letters of the Duke of Newcastle. He concludes:

Of bribery, corruption and intimidation, there is good evidence in these letters. Of all the forms of indirect corruption here exemplified, the most remarkable and the most inexcusable is the system of tampering with sentences on prisoners.

William Hogarth's view of voting at an election
Detail from 'The Polling' 1755

It seems that John Collier was directly implicated in this. Mr Williams uncovered a letter from him in August 1733 to Robert Burdett, a fellow election agent for the Duke in and around Lewes. Collier forwards a petition from sixty freeholders on behalf of a man called Thomas Black of Hastings who faced a sentence for some crime, quite possibly smuggling. The suggestion was that, should the Duke intervene on Black's behalf, the signatories to the petition would agree to vote for Pelham. Nothing in Collier's own correspondence appears to have survived to show how the petition was received or whether it was successful.

In the run-up to the election further concerted efforts were being made to widen the Hastings' franchise, as Collier noted in a letter to Newcastle on 18 April 1734:

> *Monday last in the afternoon 13 freemen's sons came to the Mayor when I was with him and demanded their freedom on the pretended usage. In an hour after, a person went round to the mayor, jurats etc and all the freemen with an invitation to meet Mr Webster at Chambers's next day .... Mr Eversfield came with Mr Webster to town; they came down last Saturday together from London by posthorses, and Jack Fuller came hither a little after them. The two former came to the Swan, sent out for the mayor, drunk a bottle of wine and expostulated ...that night there were 22 freemen's sons summoned together ... to demand their freedom.*

The Hastings Court of Record – basically the Corporation - that year dismissed their claims for freedom, and even John Sargent's application was deferred for a further two years – despite his successful Mandamus.

Then, the following year Sir Thomas brought the case of Henry Moor before the court. This turned out to be the most extraordinarily divisive event to hit Hastings perhaps in the whole of Collier's lifetime and resulted in a lengthy trial that occupied both Cranston and Collier for more than a year and led to the resignation – albeit temporary - of a number of Jurats and freemen.

Once again the question was, could a son of a Freeman automatically demand the freedom of the borough as a right? The official court transcript outlined the case:

> *Henry Moore is the plaintiff; and the mayor, jurats, and commonality of the town and port of Hastings, are the defendants ... this is a Mandamus, directed to the defendants, the mayor and jurats of that town and port, to admit and swear in the plaintiff Henry Moore into the place and office of one of the freeman of this town.*

But how to establish where such a right legally existed or whether it was up to the elected members of the corporation to decide? All the Cinque Ports maintained a Custumal – a record of traditions and privileges often going back to Norman times – or, at any rate, being written in Norman French.

Counsel for Henry Moore, the plaintiff, told the court that it was on the Custumal that their case hung:

This Customal is the rule and law of all the Cinque Ports. Gentlemen, this Customal is so old, and goes so far back as the year 1573; it contains 59 Articles ... by this 34th Article of this Customal you see what the ancient law and usage was; that the eldest son of every freeman, under these circumstances, is intituled to his freedom; and therefore, we say, that the plaintiff Henry Moore, as the eldest son of Samuel Moore, has, and he is undoubtedly intituled, under this right, to his freedom.

By today's standards the 'Case of Henry Moore, Plaintiff, against the Mayor, Jurats and Commonality of the Town and Port of Hastings' is a singularly long-winded affair turning on a very narrow point of 'custom and practice' rather than any statute. But that, of course, is the very basis of English common law and we are fortunate to have, through Collier's correspondence as well as the trial transcript, an insight into just how this worked in the early Georgian period. It had all started the previous year when, as Collier noted in one of his regular letters to a letter to Mary on 17 June 1735:

As Sir Thomas Webster goes on with one of his mandamus's (I) believe I can't come home without the greatest of hurry and fatigue until that is over. I find by your letter that it is the subject of conversation in Hasting and that his creatures have stamped success on the trial before it's over. I will not take upon me to be so positive but don't at present see any reason to despond...

So the corporation prepared its case and arranged for witnesses to attend the trial. A problem quickly emerged. Those in the best position to testify as to the prerogative of the town to confer freedom, would almost invariably be freemen themselves, and therefore barred from testifying because of the conflict of interest. So it was decided that a group of Jurats would resign for the duration of the case – in the hope and expectation of being later readmitted.

However, on the 27th June, Collier heard that *"Thomas Webster's heart failed him"* and he had withdrawn the case. Collier and Cranston immediately sent the express letter to Mayor William Coppard referred to in chapter 7.

Mayor Coppard now adopted a somewhat questionable ruse to find out who really opposed Collier and Newcastle and were thus in favour of admitting more freemen. The assembly had convened on the morning of 29th June. The potential witnesses duly offered their resignation and the Assembly adjourned for lunch. During the break Coppard was told about Collier's express letter, but deliberately failed to inform the reconvened meeting in the afternoon that Webster had withdrawn the case. A vote was held on a proposal to accept the resignations and allow the freemen to travel to London as witnesses. The result would clearly be irrelevant since the case was no longer happening, but by knowing who had voted against and 'refused to sign the book' provided the necessary information. That evening William Coppard wrote to Collier to inform him of events:

> *We adjourned until 2 in the afternoon. While we was at the Sawn ... received your express but determined to keep that*

as a secret till our going again to court [the assembly chamber] *that we might then know by their signing or refusing who were our friends and who not ... Captain Moore in a great passion in court stretched out his arm at full length and declared he would have his hand cut off rather than he would sign it.* [Coppard in Hastings to Collier in London 28 June 1735]

An analysis of the list of non-signatories is interesting in that it reveals that the factions were not necessarily divided along party lines. Thomas Moore himself (no relation to Captain Moore) and four of his supporters had, in fact, voted for Pelham in the '34 election, and not the Tory, Whistler Webster.

The court case to determine eligibility to be a Freeman of Hastings was relisted for the following summer and it was William Cranston who certified all the court documents and arranged for the ancient Hastings Custumal to be laid before the court. Once again witnesses - some of whom were of an advanced age - had to be got from Hastings to London as Mayor William Thorpe wrote to John Collier in July 1736, this was a major undertaking:

I hear Colbrun is ill and can't attend. Mrs Milward is set out in the wagon this afternoon for town... there's with her Shingleton, Joy, Evenden, Sargant, White: they have sent to Apledore after Couseens. Mrs Meadow is gone in a chair, and Boyket to attend her. John Hussey is expected in the road every hour... Dr Carelton set out yesterday....

William Hogarth's view of an election victory parade
Details from 'Chairing the Member' 1755

They all apparently arrived safely and joined the queue to testify that, in their experience and to their knowledge, there was no automatic right for the son of a freeman to become one himself. The Custumal appeared to say otherwise, and so defence counsel did all he could to challenge its authority, arguing that it was not an original document and appeared to be common to all the Cinque ports and not just Hastings alone:

> *I submit it therefore to your lordship, in the first place, that as, upon the face of it, it appears to be only a copy of a thing; and as it appears that thing does not relate to this borough in particular; and as it does not appear what book this is, nor how it came amongst the books of the corporation; and as it is only a collection of useless miscellaneous papers; I think it ought not to be read.*

In a rare moment of levity the Judge Lord Hardwicke agreed that it might, indeed, be preferable if he didn't have to read it all .... though he concluded it was probably his duty to do so!

> *If I could get off from reading this book lawfully, yet from the nature of this cause, I must look upon the book. In cases of this nature, I think it, prima facie, proper to be read in evidence.*

Having done so, and listened to the lengthy submissions, Hardwicke concluded that a right to the freedom of the borough had been properly established over time and that Moore was entitled to his Mandamus.

So Hastings lost the case, but rather more importantly for historians, it also lost the Custumal itself. At what stage it disappeared is not clear. But certainly it never returned from London and scholars have subsequently had to work from tattered papers in the borough archives, or from a copy found in Rye in Norman French.

Writing some half century later, the political historian Thomas Oldfield suggests a more sinister motive in the disappearance of the book whose loss he says was only uncovered when it was ordered to be produced in a court case involving neighbouring Seaford:

> *In the course of the Seaford contests it became important to some of the parties to inspect the [Hastings] custumal and a rule was accordingly obtained from the Court of the King's Bench for that purpose; but lo! It was missing and not to be found! Through fear that some future claimant of a freedom should seek to accomplish what Moore had left undone it was thought expedient to commit this highly important and venerable record to the flames.*

There doesn't seem to be any corroboration that the historic record was deliberately destroyed by the Corporation. Indeed J.M. Baines who devoted a whole chapter to the Custumal in his *Historic Hastings* says simply of the court case that:

> *This suit had disastrous consequences for the corporation quite apart from the expense involved, for the ancient copy of their custumal was taken up to London to*

*be produced in evidence and has never
been seen since.*

The divisions within the Hastings Corporation over the affair were slow to heal. An appeal was mounted and lost. The Town's Jurats failed to admit Moore at the following Court of Record and it was only when Sir Thomas Webster arrived with Moore at the Hastings Assembly on 14th May 1737 and produced yet another Mandamus directing them to admit him to the freedom forthwith, that the corporation gave in. Tradition demanded that a newly admitted freeman kiss the cheek of the Mayor. The man holding that office in 1737 was John Collier. According to historian J. M. Baines he did not attend the assembly having travelled to London the previous day and so *'Moor had to kiss the cheek of the deputy mayor instead'.*

If the prime motive for opposing the widening of the franchise was to prevent the Tories winning in Hastings, Newcastle, and Collier, might have saved themselves the trouble and the expense. The Whigs ended up controlling the seat for decades despite losing the case. But the legal battle was probably as much, if not more, about Cinque Port pride and politics. Prerogative and tradition clearly ran deep in Hastings.

§§§

Thomas Pelham-Holles, Duke of Newcastle. Whig. Elder brother of Henry Pelham. Statesman. Secretary of State. Prime Minister 1754-1756

Henry Pelham. Whig Prime Minster 1743- 1754

Thomas Pelham (of Stanmer) Whig. MP Hastings 1728-41, Lewes 1741-43

Sir Robert Walpole Prime Minister Whig

James Butler Successful Whig candidate in 1734 Sussex County Election

Sir Thomas Webster clothing manufacturer, elected MP Colchester 1705 and 1711. Subsequently expelled from Parliament on both occasions. Financed legal action against Hastings Corporation

Whistler Webster, son of Sir Thomas. Unsuccessful Tory candidate for Hastings in 1734 election

John Fuller 1680-1745) Brightling Ironmaster. Unsuccessful Tory Candidate for Sussex in 1734 election

Sir Cecil Bishop unsuccessful Tory Candidate for Sussex in 1734 election

John Sargent claimed Freedom of Hastings on grounds that his father had been a freeman, and successfully took Hastings Corporation to court in a lawsuit financed by Sir Thomas Webster.

Sir William Ashburton (2nd Baronet Ashburnham of Broomham) Whig. Hastings MP 1710-13, 1727-34, 1735-41

Henry Masterman leading London lawyer acting for John Sargent.

Richard Saville. Historian. Editor of 'The Letters of John Collier of Hastings 1731-1746'

Judge Lord Hardwicke - Philip Yorke, 1690 –1764 . Barrister1715. MP for Lewes (Whig) 1719. Solicitor-General and knighthood 1720. Lord Chief Justice of the King's Bench 1733 with title Lord Hardwicke. Lord Chancellor in Walpole's cabinet 1737. Friend and Confidant of Duke of Newcastle.

Henry Moore claimed Freedom of Hastings on grounds that his father had been a freeman, and successfully took Hastings Corporation to court in a lawsuit financed by Sir Thomas Webster.

Thomas Moore, Captain, ship owner, freeman. Opposed corporation's position over eligibility for freedom of town.

Basil Williams historian. Author 'Duke of Newcastle and the 1734 election' published in English Historical Review 1897.

Robert Burdett Newcastle's election agent in and around Lewes

Thomas Black Hastings felon, probably a smuggler.

William Coppard Hastings Mayor, 1727, 1735, 1742, 1746, & 1751

William Thorpe Hastings Mayor 1736, 1743, 1748, 1752

Chapter 10

Smuggling Ways.

The scene is Bedford Jail. The date 1750. A man is led from his cell, marched to the prison yard and forced to climb upon a cart. A noose is placed round his neck and, after a few words, the horses are whipped, the cart jolts forward and the man is left swinging on the end of the rope until he chokes to death. There is probably quite a crowd cheering the events. Public executions were extremely popular 'spectator sports' at the time. Indeed it would be another hundred and eighteen years before the last public hanging in England - Michael Barrett was put to death on Tuesday, the 26th of May 1868 at Newgate in front of a huge crowd that stretched from 'St. Sepulchre's Church and almost into Smithfield'.

We don't know how many were at Bedford Jail to see Gabriel Tomkins meet his end in 1750, but we do know that he was a notorious smuggler who had been operating in Kent and Sussex since at least 1717, latterly riding with the infamous Hawkhurst Gang. Tomkins features rather frequently in John Collier's correspondence, though curiously not so much for being a smuggler as for working as a revenue officer. The poacher had become gamekeeper in 1734 when, to save himself from the gallows, he turned Kings evidence and was rewarded with the post of riding officer and keeper of the Dartford Customs House in north Kent.

This brought him into direct contact with Collier who was Surveyor-General of the Riding Officers of the Customs for the County of Kent. It was a post that had been bestowed upon Collier by Thomas Pelham-Holles, The Duke of Newcastle, for his services in securing and maintaining Hastings for the Whig cause. But it was doubtless also partly for Collier's work over many years as a lawyer bringing successful prosecutions against smugglers.

All of this needs some context. In an era before income tax, most of the government's revenue was raised by levying duties on the import and export of goods. But some items faced even greater trading restrictions. Take wool for instance. In order to preserve the domestic English cloth industry it was forbidden to export raw wool at all for long periods during the 17th and 18th centuries. By the mid 1660s two-thirds of England's foreign commerce was the export of textiles made from domestic wool.

In the periods when the ban was lifted farmers were only allowed to export their fleeces through a handful of designated 'Staple' ports which imposed a duty making the product artificially expensive abroad. Even at home the purchase of wool was restricted to one company. These cartels meant that farmers received artificially low prices. Rearing sheep was an important business in Kent and Sussex and, on a clear day, farmers around Hastings could actually look across the sea to the shores of France where their product was being sold at inflated prices from which they derived no benefit. How much simpler – and more profitable - to load a boat with bales of their wool, sail it over the channel and sell it at the market price while avoiding export duties? So it was that in the late 1600s and early 1700s the practice of 'Owling' flourished – so called because the illicit export of wool was usually conducted during the hours of darkness and the smugglers reputed to use hoots to communicate.

If it was costly to sell goods abroad, it was even more expensive to import certain items – particularly tea, tobacco, spirits including brandy and rum, and luxuries like lace. All had hefty tariffs placed on them. Speaking in the House of Commons in 1734 Walter Plumer, told his fellow MPs:

> *"In that part of the country where I was, tea is generally sold by retailers in their shops at 5/- a pound ... and as the duty amounts to about 4/9d a pound, I leave it to gentlemen to judge, whether it is possible to sell by retail at 5/- a pound any tea upon which the duty has been honestly paid. It is easy to guess from whence all this tea comes, the smugglers buy it in Holland at 2/- a pound".*

The practice of smuggling affected the economy in other ways too. The official rate of pay for a casual labourer outside harvest time was just 8d a day. According to Walter Plumer, in areas of the country where smuggling was rife, employers were having to offer 18d a day and even then couldn't find enough people to work for them:

> *"... and how can it be otherwise? For all the young, clever fellows of the country are engaged and employed by the smugglers, from them they have 2/6d a day, while they wait upon the sea coast for the landing of the goods, and as soon as the goods are landed, and they mount on horseback, to go about the county to dispose of them, they have a guinea a day."*

At the beginning of the 18th century smuggling seemed to have been regarded fairly benignly by large sections of the population. It appeared a victimless crime and one that either kept you in cheap goods or provided you and your family a handy additional income. But it clearly didn't suit the government which was losing large amounts of revenue.

Throughout this period ever greater efforts were made to combat the smugglers. In 1671 Charles II established a Board of Customs to replace the former system whereby collection had been 'farmed out' to private individuals. By the end of the 17th century a force of mounted customs men called Riding Officers had been formed.

This must have been one of the most miserable jobs available. Even though they were paid relatively well – between £20 and £40 a year – from this they had to provide, feed and house their own horse. They were expected to patrol an area of coastline – often 10 miles or more – in all weathers, armed only with pistol and sword.

By the mid 18th century, gangs numbering up to 50 smugglers at a time were not uncommon. What could one lightly armed riding officer do if so hugely outnumbered? Since smuggling was, ultimately, a capital crime, the penalty for murder was no greater. Thus there was little incentive for a smuggler not to violently resist any law officer who might turn him in. So it was for any Riding Officer an extremely dangerous, not to say unpopular, profession, particularly if the job was conducted with an excess of zeal.

One such officer well known to John Collier was Thomas Carswell. He was a Freeman, Jurat and, in 1734, Mayor of Hastings. He supported Collier in his

The Hawkhurst Gang breaks into the Customs House at Poole which contains seized tea

longstanding campaign on behalf of Newcastle and the Whigs to restrict the number of Freemen voters in the town (See chapter 9), and he appeared as a witness for Collier in his legal battle over the water supply (see chapter 14).

However, on Christmas night 1740, Carswell was on duty and successfully seized about 15 cwt (750 kilos) of tea from a barn in Etchingham near Hurst Green. It is probable that the officers had followed the smugglers – members of the Hawkhurst Gang – up from Bulverhythe where the tea had been landed. Thinking their cargo safely concealed the smugglers repaired to the local inn, only later to see Carswell and a squad of Dragoons - mounted soldiers - trundling past with 'their' tea piled upon a cart, clearly heading back to the Hastings Customs House. A senior member of the gang, 'Trip' Stanford, rapidly recruited up to 30 other men and set off in pursuit of the law officers. They caught up with them on Silver Hill, leading down to Robertsbridge. The Dragoons opened fire but managed to miss their targets. The smugglers returned fire and Carswell was hit in the head and killed outright. Four soldiers were also badly wounded. The law officers fled, abandoning the smuggled goods.

The use of Dragoons to aid the customs officers was itself not without problems. In a letter to Collier the Commissioners of Customs outlined how the troops stationed at Romney and Lydd would seize brandy and horses from smugglers. The horses they would sell back to the smugglers for one guinea each, while the brandy they passed on to an 'officer of the Excise', from whom they received two shillings for each half anker barrel (about 4 gallons or 18 litres). The letter continues:

> *It appears that dragoons quartered at Folkestone frequently made seizures without any officer and carried them to Thomas Jordan, officer there, who always gave them half a crown for each half anker of brandy and twenty shillings for every bag of tea.*

And it wasn't just the Dragoons who were corrupt or corruptible. The riding officers too were known to take bribes from the smugglers. A few years later, in 1749, Collier's law partner William Cranston wrote to him about evidence that 'Trip' Stanford was providing the authorities following his arrest:

> *... finding his Tryall fix'd as far as I understand it [Stanford] begins to Squeek – 'tis what I know they have wanted him to do & it is hinted to me that his first Discovery will be of their keeping a good understanding for a valuable consideration with many of the riding officers along the coast and higher up in the country & just in the neighborhood of town and if true will make sad work.*

In other words the 'understanding' involved smugglers bribing or paying off riding officers throughout the area. Stanford, it will be recalled, was one of the gang involved in the killing of Thomas Carswell nine years earlier.

It was into this murky world that John Collier arrived when he was appointed Surveyor General of riding officers in Kent in November 1733. It does not seem to have been a particularly onerous job, requiring mainly one annual tour of all the Customs Houses in the county, usually lasting around three weeks. Yet it paid upwards of £200 a year. There's no doubt that Collier took his duties seriously, reporting back at length to the Commissioners of His Majesty's Customs in London. In his first year in the job, 1734, he set out on 16th September on horseback and visited Rye, Lydd, New Romney, Dymchurch, Hythe, Folkestone, Dover, St Margaret's, Deal, Sandwich, Ramsgate, Broadstairs, Birchington, Margate, Herne, Whitstable, Canterbury, Faversham, Sittingbourne, Milton, Isle of Sheppy, Rochester, Hoo, Dartford and Tunbridge Wells. He interviewed every Riding Officer and all other customs officials and reported back his views and recommendations:

"The officer at Birchinton whose name is Richard Thunder, a poor, indolent man and one who I believe does little duty. I humbly observe to your honours that Broadstairs and Birchinton is about six miles distant and therefore very inconvenient to the officers and in great measure prevents them from going out on duty together, and in regard their district is so long I humbly propose that the Ramsgate officers should extend their ride to Margate. That Cowper should be removed to Birchington and the ride of him and Thunder be from Margate to Reculvers and they may then go out on duty together."

The commissioners approved his note of recommendation and, we assume put his general warning about the state of affairs further south on the Kent coast:

> *I humbly observe to your honours that the Smugglers in Romney Marsh are associated into very large formidable Gangs and that without the assistance of Dragoons believe the Riding Officers will not be able to guard the coast to prevent clandestine running of goods."*

Of some particular interest are Collier's observations once he arrived in Dartford where he found one Gabriel Tomkins in charge. A brief chronology of Tompkins career might be useful here. He was born in Tunbridge Wells around 1700 and before he was twenty was reputed to be leading a smuggling gang in Mayfield. He was indicted and subsequently acquitted for the murder of Riding Officer Gerard Reeves in 1717 and he was identified as part of a group of smugglers involved in a skirmish at the Swan Inn in Reigate in 1721. That same year he 'rescued' two fellow smugglers who had been detained by revenue officers at the George Inn in Lydd, before being captured at Nutley and sentenced to seven years transportation to Providence in the Bahamas. He returned early from the American colonies which was a capital offence and had a £100 reward posted on his head. In 1728 he was again arrested and, to avoid the gallows, turned King's evidence and testified to a commission under Sir John Cope enquiring into the Customs service. As a 'reward' for this he was appointed Bailiff to the Sheriff of Sussex and Surveyor of Riding Officers in Dartford.

It seems that Collier is aware of Tomkins' colourful past, having, it is informed, prepared the

152

Crown's case against him in the Gerard Ree murder thirty or more years before. However, he made no reference to it in his reports. His 1735 submission says only that:

> I examined into Tomkins' behaviour and put him into a method of keeping a journal and directed a more frequent visiting the officers under his inspection.

The following year Collier was rather more complimentary on his visit to Dartford:

> Here resides Mr Gabriel Tomkins, surveyor of the riding officers on the Kentish side of the Thames from the buoy at Nore to Longreach. And also George Ellis, a preventative riding officer whose district is from this place to Chalk. They are both Young, active, stout men capable of performing the required duty for which purpose they keep good horses and arms.

By 1740 Collier has evidently lost faith in Tomkins. Asked to deliver his 'Journal Book', the Dartford Surveyor was unable to present it. And Tomkins had also failed to meet Collier's requirement to secure a residence in Chalk for two preventative officers who had disappeared to Rochester. As Collier reported:

> As I was not apprized of this removal I enquired of Mr Tomkins the Surveyor whether there was any order for the same from the board but did not find any upon

hich I blamed his conduct and reprimanded the officers the surveyor said could not find (a) house at Chalk to dwell in.... I gave Mr Tomkins instructions in writing to supervise .... all the riding officers under his Inspection at least twice a week and to oblige them to exert themselves in a performance of their duty.

Whether or not he carried out Collier's instructions we don't know, but Gabriel Tomkins didn't last much longer in his post. He was rumoured to be passing on information to smugglers and, after thirteen years as a revenue officer, was forced to abandon his job and leave Dartford in a moonlight flit. He next appears in official records as riding with the Hawkhurst Gang before turning to highway robbery, for which he was executed at Bedford jail in 1750.

Collier appears to have been well respected by the Customs Commissioners for his efforts, but it seems that he, personally, didn't relish the long tours of duty and the fawning officials. He wrote to his wife Mary on 29th September 1734 from Dover:

My dearest, I arrived at this place last night being very glad to have Romney Marsh at my back as soon as I possibly could and shall be oblig'd to tarry here two or three days. I am quite fatigued to death with Compliments Respect and Ceremonies that are quite surfeiting and troublesome ... I am always surrounded by a group of officers and am obliged to hear all their complaints and magnifying of services never performed that I am heartily sick of

distinguished himself during a Naval career covering nearly five decades and was, in 1745, appointed to command the North Sea Fleet to combat the potential Jacobite invasion of Bonny Prince Charlie [see chapters 6 and 12]. South coast smugglers had a long-standing reputation for Jacobite sympathies, and Vernon positively railed against *"able bodied layabouts in the Cinque ports who have no visible way of getting a living but by the infamous trade of smuggling ... I can't but think it a national reproach to have let their villainy and treachery run to such extensive lengths"*. Vernon blamed the civil authorities of the Cinque Ports – clearly including the Corporation of Hastings.

At this point two Hastings fishermen, George Harrison and Zebelton Morphett, were arrested and accused of smuggling tea as well as running guns for the Jacobites. This was hotly denied by Harrison who was a well-known local man and a freeman of the town. Collier saw fit to write effusively to Vernon about him following his arrest and that of another man named Phillips. They were, said Collier:

> *... natives of this town and bred to the sea from their infancy and esteemed, particularly Harrison, to be good sailors and perfectly well acquainted with the French coast on this part of the channel. They have been reputed, and I believe with truth, to have followed the detestable practice of smuggling, but both fairly promise never to be again concerned thereon, and Harrison's cutter was one taken the 8th out of this road by the Badger sloop. The lieutenant came on shore to know the character of the masters, not*

*finding any goods on board... Harrison
came yesterday to me and desired I would
give him a letter to you, that if you be so
pleased to let him and Phillips go in his own
or any other cutter and put a lieutenant or
seaman on board him he is confident of
making discoveries of what is doing at
Boulogne ... At his request and at the desire
of several gentleman here I presume to
give you this epistle.*

Vernon not only appears to have ignored this
entreaty, but actually to have detained Harrison.
According to Collier the Hastings man had gone to the
Admiral with his blessing, offering to help gather
intelligence on the French-supported Jacobite forces.
Later Vernon wrote of Harrison and Morphett in a
pamphlet, entitled 'Some Seasonable Advice from an
Honest Sailor':

*Whatever calamities are likely to befall us
I am persuaded their treachery has in a
great manner contributed ... Morphett, the
traitor, is being protected by John Collier.*

Unaware for the moment of Vernon's
accusations, Collier again wrote to the Admiral pleading
Harrison's case:

*I hope you'll forgive this repeated
application on behalf of George Harrison
who I sent on board you in the Downs with
some intelligence in regard to the late
intended invasion from Boulogne etc, who,*

Romanticised view of 18th century smuggling
From an oil painting by George Morland 1763-1804

after his examination you was pleased to order on board the Badger sloop of war... where he still remains. Harrison has a wife and several children and his whole fishing craft lies neglected As I sent him with a sincere intention for the service of our King and Country and gave him assurances of not being imprisoned or detained, I humbly hope your honour will ...order ... his discharge."

It seems that Harrison and Morphett were later impressed into the navy thereby avoiding any charges. But again it is instructive to see how Collier supported them as local men and was prepared to go to some lengths to argue their case against the authorities. It wasn't until after the turn of the year that Collier learned of Vernon's accusations against him but decided not to respond publicly. He did, however, attempt to clear his name in a letter to the Prime Minister Henry Pelham:

I had his [Admiral Vernon's] *thanks but when he thought proper to print his Seasonable Advice he takes notice of a letter I sent him, with a sort of insinuation of my being an Encourager of Smuggling but ungenerously ... leaves out that part that I think would clear me from such an imputation. I would not presume to trouble your honour with it but sent a copy of that whole letter to Mr Stone and to several Gentlemen of the town in my own vindication.*

John Collier continued to combat the practice of smuggling and was in regular correspondence with the Customs Board and other authorities. However, by 1756 he was regretfully declining any assistance that involved travel. In April 1756 he wrote to Mr Wood, the secretary to the Commissioners of Customs:

> *It is my misfortune and great concern that my situation as to lameness renders it at this juncture impossible for me personally to obey the commands of their lordships and the Hon. board in making a survey on the coast, by the fatal stroke of my paralitic disorder in my left foot which had greatly increased this inclement weather with intense pain not having a due circulation in the bloud of my toes that the surgeons were in some apprehension a mortification might ensue.*

That same year he resigned his post as Surveyor General and, on his recommendation, was succeeded by his son-in-law Edward Milward. It brought to an end a lifetime of service to the government both as a prosecuting lawyer and senior customs officer. His correspondence on the subject of smuggling and smugglers has been hugely important for historians of the subject and period. Personally, it shows Collier first as the righteous upholder of the law and a dedicated opponent of such law breakers. But his subsequent actions in support of those he felt had been mistreated by the authorities demonstrate another more humane side to his character. His functional dealings with people like Tompkins perhaps testify to the ambivalence of the age. Smuggling was popularly seen as a crime of statute rather than morality and one that benefited, directly or indirectly, large numbers of people. The government's increasingly severe penalties in an attempt to stamp it out it were, by and large, unsuccessful. It was only following the Napoleonic Wars more than half a century after Collier's death that Parliament removed most of the duties on imported goods and widespread smuggling finally ceased.

§§§

Gabriel Tomkins. Convicted Smuggler. Reputed leader of the Mayfield Gang from 1717. 1733 Testified before Sir John Cope's inquiry into the Customs service. 1734 and joined the Revenue Service as riding officer in Kent, keeper of the Dartford Customs House and Bailiff to Sheriff of Sussex. 1750 executed Bedford Jail for highway robbery .

Duke of Newcastle – Thomas Pelham-Holles. 1693-1768. Whig statesman, party manager and fixer. Sussex Land owner. Elder brother of Henry Pelham. Secretary of State for 30 years . Prime Minister 1754-1756 & 1757-1762. Benefactor of John Collier

Walter Plumer MP. 1682-1746 Whig politician later member of the opposition or 'Patriot' Whig faction. Campaigned in parliament against the Salt Duty,

Thomas Carswell Hastings Freeman and Jurat. Mayor 1734. Riding Officer, killed by smugglers of the Hawkhurst gang near Hurst Green on 26th December 1740.

James Stanford alias Trip or Tripp. Wealthy smuggler. Member of Hawkhurst Gang. Reputedly involved in the murder of Thomas Carswell.

Andrew Stone 1703–1773. Private secretary to the Duke of Newcastle. Confident of Pelham family. MP for Hastings 1741 to 1761. Government minister. Royal advisor, tutor secretary and treasurer under George II and George III.

William Cranston – Mary Collier's younger brother. John Collier's legal partner based in London. John Collier always refers to William as 'my brother' rather than brother-in-law.

Admiral Edward Vernon 1684 –1757. MP. Distinguished naval officer particularly in War of Jenkins' Ear where he captured *Porto Bello* but failed to take *Cartagena de Indias*, despite long siege. Subsequently author of two pamphlets critical of Admiralty: "A Specimen of Naked Truth from a British Sailor" and "Some Seasonal Advice from an Honest Sailor", leading to his dismissal from the Navy in 1746.

Edward Milward 1723 -1811. Collier's son-in-law (via marriage to his daughter Mary in 1754). Mayor of Hastings 1750 and every alternate year from 1753 to 1801. Succeeded Collier in 1756 as Surveyor-General of the Customs for Kent. Became a man of considerable property and influence in Hastings, though he was not universally liked.

Chapter 11

Stuck in the Middle - Social Standing

For the son of a fairly humble Eastbourne innkeeper, John Collier had come a long way by the mid 1730s. He was a leading – though not always popular – citizen of Hastings. He was the town clerk, a freeman, a jurat and oft-times Mayor. He was the Duke of Newcastle's election agent and estate agent to both the Duke and his brother Henry Pelham - a leading government minister. He was a senior officer in the Customs service - a prestigious position though one that also might not have overly-endeared him to a number of Hastings' seafarers. He was owner of one of the town's finest houses and was yearly increasing his land holdings. With a legal practice both locally and in London he was almost certainly one of the richest men in Hastings able, from the mid 1730s, to send his sons to the exclusive and expensive Westminster public school and his daughters to private London academies. In short he was a man of some standing in his community.

However, in the social strata of Georgian England, for all his acumen and achievements Collier remained one of the 'middling sort'. At the top were the aristocracy, followed closely by the landed gentry. They were not synonymous. If you had a title you had position and respect – even if you did not have vast wealth. If you had the wealth, you acquired a large degree of respect even if you didn't have a title other than a knighthood. A few people like Sir Thomas Webster, either personally or through their families, became so rich as manufacturers or traders or businessmen that they could effectively buy a parliamentary seat – as well the respectability of country estates and a knighthood. But they were certainly the exception. The middling sort encompassed most traders, merchants, manufacturers, civil servants, professionals – all in fact who occupied the strata beneath the gentry and above the labouring or servant classes. Through his income Collier may have been in the top echelons of this group but he was still unquestionably within it. And however much the middling sort may have wished to *emulate* their superiors, upward social mobility was a rarity. Which goes some way to explain Collier's almost deferential admiration of gentry, aristocracy and royalty.

Take his letter home to Mary on 19th May 1737 in which he sounds a little like a child in a sweetshop:

> *I dined yesterday at the Duke of Richmond's where there were 27 Sussex gentlemen amongst the rest, the Duke of Newcastle, Earl of Wilmington, Lord Abergaveny, Lord Ossulston, who is Earl Tankerville's son. The entertainment was very splendid and served all in plate, dishes and all, and a fine dessert. There were 24 footmen waiting at table and as he is master of the horse to the king, 16 of them in the king's livery, and the rest in his own, which is very handsom. In short the dinner, side board, desert and grandeur, surpassed almost everything I ever saw and the house vastly rich furnished. We tarried till 12 a clock dining at half an hour after 4.*

Charles Lennox, 2nd Duke of Richmond 1701-1750

Collier's attitude to the upper classes is also apparent in his comments about London's theatre *'I never saw a more crowded audience of good company'* he says of the Duke of Cumberland and the Princesses Amelia and Caroline who were at Drury Lane when he went to see David Garrick perform in 1742. And he had a similar attitude to visitors to the Pleasure Gardens: *'there were an abundance of people but not many of the Tip Top company'* he said about a visit to Vauxhall in 1738. (See Chapter 8).

His relationship to those members of the aristocracy who employed him is also interesting. Collier was steward to the manors of Ashburnham, Broomham Parkgate, Broomham Allfreys, Penhuest and Hasleden in Sussex, properties belonging to the Earl of Ashburnham. Prior to inheriting his brother's baronetcy in 1710, John Ashburnham was one of Hastings' two MPs and thus of a roughly similar social standing to Collier. Once he became a baron and then an earl that all changed. But Collier clearly remained on friendly terms with his lordship – though seldom lost an opportunity to mention it when invited to his table: *"I hear Lord Ashburnham, with whom I dined a Sunday, this day was to kiss the King's hand"*, he told Mary in November 1731. Two years later: *"...this day Lord Ashburnham invited me to dinner and with a strict charge to bring him* (his son Jemmy) *with me".* Two days later: *"Jemmy dined with me today at Lord Ashburnham's and he gave him a guinea."*

His lordship, however, was not a well man, and in 1737 Collier began to chart his final decline in letters home to Mary: *"Poor Lord Ashburnham is quite emaciated and sunk though he has been something better for 2 or 3 days."* He wrote on the 17th of February 1737. And again a few days later: *"One of the Daily papers said yesterday that Lord Ashburnham was very dangerously ill* and his life not expected to hold out long." By March he had declined further:

> I went out ... yesterday to Col Pelhams and thence to Lord Ashburnham who is a most shocking sight... I can't think it possible he can live, neither can I give any description of him for he is quite emaciated his spirits sunk and his speech much altered. He is carried out for about 2 hours in the middle of the day to see if air can contribute relief. He asked me and pressed to dine there which I did ....

By the end of the month Nathaniel Lamb, executor for the recently deceased Lord Ashburnham was writing to Collier asking about the estate:

> I would be glad to know if you had any concerns about the late Lord, and if you know of anything in the country that is proper we, that are the executors, should be acquainted with...

Collier's work for Ashburnham is detailed in his accounts for the executors and gives evidence of his fees to administer the estate:

> ... two years' allowance for my salary £10 10s 0d – collecting Lord's rents, seizing heriots £3 10s - £2 10s journey to Ashburnham and staying overnight £1 11s.

It's notable that after the death of the first Earl, the

Colliers remained on friendly terms with the Ashburnhams. Jemmy, it seems, was a contemporary and an intimate of his successor, also called John, and Collier father and son continued to dine with the second Earl in London from time to time.

If John Collier enjoyed meals with the Ashburnhams, the same cannot quite be said for another member of the aristocracy who gave him work, Lord Wilmington. Born Spencer Compton in 1673 he was an MP and Speaker of the House of Commons. In 1728 he was created a baron and, two years later, the first Earl of Wilmington. As a prominent Whig, a cabinet minister and a member of the Aristocracy, he might have been exactly the sort of person Collier would want to cultivate. It seems, however, the idea of dining with him was not greatly to Collier's liking:

> *The Doctor* (Carleton) *and sons are to dine in Johnsons Court tomorrow by appointment and I have now received a message to dine with my Lord Wilmington and am afraid I can't avoid it which vexes me not a little.* (9.7.1734)

And, two days later:

> *My Dear, I was obliged to dine at Lord Wilmington's yesterday to my mortification as missing the Doctor and his sons etc. I am afraid I must goe to Mr Pelhams a Saturday and not return till Munday.*

Wilmington had estates in Sussex and it seems Collier ended up representing his Lordship in a lawsuit,

Wilmington v Garland, involving an evidently complicated dispute over the boundaries of Stonebeach Manor and 800 acres of land. He wrote to Mary in June 1735:

I ... am much concerned that I am obliged to tarry so long in London. I fully expect my Lord Willmington's cause [case] to be over tomorrow.

But it wasn't. It was postponed and Collier notes that he had been worried he would have to spend time preparing the case around Christmas 1735:

Lord Wilmington's cause with Mr Garland is in a fair way of being fully concluded which I am heartily pleased with for I could not avoid going through with it which would have been long and tedious.

Many of Collier's letters mention the Royal family which was clearly an area of considerable public interest and speculation in the 18th century. This was doubtless partly as a result of the execution of King Charles I in 1649 by Oliver Cromwell and the Parliamentary forces. This cataclysmic event occurred just 36 years before Collier's birth and was still within the living memory of some elderly citizens in the early Georgian period. Indeed as we have seen, the battle to establish a secure Protestant monarchy had lasted beyond Queen Anne's reign and into the Hanoverian succession. And as we will see in the next chapter, it was not yet utterly settled as the Young Pretender, Bonnie Prince Charlie, was still alive and well and plotting to restore a Jacobite to the throne.

So even though Hanoverians had, initially, little connection with Britain, and George I spoke no English, they were nonetheless the only Royal family available and therefore garnered the respect and fealty of the British people. But even at that date the behaviour of the 'royals' seems to have been a matter of no little interest, speculation and gossip among their subjects – including it seems John Collier himself. In November 1717, in his first letter from London to his new wife Mary back in Hastings, Collier relates the strange tale of the christening of Prince George William – Grandson to King George I:

> *The young prince is not as yet christened there being a dispute ... viz the Princess before she was brought to bed sent to a foreign prince and princess to stand* [as godparents] *for ye child... and the King, as soon as it was come* [born], *resolved that ... the D. of Newcastle and the Duchess of St Alban's would stand for it and send the D. to acquaint the Princess of it – the princess told him as above, on which he went away displeased...*

In fact the incident became even more serious than Collier had suggested. The Prince and Princess of Wales had chosen Louis as the name for their son and wanted the Queen of Prussia and the Duke of York as his sponsors at the christening. But his grandfather, King George I, insisted on the name George William, and chose as godparents the Duke of Newcastle in his capacity as Lord Chamberlain, along with Diana Beauclerk, Duchess of St Albans. At the ceremony itself

Newcastle was, apparently, called out by the Prince of Wales who told him: "You are a rascal but I shall find you". Due to the Prince's thick German accent, Newcastle thought he'd said "I'll fight you" and assumed he had been challenged to a duel. The King was clearly furious with his son and daughter-in-law and banished them from court, retaining custody of the young prince, as Collier noted on 3rd December:

> *There is a Terrible distraction at Court, &*
> *they are all in an uproar- the Prince and*
> *Princesse are commanded from St James's*
> *and last night left the palace.*

By the following February Collier notes the sad death of the infant Prince George William.

> *The breach between the King and Prince*
> *widens every day ...the death of the Young*
> *Prince has taken off the care of the D. of*
> *Newcastle in bringing up his godson.*

The relationship between George I and the future George II never recovered from the row over George William's christening and subsequent death ... neither did the relationship between Newcastle and the Prince of Wales.

George I reigned for a further ten years before suffering a stroke in his native Hanover and dying at Osnabrück on 11 June 1727. He was succeeded by the Prince of Wales and preparations were quickly put in place for his coronation.

The Coronation Canopy
Detail from a contemporary print showing the Coronation Procession of George II

176

A curious tradition had prevailed - possibly since the reign of Edward the Confessor (1042-1066), but certainly since 1236 in the reign of Henry III - that Barons of the Cinque Ports could claim the privilege of bearing a canopy over the King and the Queen at their coronation. As all freemen were barons, each port elected a small group from among their number for the privilege. In 1727 John Collier was one of the joint solicitors of the Cinque and, according to WV Crake, it was he who formally made the application:

> *The Barons of the Cinq Ports having made the following claim, viz:- to have the usual office of carrying two canopies ... sixteen Barons to a canopy, to have the said two canopies for their fee ... To have the privilege of dining in the Hall at a table on the right hand of the King's table.*

The certificate was duly granted. And, whether because of his role as Solicitor, or because of his longstanding civic service as clerk, and then as mayor in 1719 and 1722, John Collier himself was elected to be one of the six Barons from Hastings to assist in the duty. This was, clearly, an enormous honour as he wrote to Mary on 5th October 1727:

> *It is expected that the coronation will exceed all that ever were in Magnificence & Grandeur. The Queen's Cloaths is to be the richest possible, & all Covered with Diamonds.*

In the same letter he gave what details he could of the arrangements:

I have not been able to learn many particulars about our Coronation affair ... there is to be a meeting of the Barons next Munday to settle who are to support over the King and over the Queen in p'ticular. I have made no progress on my robes, nor shall not till I see what Others provide ...

As a result of that meeting it was determined that another oft-elected mayor, Edward Dyne, along with MP Sir William Ashburnham and Thomas Pelham of Stanmer would help carry the King's Canopy, while Collier, along with the town's other MP, Thomas Townsend, and Colonel Pelham, would be among those carrying the Queen's.

There is a fascinating little detail also contained in this letter which provides a window into the world of Georgian London:

Candles are risen 2s 6d a Dozen just at this time, on account of the Vast Quantity bought up for the Coronation Illumin- ations...

The question of his 'robes' for the ceremony was clearly exercising Collier a good deal. Whatever was decided would inevitably be expensive. He noted that a full bottom wig in his 'complexion' would cost '15 Guineas'. A not inconsiderable sum given that his salary as Town Clerk was still around £10 a year, and he told Mary he would be 'much vex'd' if he was forced to buy one. So borrowing or even hiring one was a preferred option.

I am in a little Dilemma about my robing, but Lord Ashburnham yesterday offered me a Shirt and neckcloth for the Ceremony, that is to lend it to me, which I accepted ...we have Scarlet Robes lined with crimson Sattin, Waistcoats of the same Sattin, breeches of the same cloth, Scarlet wosted Stockings because silk will not take soe good a dye, black velvet shoes with red heels, black velvet Caps, white Gloves, of which the Topps are faced with Crimson, we are to wear swords ...

It was obviously a momentous occasion and Collier quickly wrote again to Mary to give her the full details:

...the whole was of the Greatest Splendour and magnificence it's possible to be thought of. I was at the Queen's canopy, much to my satisfaction, and the procession was very agreeable tho' vastly fatiqueing and I had the happiness of escaping without a cold ...I can't forbear telling you that the Queen was exceedingly obliging in the procession & talked very much to our corner of the Staves, viz Pelham and Townsend & so I came in for my share. Her train was born by 7 ladies, (3 of them Princesses), Dressed a fine as it is possible to be thought of & in coming back the 3 young Ladyes ... put on the same obliging airs & were very merry.

179

The Hastings Corporation Punchbowl commissioned by John Collier in 1727 from the silver staves of the coronation canopy. The inscription reads: Canopy Bearers to the QUEEN The Hon Tho. Townshend esq, James Pelham esq, John Collier esq.

Part of the tradition was that, in lieu of any fee, the Barons would keep both the canopy and the silver staves that held it aloft. The Hastings contingent decided that the metal should be melted down and turned into a ceremonial for use at Corporation functions. The work was carried out by a London silversmith Joseph Ball and the result is simple but elegant, with inscriptions round the sides:

This silver bowl was presented to the Corporation of Hasting ye premier Cinque Port by ye gentlemen whose names are hereon inscribed who had ye honour to be unanimously elected ye Barons of ye said town to support ye canopy over their sacred royal Majesties King George ye 2nd and Queen Caroline at the solemnity of their inauguration at Westminster the eleventh day of October 1727. And ye same was made out of their shares and dividend of the silver staves &c belonging to the said canopy.

For many years the bowl was used at civic functions. But by 1824 William George Moss in his history of Hastings noted:

as punch has long ceased to be a fashionable liquor, and the corporation preferring wine at their public festivals, a framework of wood has been made to fit inside the bowl to hold decanters.

Even that function fell into disuse and the bowl was then, for many years, exhibited at the Hastings Museum.

But curators there eventually deemed it insufficiently interesting for visitors and it was removed to a vault in the council offices. Now, upon application, it is occasionally brought out to be viewed or photographed.

As for Collier, it's probable he dined out on his role at the coronation for years. Certainly he didn't fail to tell Mary of the aftermath – once again gently boasting at his hobnobbing with dukes and knights:

> *I dined today at the Duke's by a particular invitation, with my Bro: Co-baron Dyne who took his pipe according to custom after dinner & I am just now come back... Mr Pelham, Colonell Pelham, Mr Pelham of Stanmer, Sir Wm Ashburton and Sir Wm Gage &c dined with us, where we have been Exceeding merry and without hard Drinking ...*

§§§

Who's Who Chapter 11, Stuck in the Middle

Duke of Newcastle – Thomas Pelham-Holles. Whig statesman and political fixer. Sussex Land owner. Elder brother of Henry Pelham. Secretary of State. Prime Minister 1754-1756. Benefactor of John Collier

Henry Pelham. Whig Prime Minster 1743- 1754. Brother to Duke of Newcastle. Employed Collier to manage his estates.

Sir Thomas Webster clothing manufacturer, elected MP Colchester 1705 and 1711. Subsequently expelled from Parliament on both occasions. Financed legal action against Hastings Corporation

Duke of Richmond, Charles Lennox, 1701–1750 MP for Chichester 1722 before inheriting title in 1723. Courtier. Served as army General against 1745 Jacobite uprising. Led campaign to prosecute Hawkhurst Gang of smugglers. Owned Goodwood estate in Sussex. Notable for correspondence with Duke of Newcastle. Early patron of Cricket.

Earl (1st) of Asburnham - John Ashburnham 1687 - 1737. Hastings MP 1710. Resigned seat same year after inheriting brother's Baronetcy. Collier was steward to his estates in Sussex and was on dining terms with him. Became a courtier, Lord of Bedchamber 1728-31. Created Earl of Ashburnham 1730.

Colonel **James Pelham** of Crowhurst. Aka Jemmy. Cousin to D. of Newcastle. Coronation canopy bearer with Collier 1727. Hastings MP 1741-61

James Collier. John and Mary's second son nicknamed Jemmy. Died 1747 aged 26

Lord Wilmington – Spencer Compton – 1673-1743. Whig statesman, Speaker of House of Commons, and minister under Walpole but fell out with him. Created Baron 1728, associated with Patriot Whigs. Prime Minister 1742-3. Owner East Borne estate Sussex, (later Compton Place). Collier represented him in a land dispute.

Dr Henry Carleton. The Collier's friend and physician in Hastings. A former Mayor and deputy Mayor.

Queen Anne (1665 –1714) Daughter of James II but raised a protestant and succeeded to throne following death of King William III in 1702. Most notable for creating the United Kingdom following Act of Union with Scotland in 1707. Married to Prince George of Denmark

Charles Edward Stuart (1720 –1788) 'The Young Pretender. Aka Bonnie Prince Charlie. Great grandson King James II. Jacobite claimant to the throne. Led the 1745 uprisings. Defeated at Culloden April 1746. Escaped from Scotland and lived rest of his life on continent.

King George I of England (1660-1727). Born Hanover. Great grandson James I. Succeeded Queen Anne in 1714.

King George II George Augustus (1683-1760) Succeeded George I in 1727. He was Duke of Brunswick-Lüneburg (Hanover) and a prince-elector of the Holy Roman Empire. Married 1705 Caroline of Ansbach.

Queen Caroline 1683 – 1737. Wife of George II. Formerly Caroline of Brandenburg-Ansbach. Supporter of Robert Walpole's Whig faction. Popular queen widely mourned following her death in 1737.

Prince George William (1717-1718) Second son of George Augustus, Prince of Wales, later King George II and Caroline of Brandenburg-Ansbach later Queen Caroline. Prince George was the subject of a family feud after King George I overruled his son's choice of name and godparents for his grandson. Prince George died aged 3 months 4 days from a polyp on the heart.

Diana Beauclerk (1679-1742) Duchess of St Albans, born Lady Diana de Vere, Courtier. Mistress of the Robes to Caroline, Princess of Wales from 1714 to 1717. Chosen as godparent to Prince George William by King George I, against the wishes of his parents, Prince and Princess of Wales. Married 1694 Charles Beauclerk, 1st Duke of St Albans

Edward Dyne. Hastings Jurat 1708, Mayor 1720,1724,1726,1728. Coronation canopy bearer with Collier 1727. Died 1732

Sir William Ashburnham (of Broomham). Hastings MP 1710-1713 and 1722-1741. Coronation canopy bearer with Collier 1727

Thomas Pelham Whig. MP Hastings 1728-41, Lewes 1741-43.

Hon **Thomas Townsend**. 1701– 1780. Elected MP Hastings 1727 but chose to represent Cambridge. Nephew to Duke of Newcastle. Fellow coronation canopy bearer with Collier 1727

Colonel **James Pelham** of Crowhurst. Aka Jemmy. Cousin to D. of Newcastle. Coronation canopy bearer with Collier 1727.

William George Moss. Historian, draughtsman, author of: The History and Antiquities of the Town and Port of Hastings 1824.

Chapter 12

War and Rebellion

On Sunday 12th April 1744 news of England's declaration of war against France reached Hastings. The King's order was conveyed by an officer of the Lord Warden of the Cinque Ports and a proclamation had then to be made to the people of the town. John Collier was disparaging about the way this was done in their neighbouring Sussex town. *'They proclaimed it at Rye a Saturday before their order arrived and we hear fired guns. This we thought not proper.'*

So the Hastings' elders met on the Sunday night at their club to discuss how it should be done there. Although Nathaniel Cruttenden was mayor that year, John Collier had by then held the office five times – most recently in 1741. Thus he was among the senior Jurats whose duty it was to make this announcement to the citizenry. From a letter he sent to Mary in London a couple of days later we have an extraordinarily vivid picture of the occasion.

On the stroke of two o'clock on Monday afternoon a corps of 110 men assemble in 'The Fishmarket' - probably at the bottom of today's High Street - under the command of a captain and other officers. They are resplendent in their uniforms – described by Collier as *'all clean and powdered'*.

Once they are mustered, the dignitaries give notice to the Captain to begin the march. Three sergeants and 12 men with the drums carry the colours. Collier is among those to make the official salute to the officers who proceed with six mounted dragoons clearing the way with swords drawn.

Then the Mayor and Jurats, followed by Capt. Scott and the whole body two drums in the front after one rank, the colours in the middle carried by Maul and Ensign Thomas brought up the rear. Marched as slow as possible and the soldiers drawn up at the old Market, Patrick read the Declaration, with the usual previous proclamation, then three loud huzzas.

The whole entourage then march back to the Fishmarket where the proclamation is again read. The soldiers are offered drink while the dignitaries adjourn to the Swan. It was, Collier told Mary, *'a very fine afternoon, though foul weather... a prodigious number of people present'.*

It is, perhaps, no great surprise that a declaration of war should have been announced in such a grand manner, even in a place as small as Hastings. But, as we've seen, the people in early Georgian England were greatly in thrall to the crown, and ceremony was much revered. But the fact is that *this* war was fairly unremarkable. Since the beginning of the 18th century Britain had been involved in a seemingly ceaseless round of conflicts, starting with the War of Spanish Succession 1701–1714, The Great Northern War 1700–1721, and the so-called War of Jenkins' Ear against Spain which began in 1739 and wasn't fully concluded until 1748.

However the events presaged by the declaration in Hastings in April 1744 were perhaps more significant than any of these, and would lead to a direct threat to the protestant British monarchy.

The war of the Austrian Succession had actually

begun a few years earlier in 1740 and was to involve most of the great powers of Europe. As a woman, Archduchess Maria Theresa was not legally able to succeed to the Hapsburg throne, enabling France, Prussia and Barvaria to challenge the Hapsburg dynasty. Opposing them were Britain, the Dutch Republic, Sardinia and Saxony, all of whom sided with the Archduchess.

King George II, as Elector of Hannover, was rather closer to the dynastic European infighting than many in Britain and, in the face of some political dissent, managed to persuade the British Parliament to allow him personally to lead an army of 37,000 British soldiers on the continent. The ensuing battle of Dettingen on June 27th 1743 was to be the last time in British history that a monarch commanded his troops in battle. Despite losing his horse and being forced to advance on foot, George and his soldiers of the so-called 'pragmatic army,' narrowly emerged as victors.

But while he was tied up in Bavaria, the French were amassing a fleet in Calais preparing to invade Britain. And this would have immediate consequences for John Collier and the people of Hastings.

The problem for England was that France was actively supporting the Catholic Jacobite cause which was now headed by the Young Pretender. Charles Stuart, popularly known as Bonnie Prince Charlie, was the son of James Francis Edward Stuart, thus grandson of James II. We saw in Chapter 6 how unsettled Britain was by the attempts to return it to Catholicism but the defeat of James Stuart, the Old Pretender, in 1715 seemed to have established a period of certainty under the protestant Hanoverian monarchs. Now, in the 1740s, the Stuarts were again threatening the stability of the state.

James Collier wrote to his father from London on the 16th February 1744:

> *A message from the King was yesterday delivered to the House of Lords signifying that the pretender's eldest son was now in France and that an invasion was intended, supported by the French Fleet cruising on the British coast ... when the Lord Chancellor read this message the Duke of Marlborough rose up and declared he would spend the last drop of his blood in support of the present Royal family and moved an address to his Majesty to assure him that the Lords would stand by and support him and his family with their lives and fortunes.*

So England was already on a war footing even before the formal declaration as made. John Collier, as Solicitor for the Cinque Ports and agent for the Duke of Newcastle was asked to help raise troops for the local Militia. Around the 26th February 1744 he received a letter from Sackville Bale in Whitehall – presumably a civil servant – conveying the Duke's compliments and asking Collier to provide the *"names of three gentlemen that are fit and willing to serve as captain, lieutenant and ensign in the company belonging to your port"*. Bale further asked for recommendations for three "proper" persons for Winchelsea and for Pevensey and wondered whether there were *"arms, drums or colours belonging to the companies of those three places"*. The letter concludes by saying that the Government was awaiting news from Admiral Sir John Norris – Commander in Chief of the

George II at the Battle of Dettingen, 27 June 1743
The last time a British Monarch led his troops into
battle

Channel Fleet – concerning fifteen French ships which had been seen lying off Dymchurch the previous morning.

Another letter, this time from the Duke's private secretary and Hastings MP Andrew Stone, was written to Collier on the same day as Bale's, recording that the French squadron is *"gone westward"* and that Sir John Norris was following them. Collier was now asked to *"employ some proper persons to keep a good look out upon the coast and when they shall see either of these squadrons, or any part of them, that you will send immediate notice of it by express to my lord duke."* This he duly did, reporting back to the Duke at length the following day that 15 French Men of War had sailed past Hastings and were believed to have anchored at Romney Bay to the east of 'Dengeness' point. Sir John Norris and the British fleet were approaching when *"there was a violent rain that evening and the wind changed"*.

In fact what Collier had witnessed was nothing less than a full-scale invasion plan. The French intended to install the Jacobite Stuart on the throne as James III who would end Britain's anti-French alliances with Austria and the Dutch. A French army estimated at between 6,000 and 15,000 men had assembled at Dunkirk which would equal or outnumber the standing British Army stationed in the south of England. By the 26th February French transport ships had sailed from Dunkirk and were on their way to Maldon in Essex which had been selected for the landings. But their covering squadron under French Admiral Roquefeuil miscalculated the location of Norris and his Channel Fleet, believing them to be in Portsmouth. Once the British war ships appeared at Romney Bay the French withdrew, and Norris followed in pursuit. As with the Spanish Armada 150 year earlier, it was the weather that ultimately saved England. The violent rain and the change in the wind that John Collier had noted turned into a major storm. Twelve French transport vessels were sunk, more than half going down with all hands. The rest were severely damaged and forced to limp back into Dunkirk. Roquefeuil's Men of War were dispersed by the storm, finally making it back to their home port of Brest badly battered. The British fleet, having found shelter in South Coast ports, remained mainly undamaged and the French invasion plans were cancelled. Admiral Norris retired the following year to his estates at Benenden in Kent. A memorial to him in the local church reads in part:

> *... there never breathed a better Seaman, a greater Officer, a braver Man, a more zealous wellwisher to the present Establishment, nor consequently a truer Englishman than this Sir John Norris'.*

If the immediate threat of invasion was over, normality did not entirely return to the citizens of Sussex. For a start they were forced to billet a growing number of soldiers. The Prime Minister, Henry Pelham, himself recognised the problems this was causing when he wrote to Collier about estate business:

> *The great assembling of troops at present has been on account of the late threatened invasion, a little time must clear up these affairs and when the government is safe you may be assured the people will be eased.*

We don't have any direct reports from the letters of just how greatly the people of Hastings were incommoded by these troops, but we get a hint of it from an ironic line in a letter from William Cranston to Collier in March 1744:

> *Your situation as to soldiers is truly miserable but there's no help for it, better them than Frenchmen.*

A fortnight or so later the troops quartered in Hastings were sent to Canterbury. Apparently they were eager – if not desperate - to get away, as Collier had earlier observed to Mary:

> *Munday there is to be a draft of ten men of a company out of this regiment, so 100 in all and the same out of every regiment in England, to go directly to Flanders. This is very far from being disagreeable to the soldiers, or occasion any desertion, for there's more than 30 in each company have given their names to be of the number, and some threaten to desert if they don't go.*

The problem, as Collier observed, was that those who replaced them in the town seem to have been even worse:

> *The soldiers marched this morning towards Canterbury but 3 companies of Lord Henry Beauclerk's who have been at Portsmouth, supplied their places ...and I suppose we shall have the pleasure of their*

company till Munday. They seem a parcel of ill cloathed creatures ... all these marches have been made without due consideration to this country as to quarters, lodgings etc. The poor creatures, especially the women have a terrible time of it, not beds for a quarter.

But many those who did finally get to Flanders may have ended up regretting their enthusiasm to be out of England. The second large battle of the War of the Austrian Succession in which British troops played a major part took place the following spring in Fontenoy in Belgium near Tournai. The French army of 50,000 was confronted by the slightly larger 'pragmatic' allied army under the command of the Duke of Cumberland, the youngest son of George II. It was not a notable success. In fact the British contingent suffered 4000 casualties including 200 officers. Cumberland had to withdraw towards Brussels, which left the French to take control of most of Flanders.

News of the scale of the defeat filtered through to Hastings over the succeeding days. William Cranston wrote to Collier from Johnston's Court:

As the numbers lost is uncertain so is their quality also, some affirming that Lord Albemarle and his elder son Lord Ancram are dead, Campbell, Cope with one leg each, the Duke and Lord Crowford wounded, the former losing two horses from under him.

This report is notable for its inaccuracies – doubtless the product of the frenzied rumours reaching

London just four days after the battle. Lord Albemarle was wounded not killed, and his son didn't take part in the battle as he wasn't born until 1772. Lieutenant-General Sir James Campbell lost more than a leg, being fatally wounded in the fighting.

Collier's future son in law Captain James Murray, who was soon himself to serve in Flanders, was equally wayward with the casualty figures suggesting *"our loss can't be less than 10,000"*, when he wrote to Hastings on the same day as Cranston, praising the British allies: *"the Dutch behaved with unexpected resolution and zeal, their numbers lost are proof of this."* By the following week, while more accurate information was being conveyed, the story of Cumberland's disastrous defeat was already beginning to be rewritten. James Collier penned a letter to his father 11 days after the battle mentioning George Worge, Collier's son-in-law through his first marriage:

> *Mr Worge was very uneasy about his brother and is glad to find he is only wounded. It is generally agreed that if the Dutch horse had behaved, as they ought to have done we should certainly have succeeded in our attempt. The Duke of Cumberland's behaviour was such that he is now the toast of all companies and the event appears not so fatal as was first apprehended.*

These differing accounts of the battle are illustrative of the way news travelled in the mid 18th century, before the advent of national newspapers or electronic communication. The difficulty of getting reliable information became even more apparent in 1745, as rebellion again threatened the stability of the realm. As with the near invasion the previous year, the French were again assisting the catholic Jacobite cause by actively supporting the Young Pretender Charles Edward Stuart. But the extent of any actual military intervention was unknown. And without tangible French support, the Jacobite Scots were unwilling to rebel. Charles however decided to press on and, in August, landed in Scotland with two French ships and around 100 volunteers from the French Army's Irish Brigade.

By September he had persuaded a number of Highland clan chiefs to his cause and entered Edinburgh where a reputed 20,000 cheering citizens greeted the Jacobite army. The Old Pretender was declared King James VIII of Scotland, and Charles made plans to launch an invasion of England. The first indication of the impending crisis in the Collier correspondence comes in mid-October when Cranston writes to Hastings giving somewhat opaque news that:

> *upon the late success of the rebels their neighbours in the highlands who were before esteemed well affected, had imprisoned their chiefs and were marching to join the pretender.*

In fact by then things had moved on rather faster than Cranston seems aware. The Jacobite army had fairly comprehensively defeated the English under Sir John Cope at the Battle of Prestonpans in East Lothian. Around 500 English were killed and the same number wounded, while Charles Stuart's forces lost only about 40 killed and 80 wounded. It opened England up to the Pretender's march south and, if it did nothing else, it sent shivers through the financial markets as Cranston told Collier on 22 October, a month after the battle.

The effect this rebellion has already had upon credit is almost past belief and could not have guessed it but by being amongst it. I was in company last night with 2 top Lancashire and Cheshire agents. Who assured me neither of 'em had made out a writ in either county for near six weeks past so but a gloomy prospect for the law. No new birthday clothes for the ladies, the looms being all at a stand.

In November Carlisle fell to the Jacobite army. The government seemed slowly to be realizing the gravity of the threat and recalled The Duke of Cumberland from Flanders along with 12,000 troops, suspended Habeas Corpus and increased the recruitment and activities of local militias. A fact noted by James Collier as he wrote home to Hastings:

The City Militia are constantly exercised and part do duty every night in several places; a six o clock 100 march with beat of drum and fix their headquarters in St Dunstan's vestry room from whence at ten a party of them are detached to take post at temple bar and relieved every two hours. They stand on each side of the way with their bayonets fixed challenge every foot passenger and stop every coach and open the doors to see that no arms are concealed. [James Collier in London to John, 7 November 1745]

James also mentions to his father the 'Deptford Procession'. This serves as an interesting illustration of

'Bonnie Prince Charlie'
Charles Edward Stewart - 1720-1788

the apparent attitude of the English people to the threat of the Jacobite rebellion. To mark King George's birthday the south London borough of Deptford, then a separate town, performed a mocking imitation of Catholicism with a procession of effigies portraying a Highlander, a Jesuit, two Capuchin friars, the Pretender, and the Pope. According to historian Laura O'Friel,

> *The Capuchins, complete with flogging rods and rosaries, carried a sign titled "Indulgences Cheap as Dirt," listing various sins and required sum for forgiveness. Murder cost 9 pence, reading the Bible a thousand pounds, and engaging in Rebellion cost nothing at all but gained sinners a reward in Heaven*

Support for the King seems to have been widespread, certainly in the shire counties. Colonel Pelham, Hastings MP and cousin to both the Prime Minister and the Duke of Newcastle, wrote to Collier in November suggesting this should be shown in some tangible form

> *I forgot to acquaint you last post that his grace and we all think there should be an address to His Majesty from our corporation, since they are so general. We are time enough and no reason to fear our loyalty and zeal for the government can be suspected.*

The tide seemed to be slowly turning against Bonnie Prince Charlie and the Scottish rebellion. By 4th December they had penetrated as far south as Derby, but two days later decided on a withdrawal to to Scotland. Cumberland's army arrived at Carlisle on 22 December, forcing the garrison to surrender a week later, removing any Jacobite military presence below the Scottish border. But in the south fears had been rising about another cross-channel invasion by the French in support of the Jacobite army in the north, as Cranston told Collier on 7th December...

> *We are in a good deal of consternation in town more from an assurance of a large embarkation from Dunkirk than from the rebels, who may now be said to be flying from the Duke's army ....but the apprehension of a landing in Suffolk, Norfolk, or Lincolnshire and of the rebels going thither to join 'em and towards which countries the are supposed to be pointing , greatly alarms us ... pray god send us out of these difficulties speedily.*

If divine intervention was to happen, it was not to do so immediately. Two days later Cranston is writing to Collier that the invasion seemed to have happened:

> *The alarm the town was in this morning, and especially the great ones, is not to be expressed, occasioned by a messenger from Mr Harrison of Seaford ... that there were a number of French ships actually in Pevensea bay, and the soldiers landing...*

The report was dispatched to London, arriving at the Duke of Newcastle's at 2.00 am. He got up and took it to St James's by 3.00 where:

Lord chancellor, Lord Harrington etc etc etc all assemble in council by 4.00. The guards of all kinds instantly called up and assembled in the park ... between 8 and 12 all this news flew like wild fire through the streets of the city. The two chief justices then actually sitting at Guildhall rose from their benches in the middle of their causes.

But it turned out to be a false alarm and Mr Harrison of the Seaford Customs house rather sheepishly admitted that he was 'misinformed' and that the ships that had been spotted were in fact British cutters sent out by Admiral Vernon. Nonetheless Cranston's account provides a vivid picture of the extent of the crisis and the fear circulating even in the highest government circles. Notwithstanding the error, The Duke of Newcastle wrote directly to John Collier on the 13th December saying intelligence had been received that preparations *'are being made at Dunkirk and other parts in France, for making an immediate descent upon some parts of the coast."* Collier replied the following day:

....in humble obedience to your commands [I] immediately dispatched directions to all Customs officers on the coast of this county and in Kent to keep a good lookout and constantly patrol day and night ...we have a constant double watch patrolling the coast at this place and proper persons at Farleight church and the summit of all the hills near the town to observe and give intelligence ...

Collier is as good as his word and has two Hastings fishermen convey the various reports to Admiral Vernon and the Channel fleet. Unfortunately since the bearers, Harrison and Phillips are reputed smugglers, they are immediately detained and, in Harrison's case, actually clapped in irons by the Admiral. There then ensues the testy war of words outlined in Chapter 10 between Collier and Vernon.

By the 21st December James Collier is writing to his father in Hastings that:

> *Tis generally believed here that the invasion will not take place in the south part of Great Britain but they will attempt to land their forces at Melrose. I am in great hopes that tomorrow will prove a more favourable day than this which has been the most disagreeable this season.*

Over the Christmas period Cumberland, the King's son, marched the English army from Carlisle across to Edinburgh, reaching the Scottish capital on 30th January. But in the meantime General Hawley, commanding the King's forces in Scotland, left Edinburgh in an attempt to relieve Stirling Castle, and suffered a serious defeat at the hands of the rebels whose army had now swelled to around 8,000. A portion of Hawley's troops fled in the heat of battle. Sir Thomas Webster wrote to Collier on 27th January:

> *Our unaccountable miscarriage in Scot-land causes great consternation, these repeated pannicks, and ill behaviour of so many of our troops, becomes serious and*

big with just apprehensions of bad consequences.

Two days later John Collier found himself caught up in a fascinating affair which well illustrates the mood of the country, and especially those on the South Coast at this stage in the Jacobite uprising. Three men in a small boat were driven ashore at Eastbourne by a storm. They arrived at an alehouse in Pevensey seeking a fresh boat to carry them across the channel to France and were directed to another Inn in Hooe which was a known smugglers haunt. However their behaviour not surprisingly aroused suspicions given the state of the hostilities with the French and they were detained by a group of locals who sent word to Collier in his capacity as a law officer in Hastings. He wrote to the Duke of Newcastle on 29th January 1746:

> *I sent a party to take care of and bring them hither, which they did about 10 this morning. I examined several persons who swear positively as to their desiring a boat to carry some of them to France...One of them calls himself James Bishopp, brother to Sir Cecil Bishopp of this county aged about 30. Another his servant named James Cravellion ... the third one Abraham Ibbotson ...they acknowledge themselves Roman Catholics.*

Collier confined the three men in custody of the troops quartered in Hastings under a Captain Campbell and asked Newcastle what he thought should be done about them. The matter was delicate as Bishopp was the younger brother of a Sussex landowner and MP and baronet, Sir Cecil Bishopp. The Duke's secretary Andrew Stone replied that the Duke would send for them to be brought to London in custody and examined as possible traitors. Two days later the Duke himself wrote to Collier:

> *His majesty very much approves the zeal and attention you have shewed for his service on this occasion. You will send me an account of any expense you have been or shall have for the subsistence of the prisoners.*

Ibbotson, Bishopp and his servant were duly transported to London under guard, and examined by Newcastle. They were then granted bail of considerable sums - £4,000 and £1,000 respectively – to appear in court. One of those who guaranteed Bishopp's surety was Lord Thomas Gage, a Roman Catholic who'd inherited a Baronetcy that had originally been purchased from James I. The Duke of Richmond, writing to Newcastle on 28th February 1746 says with some irony, that Bishopp's *'designs must have been treasonable because my Lord Gage assured me they were not.'* The letter also asks what became of the examination of Mr Bishopp? There is no answer from Newcastle and whether they ever stood trial or what the outcome was is, unfortunately, not readily to be found in contemporary records. One postscript however shows Collier in decidedly human light. Writing after the three men had left is custodial care in Hastings he complains bitterly:

> *Mr Bishopp in his last moments at this place did not keep up the character of a*

Gentleman. He was used as such though under suspicion of being a traitor to his country, permitted to remain under guard in an inn, directed his own provisions, wine etc, and during the whole time intimated discharging the same, but at his departure refused paying a shilling said he was a state prisoner and therefore could contract no debt nor none would pay and indeed went off in a surly, abrupt manner.

Fortunately the rebellion was drawing to a close. After Cumberland's Army reached Edinburgh the main Jacobite force retreated to Inverness. The English troops advanced along the coast, entered Aberdeen on 27 February and approached Inverness a fortnight later. There the Battle of Culloden on 16 April proved a decisive defeat for the Young Pretender and the Jacobite cause. Charles Stuart narrowly escaped and evaded capture before being helped to flee by boat to Skye dressed as the maid of Flora MacDonald.

Writing to Collier from London, William Cranston probably summed up the feelings of the nation:

I think an happy occasion is at last arrived when we may fairly congratulate one another. The victory seems to be compleat and the rebels totally demolished. We have had nothing but bells, guns ere since ten this morning. Those of the tower and in the park led the van, and, whilst I was on the water the standard was put up at the tower...The joy seems to be universal.
[Cranston to Collier 24 April 1746]

It wouldn't be the last time for John Collier that an enemy would threaten the way of life of those in Hastings and the country at large, but the French backed '45 rebellion was clearly as immediate and as frightening an event as any in his lifetime.

§§§

Who's Who in Chapter 12, War and Rebellion

Nathaniel Cruttenden. Hastings Mayor 1733, 1738, 1744, 1749. Brickmaker, land owner, Commissioner for Sussex Land Tax, Commissioner Hastings' Land and Window taxes

King George II - George Augustus (1683-1760) Succeeded George I in 1727. He was Duke of Brunswick-Lüneburg (Hanover) and a prince-elector of the Holy Roman Empire. Married 1705 Caroline of Ansbach.

James Francis Edward Stuart. 1688 - 1766, The 'Old Pretender'. Catholic. Son of James Stuart. Half-brother of Mary.

Charles Edward Stuart 1720 –1788 'The Young Pretender" aka Bonnie Prince Charlie. Great grandson King James II. Jacobite claimant to the throne. Led the 1745 uprisings. Defeated at Culloden April 1746. Escaped from Scotland and lived rest of his life on continent.

James Collier. John and Mary's second son. Nicknamed Jemmy. London lawyer. Died 1747 aged 26

Sir John Norris 1670 -1749 – Admiral of the Fleet. Served during Nine Years War, War of Spanish Succession, Great Northern War, and War of Jenkins' Ear. Commander of the Channel Fleet in war with France and Jacobite rebellion 1744-1746.

Andrew Stone 1703–1773. Private secretary to the Duke of Newcastle. Confident of Pelham family. MP for Hastings 1741 to 1761. Government minister. Royal advisor, tutor secretary and treasurer under George II and George III.

Duke of Newcastle – Thomas Pelham-Holles. 1693-1768. Whig statesman, party manager and fixer. Sussex Land owner. Elder brother of Henry Pelham. Secretary of State for 30 years . Prime Minister 1754-1756 & 1757-1762. Benefactor of John Collier.

Duke of Richmond – (2nd Duke) **Charles Lennox.** 1701–1750 Courtier and Politician and regular correspondent of Duke of Newcastle.

Henry Pelham. 1694-1750. Whig Prime Minster 1743-1754. Brother to Duke of Newcastle. Employed Collier as steward to manage his estates.

Duke of Cumberland Prince William Augustus, 1721 - 1765), third and youngest son of King George II and Caroline of Ansbach. Commanded defeated allied army battle of Battle of Fontenoy 1745. Commanded loyalist British forces against 1745 Jacobite rebellion. Defeated Young Pretender Charles Stuart at Battle of Culloden 1746. Dubbed 'butcher' for his subsequent ruthless pursuit of Jacobites.

James Murray 1721-1794. John Collier's son-in-law having married Cordelia Collier in 1748. Son of Scottish

Roman Catholics. Successful army career, Captain 1742, Major 1745, Lt Col 1751, Major General 1762. Served with General Wolfe in Canada. Governor Qubec 1760-68, Deputy Govenor Minorca 1774-84. Owner Beauport Park Hastings.

George Worge. Collier's son-in-law (as husband to Elizabeth Collier –his daughter from his first marriage). Solicitor in Battle. Confident and friend.

Colonel **James Pelham** (Jemmy) of Crowhurst. Cousin to D. of Newcastle. Hastings MP 1741-61. Coronation canopy bearer with Collier 1727.

General **Henry Hawley** 1685 –1759 British army officer, served at Battles of Dettington and Fontenoy. Military commander in Scotland during Jacobite uprising. Defeated at Falkirk but commanded cavalry under Cumberland at Culloden 1746

Sir Thomas Webster clothing manufacturer, elected MP Colchester 1705 and 1711. Subsequently expelled from Parliament on both occasions. Financed legal action against Hastings Corporation. Correspondent of John Collier

James Bishopp. Apprehended in Hooe and questioned by Collier (and later Newcastle) as alleged Jacobite traitor. He was younger brother of Sir Cecil Bishopp - 6th Baronet of Parham in Sussex and an MP.

Abraham Ibbotson – a farmer apprehended with James Bishopp as alleged Jacobite traitor.

Thomas Gage, (1st Viscount Gage) of Firle Place Sussex, MP for 33 years between 1717 and 1753. Roman Catholic whose inherited Baronetcy had originally been purchased from James I.

Chapter 13

An Impecunious Jacobite son-in-law.

In 1760 Collier was in the last year of his life. His health had been extremely poor for some time. It seems he had suffered a stroke several years earlier and he was now plagued with gout. But according to his descendent Charles Sayer, by 1759 his mental faculties had 'recovered' and so it is likely he would have been able to receive, and understand, the most extraordinary family news .... his son in law had just been appointed Governor of Quebec having distinguished himself in battle, serving under General Woolf in the famous siege and capture of that city the previous year.

That Collier could get and comprehend this news would have been a source of some satisfaction to Colonel James Murray who, in 1748, had married Collier's eldest daughter Cordelia. Murray's rise up the military ladder had been greatly aided by both Collier's money and his political influence and Murray always promised his father-in-law he would do his utmost to repay him through his achievements if not thought his purse: *"I am far from despairing of success in my profession and I shall ever study to behave as your son ought to do"*, he wrote.

It must also have been of some pleasure to Collier that the youth whose politics and religion he detested and thus seriously disapproved of as a match for his daughter had 'made good'. Indeed of all Collier's descendants, James Murray was to be much the most famous – recognized nationally and internationally for his accomplishments.

Later we'll look at the not inconsiderable problems John and, after his death, Mary Collier had with their four other marriageable daughters. But in this chapter it's worth detouring down a parallel by-way to examine the particular trials their eldest, Cordelia, posed for them. And we'll take that journey at this point because it is so relevant to the previous chapter.

To begin we must travel nearly 500 miles north for an introduction to 'Bare' Betty.

Elizabeth Stirling was the daughter of an eminent Edinburgh surgeon and the town's MP, George Stirling. During a public examination this somewhat precocious schoolgirl was referred to as "Betty" Stirling. "Oh no," she is reputed to have admonished the teacher, "you can call me Mistress Betty ... or Miss Elizabeth ... but certainly not bare Betty." Naturally from that moment on she was known universally as 'Bare' Betty. In her mid-teens she met Alexander Murray, her future husband, who was a student at Edinburgh University. In fact his proper title was Alexander Murray, 4th Lord Elibank.

This Scottish peerage had been created in 1643 for Sir Patrick Murray who became the 1st Baronet, having supported the Royalist cause in the English Civil war by 'lending' Charles I considerable sums of money. This, along with five marriages and involuntary levies to the Covenanters in the Scottish Civil War, rather depleted the family fortunes. Nonetheless Alexander Murray was brought up in some splendour at Ballencrieff and was wealthy enough, after inheriting his title, to invest heavily in the stock market. This was not his wisest decision because, following the South Sea Bubble of 1720, he pretty much lost the lot.

So there's Alexander Murray, 4th Lord Elibank, and his wife, 'Bare' Betty now living in genteel poverty with four sons, all of whom need to be given - or purchased - a good start in life, when their problems are compounded by the arrival of a fifth boy, James, on 21 January 1721.

Primogeniture – the common law right of the eldest son to inherit the family land and property – was introduced into British law by William the Conqueror in 1066 and only finally abolished in 1925. While it may have been efficient in preserving intact the assets of the aristocracy or landed gentry, it was pretty rough on younger sons. By tradition they had few options but to go into the Army or the Church if they didn't want to 'lower' themselves and take up a profession. In wealthy families their plight might be eased by a remittance from the family estate, but otherwise they were pretty much on their own.

The sons of Alexander Murray tended to follow the traditional route. Patrick, born 1703, would inherit the title but initially was able to benefit from some military sinecures before studying for the law and marrying an heiress.

George Murray was born in 1706 and entered the Royal Navy at the age of 15, rising to rank of captain and serving, controversially, with Commodore Anson in his 1740s squadron that circumnavigates the globe - controversial because Murray's ship became separated from the others while rounding the Cape and returned to England without completing the voyage.

The third son, the Rev. Dr. Gideon Murray became chaplain-general to the army and a cannon at Durham Cathedral, while the fourth boy, Alexander, turned to politics and became a fervent supporter of the Jacobite cause.

The fact was that the entire family were Jacobites, but they were canny enough to avoid openly siding with Bonnie Prince Charlie in the '45 rebellion. Horace Walpole, Whig politician and man of letters, said of the two older two Murray/Elibank brothers that they were:

both such active Jacobites that if the Pretender had succeeded, they could have produced many witnesses to testify their zeal for him ... both so cautious, that no witness of actual treason could be produced by the government against them.

Anyway the fifth and youngest son James was educated by Mr William Dyce at a school in Selkirk in the Borders and, conscious he would receive little or no financial help from his family, signed up as a cadet in the Royal Scots at the age of 15. His division, the 3rd Scots, was stationed at Ypres in Flanders in the "Dutch Service". In 1740 he successfully applied for, and obtained, a commission as a second Lieutenant in "Waynard's Marines". This was a new regiment in the British Army named after its founder John Wynyard, also known as 47th Foot or 4th Marines. A Lieutenant-Colonel in that same Regiment was one Patrick Murray – the future 5th Lord of Elibank and James' eldest brother.

Patrick's army 'career' is worth noting briefly as an example of the extraordinary extent of patronage prevalent at the time. The future Lord Elibank was just three years old when he was commissioned in the army with a rank of Captain! It seems that Queen Anne, determined to shore up the Act of Union which she had achieved in 1701, allowed for a number of blank commissions in Scottish regiments which senior officers such as Colonel Alexander Grant were encouraged to award to relatives and friends so as to ensure future loyalty.

A reconstruction of Ballencrieff Castle.
Seat of the Elibanks, and childhood home of James
Murray.

Courtesy of the artist Andrew Spratt

According to Arthur C Murray, Lord Elibank's descendant and biographer, the Queen herself signed the commission of the three-year-old Patrick:

> *Still more astonishing though doubtless highly gratifying to his parents – was the military regulation which permitted the issue of pay and allowances to infant warriors of commissioned rank; the regulation being exemplified in the case of Patrick by a document dated 1711 – when the doughty soldier was eight years old – setting forth the regimental pay due to him including arrears for services in Flanders for himself and two servants! ... though nominally serving in Flanders, the youthful captain was still at his school-desk in Musslburgh.*

This helpful start in life enabled Patrick Murray to complete school studies, attend Edinburgh University and train as a lawyer, before being gazetted as a major in 'Ponsonby's Foot', part of the 37th (North Hampshire) Regiment of Foot later being appointed Colonel in the 47th Foot.

The history of the two brothers' sojourns in the Caribbean during the War of Jenkins' Ear along with their part in the unsuccessful Carthagena campaign can be studied elsewhere. Suffice it to say that in 1742 Collier's future son-in-law, James, returned to England as Captain of the Grenadier Company of the 15th Regiment of Foot and fought in Europe during the War of the Austrian Succession being, in 1745, badly wounded during the

Siege of Ostend and, the following year, distinguishing himself in the Raid on Lorient.

It was during this period – perhaps while recovering from his wounds - that Captain Murray came to be stationed in Hastings, as part of the anti-smuggling garrison whose barracks were next to All Saints Church. Immediately opposite which was the elegant house of John Collier, wherein resided his daughter Cordelia now in her early 20s.

Throughout history there have been no shortage of fathers who disapproved of their daughter's choice of husband, and not a few fathers who have, similarly, thought their son's choice of partner was unworthy. In James Murray and Cordelia Collier both families appeared united in their opposition to the romance and proposed union.

Editor of the 1907 edition of the Collier letters, and descendant of the family, Charles Sayer concludes:

> *There are many indications in the correspondence that Col Murray was on bad terms with his brother Lord Elibank (who) probably considered that Mrs Murray's fortune was not of a sufficient amount to Justify Colonel Murray's marrying out of his own rank: and a difference in politics perhaps had something to do with it.*

Heather Warne whose classification of the Collier letters is still used by the National Archives has a similar view:

> *The match was opposed on both sides, because of Murray's poor financial*

*position and by the Murrays because he
was marrying below his rank.*

Citing town records, Hastings Historian J
Mainwaring Baines reaches the much same conclusion:

> *James Murray met Cordelia Collier while
> he was stationed in the town as a young
> officer. Her father was against the match
> but when he found there was 'such an
> attachment between 'em I doubt cannot
> be got the better of' he relented and they
> were married in London in 1748.*

Collier himself seldom if ever speaks particularly
warmly of Murray and in a letter to his Friend Thomas
Green in 1750 he is at his most candid:

> *You are no stranger to my opinion of her
> marriage, but when I found it could not
> be agreeably prevented I was desirous of
> making the best of it...*

The young soldier and suitor clearly realised his,
and his family's, Jacobite leanings were proving a major
obstacle in both his personal and professional life. As we
saw in the last chapter the '45 rebellion put the nation
on a high alert against papists. John Collier was nothing
if not a staunch Anglican and a dedicated Whig so it's
unsurprising that an impecunious Jacobite soldier was
not his first choice for a son-in-law. Indeed it's clear that,
initially, Collier refused to countenance the match: *"I told
him I could never think of marrying my daughter to the
uncertain situation he was in"*.   All of which makes his

subsequent behavior towards Murray the more magnanimous.

Collier's ledger for December 1748 shows he paid out £200 *"to Mrs Murray for her wedding cloathes"* and on the next line, *to ditto as a present for pocket money £21.00.* But it was what he was subsequently prepared to do for his son-in-law that shows him in a truly good light.

We know that the marriage took place at St Bride's in London, but not whether the respective parents attended. Alexander, the 4th Lord Elibank had died in 1736, but his widow 'Bare' Betty was still alive, and his elder brother Patrick was now the 5th Lord. Had they made the 400 mile journey south from Edinburgh? Had John and Mary Collier made the arduous 50 mile Journey north from Hastings? And if they met, what did the two families make of each other?

From the Collier letters we can see that the courtship between Cordelia and James Murray had been conducted over several years. His name is first mentioned in November 1744 when he paid a surprise visit to James Collier in London who conveyed the news to his father in Hastings:

> *Last Wednesday morning I was extremely surprised at an unexpected visit from Captain Murray who came to town the day before. He breakfasted here and we were afterwards walking in the park ... I have seen the captain since and find that he has thoughts of going to Scotland*

Cordelia Collier. She married James Murray in 1748

The following May sees Murray in correspond-dence with Collier in Hastings, and we get the first indication that he had already been seeking his help, and quite possibly, his financial assistance:

> *I am favored with both yours, for which and the trouble you have often had with my affairs, you'll please accept my hearty and sincere thanks ... As every opportunity I have of shewing my gratitude for the uncommon civilities I have met with from your family, will give me infinite joy, I hope you'll lay your commands always upon me and in the meantime make my compliments to Mrs Collier, Miss Delia and the other young ladys.*

Later that month James Collier notes that *"Captain Murray, I find by my uncle, has gone to Hastings".* So it's clear that James Murray was a regular visitor to the Colliers for a number of years before he finally married Cordelia. And if John Collier didn't help him with his debts before then, he certainly did afterwards. In 1748 Murray's regiment was due to be stationed in Ireland for a year which, it appears, was not a popular posting for either bride of groom. Indeed it seems they asked Collier if he could bring some influence to bear to get Murray excused. He couldn't. Then Cordelia wrote to her father about their financial situation if they were leaving England, along with the cost of a possible promotion for Murray. She even asked for an advance loan on strength of her wedding settlement. Collier drafted a reply declining this – though we don't know if the letter was ever actually sent.

According to Charles Sayer, Murray then took the £600 from his own savings – a fund he was building in order to purchase his way up the ranks of his regiment. It seems that Mary Collier was involved in the discussions over her daughter and son-in-law's finances as we see from the heartfelt, if somewhat angry letter, from Murray to John Collier in February 1749:

> *I can easily see from the alteration in your style that I have been unfortunate enough to incur your displeasure. I am sensible I don't deserve it, but I am born under an unlucky planet for though no man endeavors more to please, nobody ever succeeded less. My own relations blame and despise me for being so imprudent as to marry without bettering my circumstances, and by endeavoring to reconcile the affair then I am so unhappy as to add your displeasure to theirs. Some attempts too, have been made by Mrs Collier to irritate my own wife against me. This is most unchristian and barbarous. God forgive her as I do, for surely nothing but and excess of the rage could have prevailed on Mrs Collier to have forgot herself so much.*

This risky strategy – openly criticizing Mary to her husband – seems to have paid off for later that year it seems Collier did advance Murray £1000 to enable him to buy the rank of Major. In May 1750 Murray wrote gushingly to his father-in-law:

I shall not attempt to express how grateful I am, words being incapable of it for had I been your only child I could not have expected so much indulgence, after having done everything to forfet your regard: I shall only say that as you have agreed to make me the happiest of men I should be most unworthy was I not to make it the study of my life to please the best of fathers and most generous benefactor that ever man had.

But that wasn't all. There was another promotion on the offing, and again Collier was prevailed upon to help out. As he explained, writing from Bath to his friend Thomas Green in the August 1750 letter partly quoted above:

By letters last post from my Daughter Murray we have an account of their setting out for Ireland and safe arrival at Chester and we expect her here in 7-10 days. You are no stranger to my Opinion of her Marriage, but when I found it could not be agreeably prevented I was desirous of making the best of it. I have always had a satisfactory account of Mr Murray making a good husband and is very kind to her – There's the near prospect of his being Lt Colonel in his regiment & which also gets him rank"

Indeed, the next year 1750, Collier bought Murray the rank of Lieutenant Colonel for £1,900. It wasn't the last time that he was prevailed upon to help his son-in-law.

221

General James Murray,
Son of 4th Lord Elibank, husband of Cordelia Collier,
Governor of Quebec 1760, and Minorca 1774

In 1752 he interceded on Murray's behalf with Henry Pelham who was then Prime Minister. Murray thanked him profusely:

> *I can't express how sensibly I am obliged by your application to Mr Pelham and how I am vexed to the soul; that you should be put to the Blush on my account for his objection to my family is most plausible.*

Murray even cancelled a planned trip with his wife to visit his dying mother 'Bare' Betty in Scotland:

> *"I was aware that a visit to Scotland might be of no service to me in point of preferment at St James' ... and that the only proper place for me is the regiment which I shall constantly and diligently attend.*

But Murray's financial troubles continued, though it's uncertain whether it was because of his own extravagance or that, without a private income, it was near impossible for a couple to live on a Colonel's pay. In 1755 William Cranston writes to Collier about a visit he's had from Murray's friend Colonel Jorden to say that a rumour of his Regiment going abroad had brought all his creditors upon him and that he had no recourse but to sell his commission and go into the Queen of Hungary's service which said Col. Jorden would be his ruin. Cranston says: *"'tis a most unhappy affair all round & gives me much concern, & I almost bleed for Mr Murray."*

Once again Collier comes to the rescue and settles Murrays debts to the tune of £1,395. But Cranston raises an interesting point:

> *In my talk with Col Jorden about Mr Murray's affairs two of the things which occurred to you upon this occasion struck me also, - one was – why did he not apply to his own family for assistance – they had done nothing for him – you a great deal – The answer was that he was persuaded that so far from giving him any help t'wold be a matter of triumph for them to see him undone & you obliged to take his Wife from him – this is a horrid disposition & yet the Col assured me 'twas he real belief & from the little knowledge I have seen of them I don't think it at all improbable but may be true.*

At this point it's worth briefly embarking down yet another branch-line to enable us to obtain a better view of the Murray/Elibank family and in particular what their biographer Arthur Murray describes as its 'enfant terrible' - Alexander. It will prove illustrative of the feeling in the country exactly half way through the 18th Century, as well as helping to explain why Collier's help for his son-in-law was so vital to Murray's career.

Alexander, Betty's fourth son, had been born in 1712 and after an initial career in the army turned to politics and in particular to the Jacobite cause, supporting, in the 1750 Westminster election, their candidate Sir George Vandeput. Even though he secured a majority of the votes, Vanseput's rival Lord Trentham was declared victor and took the seat.

A petition to the house alleging a 'false return' so annoyed the authorities that they accused a number of people of, effectively, plotting against Trentham. One was Alexander Murray and he was summoned to the Bar of the House of Commons to answer the charge of 'menaces and seditious behaviour' from the high bailiff. A subsequent motion was passed demanding that Murray should kneel in contrition before parliament. This he refused to do, declaring:

> *"Sir, when I have committed a crime I kneel to God for pardon; but I cannot kneel to anybody else."*

The house was divided as to a suitable punishment. Eminent parliamentarians such as Henry Pelham, William Pitt, Henry Fox and Admiral Vernon all spoke in the debate which concluded with the Speaker's motion being passed that:

> *The Hon Alexander Murray having in the most insolent and audacious manner absolutely refused to be on his knees is guilty of the most dangerous attempt of the authority and privileges of this house.*

Murray was committed to Newgate jail on 6th February and denied pen paper or visitors. The case became a major cause célèbre with leaflets and cartoons circulating on the streets and in the coffee houses, condemning parliament for acting in an *"illegal, unconstitutional and unprecedented manner."* And it wasn't until the summer recess on 23rd June that Murray was finally released, albeit with the threat of being sent back to Newgate at a later date. He quietly left for France where he joined the entourage of the exiled Bonnie Prince Charlie. But it helped end the practice of prisoners being called before the Bar of the House on their knees. As constitutional historian Erskine May concluded:

> *The proud spirit of Alexander Murray revolted against this indignity. As a consequence some years later the Commons formally renounced the opprobrious usage by standing order.*

Alexander Murray's subsequent actions do not, however, show him in such a good light. While in Paris he was instrumental, with his elder brother Patrick, in planning a coup d'etat to overthrow George II. Ultimately the Elibank Plot came to nothing, though a fellow conspirator, Dr Archibald Cameron, was arrested and executed. Alexander remained in exile for a further nineteen years before being pardoned by the King's Privy Seal.

That these scandals affected the career of James Murray there can be little doubt. In 1756 he failed to get a job of Lieutenant Governor of Stirling Castle, despite Collier lobbying the Duke of Newcastle.

The following year, to encourage Murray to spend more time in Hastings, Collier arranged for him to become a freeman and a jurat of Hastings Corporation. But war intervened and Murray told Collier he had:

> *The honour to command a glorious regiment of my own training and am confident of acquiring a little reputation at least which in time may procure my preferment.... in the meantime I am put to*

great expense which is unavoidable. I have not been able to sell my horses so shall send them to Sussex to be sold there if possible.

The subsequent Raid on Rochfort – part of the Seven Year's War – was not a success, with the Army Commander Sir John Mordant refusing to commit his troops – including Murray's regiment – to battle. But the following year his chance to shine finally came as his regiment was sent to America.

The posting, however, led to a major change in family circumstances. Cordelia's health had not been of the best for some time – possibly as a result of contracting Smallpox while in Ireland - and it seems she absolutely refused to embark on the long and arduous trans-Atlantic sea voyage. So as Colonel James Murray sailed off to find fame – even if not great fortune - Cordelia remained behind in England.

In 1758 Murray was in command of a battalion at the successful siege and Capture of Louisbourg in Nova Scotia. This led the way for the British Army, now under General Wolfe, to move up the St Lawrence River to Quebec. At the famous Battle of the Plains of Abraham in which Wolfe was killed, Murray commanded the left wing of the British forces taking the most active and prominent part in the victory. He was rewarded by being appointed military governor of Quebec and then, three years later in 1763, the first civil governor of the entire province.

Eventually he was promoted to the rank Major General and subsequently became Governor of Minorca where he presided over one of those classic British military disasters which are converted into gallant successes by popular legend – defending and subsequently surrendering Fort St. Philip, at Port Mahon after seven months against impossible odds and with his own forces being daily depleted by appalling sickness.

It seems that his marriage to Cordelia barely survived the long years of separation while Murray was in Canada, but she did try to join him in Minorca, though was forced to return to England by ill health almost immediately. She died at the house Murray had built between Ore and Battle, Beauport Park, in 1779.

Murray returned to Hastings and took some part, as John Collier had hoped, in civic affairs as well as helping to organise Collier's estate after his death. He became owner of Bohemia House and Farm as well as the Swan Inn. He died at Beauport on 18 June 1794, and is buried in the apse of the now ruined Old St Helen's Church.

§§§

Who's Who Chapter 13. An Impecunious Son in Law

Charles Lane Sayer – *descendent of John Collier, transcriber and editor of The Correspondence of John Collier and his Family pub. 1907*

General James Woolf (1727-1759) British Army officer, served in War of Austrian Sucession, Jacobite Rebellion and Seven Years War. Second-in-command of expedition to capture the Fortress of Louisbourg. Commander of British forces which sailed up the Saint Lawrence River to capture Quebec City. After a long siege Wolfe was killed at the height of the Battle of the Plains of Abraham.

James Murray 1721-1794. John Collier's son-in-law having married Cordelia Collier in 1748. Son of Scottish Roman Catholics. Successful army career, Captain 1742, Major 1745, Lt Col 1751, Major General 1762. Served with General Wolfe in Canada. Governor Quebec 1760-68, Deputy Govenor Minorca 1774-84. Owner Beauport Park Hastings

Elizabeth 'Bare Betty' Stirling. Daughter of George Stirling born around 1683. Married Alexander Murray (4th Lord Elibank) February 1698. Mother of James Murray - thus Cordelia Murray nee Collier's mother-in-law - and 4 other sons and 5 daughters. Died November 1756.

Patrick Murray 5th Lord Elibank 1703-1778. James Murray's eldest brother. Jacobite. Army colonel. Wit and member of Edinburg literary circle.

George Murray 6th Lord Elibank 1706-1785. Captain in Royal Navy. Sailed with commodore Anson's squadron on round the world voyage in 1740 but became separated and his ship the Pearl returned straight to London. Accused of deliberately deserting his squadron on active service. Robustly defended by his descendant Col Arthur C Murray.

Gideon Murray (1710-1776) Rev. Dr. Gideon Murray became chaplain-general to the army and a cannon At Durham Cathedral. Was present with George II at the Battle of Dettingen in 1743. Chaplain of 43rd (afterwards 42nd) Highlanders.

Alexander Murray 1712-1778 Soldier then Politician. Nicknamed the Jacobite Earl of Westminster. Jailed for refusing to kneel at the Bar to the House of Commons following allegations of defamation during 1750 Westminster Election. Fled to Paris, joined entourage of (Bonnie Prince) Charles Edward Stuart. Co-conspirator in Elibank Plot to overthrow George II.

Arthur C Murray. Army Colonel. Biographer. Author of The Murrays of Elibank and The Five sons of 'Bare' Betty (1936).

Queen Anne (1665 –1714) Daughter of James II but raised a protestant and succeeded to throne following death of King William III in 1702. Most notable for creating United Kingdom following Act of Union with Scotland in 1707. Married to Prince George of Denmark

Heather Warne – catalogued the Collier papers for an Archive Diploma Dissertation in 1966 and wrote biographical introduction. Her classification of the Collier Letters is still used by the collection at the East Sussex Record Office

J Manwaring Baines. Hastings Historian. Author of Historic Hastings, a Tapestry of Life

James Collier. John and Mary's second son. Nicknamed Jemmy. Died 1747 aged 26.

Mary Collier. b 1710. Second daughter of John Collier and Elizabeth Elphick.

Thomas Green. Friend of John Collier who was executor of his will. Had estate in Norfolk.

Henry Pelham. (1694-1750) Whig Prime Minster 1743-1754. Brother to Duke of Newcastle. Employed Collier as Steward to manage his estates.

William Cranston – Mary Collier's younger brother. John Collier's legal partner based in London. John Collier always refers to William as 'my brother' rather than brother-in-law.

Lord Trentham (Granville Leveson Gower) 1721-1803) Brother in law of Duke of Bedford. Spent £4,400 to become MP for Westminster in 1747. Appointed Lord of Admiralty and had to seek re-election in 1750. Opposed by Sir George Vandeput, wealthy Huguenot. Bedford, supported by governing faction, rigged the election. A petition from (among others) Alexander Murray accused the High Baliff of electoral fraud but in turn Murray found himself charged with 'menaces and seditious behaviour'.

Sir George Vandeput, *second* baronet *of* Twickenham. Descendant of Henry Vandeput of Antwerp who fled religious persecution with other Protestants in 1568. Contested Westminster Parliamentary seat in 1750 and was beaten in rigged election by Lord Trentham. Supported by Lord Elibank and Alexander Murray.

William Pitt, 1st Earl of Chatham, (1708 –1778) (Pitt the Elder) Politician and leader of "Patriot Whigs" who opposed Walpole and Newcastle Whig faction. A brilliant orator nicknamed the 'Great Commoner' being usually opposed to the governing faction. A leading minster 1756 to 1761. Prime Minister 1766-1768. Known as key supporter of the Seven Years' War and for single-minded devotion to victory over France.

Henry Fox, 1st Baron Holland, (1705 –1774). Orator, politician and minister in Duke of Newcastle's government 1755. Known for scandalous elopement with Lady Caroline Lennox – daughter of Duke of Richmond 18 years his junior. Father of politician Charles James Fox.

Admiral Edward Vernon 1684 –1757. MP. Distinguished naval officer particularly in War of Jenkins' Ear where he captured *Porto Bello* but failed to take *Cartagena de Indias*, despite a long siege. Subsequently author of two pamphlets critical of Admiralty: "A Specimen of Naked Truth from a British Sailor" and "Some Seasonal Advice from an Honest Sailor", leading to his dismissal from the Navy in 1746.

Charles Edward Stuart 1720 –1788 'The Young Pretender. Aka Bonnie Prince Charlie. Great grandson King James II. Jacobite claimant to the throne. Led the 1745 uprisings. Defeated at Culloden April 1746. Escaped from Scotland and lived the rest of his life on continent.

Dr Archibald Cameron. Prominent leader in the Jacobite rising of 1745. He was a co-conspirator in the 1752 Elibank Plot along with Alexander Murray. He was the last Jacobite to be executed for high treason, in 1753.

Duke of Newcastle – Thomas Pelham-Holles. 1693-1768. Whig statesman, party manager and fixer. Sussex Land owner. Elder brother of Henry Pelham. Secretary of State for 30 years. Prime Minister 1754-1756 & 1757-1762. Benefactor of John Collier

Chapter 14

Improving His Town

Say what you will of John Collier, he was clearly a man unafraid of change and, as a Corporation official and leading citizen, was ever happy to instigate improvements for his town – or at least to try.

Schemes were hatched during his lifetime to create or upgrade roads and pavements and lighting, to provide fire-fighting equipment, and to establish a workhouse to assist the poor and destitute.

But perhaps most notable of the improvements were John Collier's own efforts to create a supply of clean water for the townspeople. However, just as a prophet is said to be without honour in his own domain, so Collier's attempts to provide 'mains' water ran into the most extraordinary problems and opposition.

We saw in the opening chapter that in the early 1700s the Bourne stream was not only the main source of water for the people – and often the animals – of Hastings but also supplied a key raw material for at least one brewery. The trouble was that it remained highly polluted for much of the time. Indeed there were floodgates at the bottom of the Bourne that had to be closed twice a week on Tuesday and Friday afternoons in order to build up sufficient head of water to flush away the detritus when they were re-opened. As Collier himself put it:

> *These floodgates are shut up close for at least 24 hours each time to let water off at once, to clense the filth and nastiness thrown into the Bourne by the poor people*

233

> *that live by the sides of it during which 24 hours, twice a week, the inhabitants can have thereby no supply of water.*

The only alternative at that time was to use a well, should you happen to have one, or the spring at the base of the cliffs at Rock-a-Nore. But if you lived in Market (High) Street, or anywhere on the north or west side of the town it was a considerable distance to carry pails or barrels of water.

So, probably mixing altruism with a bit of self-interest, Collier and a neighbour, Dr Henry Carleton, came up with an ambitious scheme to improve Hastings' water supply.

Collier owned some land up above the town onto which emerged several of the springs that formed the Bourne. The plan was to dig a small basin or reservoir there and pipe clean water down into the town...

> *...clear from the filth and slubb of the high roads and from all the common drains of the town which discharge themselves into the Bourne from the carless nastiness of the poor inhabitants.*

Collier and Carleton engaged a contractor, Robert Rossam of Herstmonceaux, and, on 3rd February 1733, commissioned him to lay *'good strong elm pipes of 4 inches bore'* from the upper stream to the High Street with four 'proper' stopcocks for use of the inhabitants. There were also to be *'fire pluggs'* for a supply of water *'there being noe conveniency of water if a fire should happen'*.

Mr Rossam's accounts detail the expenditure of £83 on pipes, stopcocks, joints, digging up paving and laying it down again. The initiators of the scheme did their best to ensure it had the support of both the corporation and the people of the town. Collier had recently completed his third stint as mayor and so asked his successor Thomas Godley to convene a special meeting or 'hall'. This had been held on 9th November 1732 ...

> *'at which there were present the whole body of mayor, jurats and freeman, except 5 or 6 freemen that were absent from the town, hindered by sickness'.*

Collier records that the scheme was met by general approbation, *'not one dissenting'*, and assurances were given that all surplus water would be returned to the Bourne for the use of anyone who did not wish or could not afford having it *'by pipes'.*

The reason we have such unusually detailed information about this water scheme is that it ended up in lengthy court cases. The main litigant was one Henry Sargent who filed a claim for trespass, alleging the defendants had maliciously intended...

> *to deprive the plaintiff of the convenience, advantage and benefit of taking water out of the said rivulet or stream ... a great part of the water of the said rivulet or stream was carried away and diverted from its ancient or usual course of channel so the plaintiff could not take water from and out of the said rivulet or stream to supply his occasions in so ample, convenient and beneficial manner as before'.*

This was particularly vexatious to John Collier because Sargent had *'often declared'* that he supported the project, saying that he intended to take advantage of the piped water. Indeed, as a local brewer he must surely have stood to gain considerable benefit from it. However local politics had clearly intervened. It would seem Henry Sargent was related to John Sargent who, as we saw in Chapter 9, had taken the Corporation to court after he had been refused the freedom of the town on the death of his father. Collier had been behind the attempt to restrict the franchise so there was little love lost between himself and the Sargent family. Moreover it seems that Henry Sargent had unsuccessfully stood for office in a recent local election which. According to Collier's affidavit...

> *finding he should be disappointed therein he and two or three more hot headed fellows stirred up the common people against it* [the water scheme] *and raised a clamour and went about the town with a paper and with falsehoods and threats prevailed a great many of the mean inhabitants to sign a paper to go to law in order for the pipes to be removed and accordingly have brought this action and three more for the same purpose'.*

Reading between the lines it would seem that Collier had made himself particularly unpopular in some quarters with his attempts to prevent the sons of freeholders from automatically inheriting the freedom of the town – and with it the right to vote. Henry Sargent had certainly sided against Collier in his ploy to get senior jurats to resign temporarily so they could give evidence in court against this ancient custom.

There may also have been a further element at work to explain the four apparently self-damaging legal actions. The Colliers lived in the grandest house in the town. The two sons had gone to an expensive public school in London, John Collier rubbed shoulders with the aristocracy, both local and national. As mayor he was a law officer, as a lawyer was a prosecutor of smugglers - a profession that undoubtedly provided additional income for many in Hastings, both mariners and landsmen alike. Now here was this 'grandee' taking the 'people's water' and diverting it for his own ends – or only offering it to them if they could pay the probably hefty suns required.

Whether his motive was one of simple jealousy, social resentment, or political difference, Henry Sargent pursued his case all the way to the Court of the King's Bench at which point Collier wrote his defence which provides us with so much detail of the case. This lengthy affidavit has been painstakingly transcribed by Richard Saville, along with a counsel's opinion which Collier and Carleton obtained from John Darnell. It was, opined the barrister: '*A most malicious action and of great consequence to the defendants*' but since they were just as entitled to the water in the Bourne as the plaintiff, and since no water was wasted as a result of going into the pipes '*I think the plaintiff cannot maintain this action.*'

But maintain it he did, as did Benjamin Meadow of Hastings who brought a similar action along with two other local men whose names are given only as Guy and Taught (probably freemen John Guy and Robert Taught). Ultimately the King's Bench transferred the cases to the Sussex Assizes and, in August 1734 and March 1735, juries found against Dr Carleton and John Collier, the former having to pay damages of five shillings and the latter three shillings. In a letter to Mary in June 1735 Collier referrers to it as the *'villanous usage we have met with about the pipes'*.

There is some mystery of what actually happened to these pipes and the whole water supply after the case. Charles Lane Sayer in his 1907 transcription of the Correspondence of John Collier refers to the 'discontinuance of the scheme'. However in that June 1735 letter Collier says to Mary he hopes *'the pipes are finished and that you have a supply of water to your satisfaction'*.

The contractor Robert Rosam was certainly paid the £200 that had been agreed for the main part of the scheme, and subsequently noted he had received *'of John Collier two and twenty pound in full of this account for laying in the pipes to his own house.'* There is also a reference five years later, in the summer of 1740, when Collier tells Mary: *'Master Bossom designs to sail tomorrow. I hope he will bring down some pipes for the water'*. The following month Collier records an *'account for waterworks'* of £2 16s 00d for 16 yards of 5 inch pipe at 3s 6d a yard.

So it would appear that the malcontents who opposed the pipe scheme and who were awarded nominal damages did not actually manage to prevent it altogether. Nonetheless it is clear that not many people took advantage of it. Nearly a century later, in 1832, the Corporation conducted a survey which found that in the St Clement and All Saints parishes only 43 houses were supplied with water while 700 were not. It presaged a new scheme to create a reservoir at the head of the Bourne valley and pipe water to individual houses –

Collier's dream - a reservoir to the north of All Saint's Church that would collect clean water and disperse it through elm pipes to subscribers on the town. The scheme attracted very considerable opposition.

exactly what Collier had proposed almost a hundred years before. At this point only 228 people agreed to take the water. Even in 1850, according to J Mainwaring Baines, only one third of Hastings' homes were on the 'mains'.

By the 1890s though the expanding town faced increasing demands for clean water and the Corporation purchased Church House Farm in Brede. They sunk three wells, built a pumping station and employed a steam engine to pump the well water to a storage reservoir at Fairlight. The waterworks opened in 1904, and the Collier inspired use of the Bourne springs to provide fresh water disappeared forever.

§§§

There is no record of Hastings having any form of street lighting before John Collier's time at the town hall. In neighbouring Rye there had been an ordinance since 1575 that constables should ensure that 'lanthorns and candles' were hung outside of houses of those that could afford them. The first evidence of street lighting in Hastings seems to be 1744, when the local MP, Colonel Pelham, gave the town a set of lamps. However the cost of igniting, maintaining and fuelling them fell on the Corporation, with the oil alone costing in excess of £14 a year and the lamp-lighter's remuneration being between £4 and £5 a year.

John Collier subsidised the cost from his own pocket from time to time, but also set out to see if there wouldn't be others who could help defray the expense. In a draft letter to the Duke of Newcastle's office in 1754 he outlines his position:

The town has been for a great many years lighted with lamps beautiful and useful to the corporation – the original gift of Col Pelham. Of late the Oyle has been by one way or other provided, but of late been managed with difficulty. I advanced the money this year and am afraid there will be a deficiency in the finances of the Corporation are low and we are in debt.

It's not certain whether this letter was ever received by the Duke, but even if it was it's unlikely that he would have put his hand in his pocket to help. As we will see later, Collier had considerable problems over many years trying to get money he was owed by Newcastle repaid at all.

Two years later things had not improved and Collier appealed this time to Colonel Pelham:

I also intended to have laid before you the annual expense of Oyle and lamps and lighting ... I have for many years managed to pay the expense out of the little revenues belonging to the town but now the corporation finances are sadly out of order and we are much in debt ...I should be sorry to see it drop after being enjoyed for so many years and design to mention it to you in the hopes that you and your colleague would supply the Annual Expense until we can manage to pay the same again ...now is the time of providing a stock of Oyle for the service of the Winter and they begin lighting soon after the full moon about Michaelmas.

Colonel Pelham and his fellow Hastings MP Andrew Stone came good and stumped up 20 guineas to cover that year's costs. But J Mainwaring Baines believes that the expense became unsustainable and quotes a writer in 1819 saying of the town *"not a lamp is to be seen to light ones way, not a soul to say goodnight to."* Eleven years later though the local paper was able to record 'This town was for the first time lighted by Gas last evening,'

§§§

We noted that Collier thought it important to provide a supply of water to be used in case of fire, and in many ways is seems remarkable that so many of the houses in the old town still exist given the incendiary dangers inherent in their construction. In Historic Hastings Baines details various ordinances passed over the years to mitigate the risks, including banning thatched roofs on any new building from the early 1600s. But even in Collier's day this was being flouted and a John Kneeves was ordered to demolish a small house he had built, on the grounds it was a public nuisance.

It was, once again, the town's MPs who came to the rescue, offering to underwrite the cost of a fire engine for Hastings. Since this wasn't the sort of machine that could be readily bought in Sussex, William Cranston in London was asked to investigate the best equipment. In January 1750 he wrote to Collier:

There is another place for ffire engines ... I shall go to this second place before I determine which to purchase of &

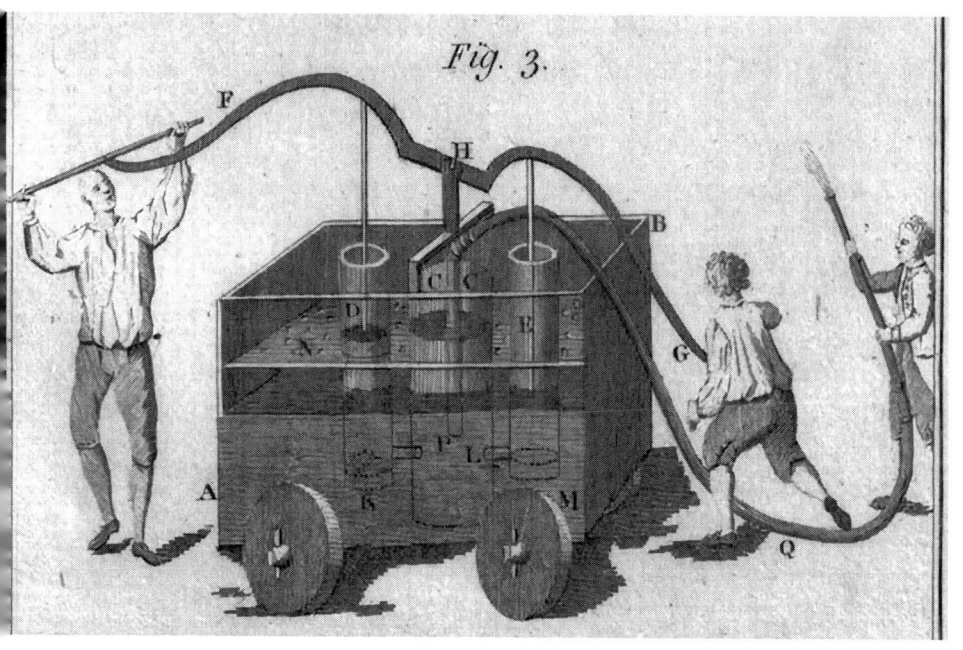

Diagram of a fire engine or pump from the early 18th century

when I do purchase think 'twill be quite right to imblazon the donors thereon – 'as a gift of the Hon James Pelham and Andrew Stone esq. to this corporation' or in any other words you thin may be proper.

§§§

John Collier was, throughout his life, a devout churchgoer. He married a vicar's daughter and attended St Clements church regularly when he was in Hastings. His memorial in that church says, in part, *'he thought the duties of religion indispensible; therefore constantly attended divine service'*. And in his will he left the poor of the town £10 to be distributed amongst them by his wife at her discretion.

The link between relief of the poor and a parish was, in the 18th century, indissoluble. Since the middle ages it had been the parish that was charged with looking after the destitute. The Poor Relief Act of 1662 specified that a parish had responsibility for its own residents – through birth, marriage and apprenticeship. Conversely a parish had no responsibility for outsiders and the Act had the effect of considerably reducing the mobility of labour and discouraging people from leaving their home parish to seek work elsewhere. It also encouraged parishes to ship people sometimes considerable distances back to their 'home'. Since poor relief was funded by parish overseers who collected 'poor rate' taxes from local property owners it is unsurprising that they wanted to be responsible for as few people as possible. In Historic Hastings J Manwaring Baines charts numerous instances of the town's parishes trying to 'export' their problems. In 1745 All Saints records show they were paying 1/6d to 'Goody Knave' and her child. So they proposed instead a one-off payment of *"2 shifts, [a] pair of shoes, an apron and 5/- on condition of [her] going off and taking her child."* An offer which, apparently, she didn't take up.

However, during Collier's lifetime the system began to change. Bristol was soon followed by a dozen other towns in having private acts of parliament to create 'corporations for the poor' which would subsequently establish workhouses for them. In 1724 an act of parliament enabled parishes either individually or jointly, to initiate their own workhouses.

In Hastings there had been some provision since 1610 when a poor house was designated in All Saints Street. This was later converted into cottages numbered 1 & 2, and then demolished to make way for the imposing steps that today lead up to All Saint's Church. By Collier's time, though, this 'hospital' for the poor of the parish was clearly proving insufficient for their needs and, enabled by the 1724 act, All Saints parish combined with St Clements and St. Mary-in-the-Castle to create a joint workhouse for the town. In 1753 they bought a building, the Pilchard House, on a site on the then edge of the town in George Street (number 42 today). £600 was raised by way of a loan for a new building but, this being Hastings, it was not without controversy. John Sargent - long a thorn in Collier's side - seemed to be behind the trouble as Collier explained to the Duke of Newcastle's Steward John Greening in a letter of April 1754:

> *After dinner there happened some noise and clamour in regard to our poor and workhouse lately built. The chief foundation was John Sargent, one of our*

freemen, impudently asserting that my Lord Duke of Newcastle and Mr Stone both promised and engaged to him at Newcastle House that they would pay the whole expense and charge of the building and furnishing it, and so had told a great many of the Freemen. Mr Stone assured me there was no such thing ever said, talked of or promised.

Andrew Stone, it will be recalled, was both Newcastle's private secretary and a Hastings' MP. He and his fellow MP, Colonel Pelham, were benefactors of the town and:

very handsomely gave £400 towards the poor and the workhouse – a satisfactory benevolence to all until this assertion.

This may all seem a bit of a storm in a teacup until one realises that 1754 was an election year, and once again Collier was managing this 'treasury' borough for the Whigs, and once again some freeholders were opposed to the way the election was being conducted. It's clear from Collier's letter that the Duke and his two MPs had been busy entertaining voters in the constituency:

When my Ld D. of N. was last here, while drinking with the Corporation, the poor house was mentioned and his Grace was pleased much to approve of it and encouraged it much to go on ...I was confined to my chamber the Election day with a severe fit of the gout or I imagine this discourse and clamour would have been prevented. The members £400 towards it and Colonel Pelham giving the material of some buildings called Pilchard houses and his ground on which they stood was very handsom and so esteemed. Col Pelham and Mr Stone discharged all the expenses of dinner and all the parade &c and &c, at the election.

§§§

As we have seen previously John Collier was actively involved in attempts to improve the roads by instigating and investing in the Flimwell and Hastings Turnpike Trust. But the Hastings Corporation was also trying to improve life for pedestrians in the town. In 1706 Dr Henry Carleton, then mayor, was granted 50 shillings by the assembly for *"raising the pavement before Richard Amyetts door, and high as the other..."* Nearly half a century later in 1751 Edward Milward – immediate past Mayor and the Colliers' future son-in-law - was writing to John and Mary in Bath about a new scheme once again financed by the town's MPs, Andrew Stone and Colonel Pelham to provide pavements:

> *Pray acquaint the Ladies that the Footwalk shall be as convenient for their footsteps and Hoops as can be made.*

Interestingly, according to a subsequent Milward letter, one source of the materials for this pavement was the ruined Hastings Castle:

I have ventured to give orders for the straggling stones fell down from the Castle and lying in the hills adjoining to be picked up and used, they being better than anyone can get.

From all this correspondence it's clear that it was hoped, and perhaps expected, that the town's members of Parliament would contribute to Corporation causes, be it the provision of pavements or fire engines or oil for the lights or land and money for a workhouse. These might be considered simple acts of altruistic generosity, but there's no doubt they did little harm when it came to attracting voters. It's also clear that electioneering involved a good deal of other expense for entertaining the electorate, and this was not always popular with political opponents. It wouldn't be for nearly another 80 years that the electoral system would undergo major changes with the 1832 reform act, and rotten boroughs would be swept away and the franchise extended beyond freemen. Of course that would mean that small towns like Hastings would lose much of their political influence, and with it perhaps the benevolence of some statesmen and politicians.

§§§

Who's Who Chapter 14. Improving His Town.

Dr Henry Carleton. The Collier's friend and physician in Hastings. A former Mayor and deputy Mayor.

Robert Rossam of Herstmonceaux. Builder and plumber employed by Collier and Carleton on their scheme to provide piped water to Hastings from 1732

John Sargent claimed Freedom of Hastings on grounds that his father had been a freeman, and successfully took Hastings Corporation to court in a lawsuit financed by Sir Thomas Webster. Member of extended Hastings family.

Henry Sargent – Hastings brewer, possibly brother or cousin to John – successfully sued Collier for trespass for taking water from the Bourne.

Richard Saville. Historian. Author of 'The Letters of John Collier of Hastings 1731-1746'

Benjamin Meadow 1671-1745. Freeman of Hastings. Sued John Collier and Dr Henry Carleton over their piped water scheme.

John Guy and **Robert Taught**, Freemen. Fellow litigants over the Water scheme

Charles Lane Sayer – descendent of John Collier, transcriber and editor of The Correspondence of John Collier and his Family pub. 1907

James Bossom, 1688-1764. Boat owner and carrier between Hastings and London. Freeman and Jurat of Hastings. Sometime friend of Collier's.

J Manwaring Baines. Hastings Historian. Author of 'Historic Hasting a Tapestry of Life'.

Colonel **James Pelham** (Jemmy) of Crowhurst. Cousin to D. of Newcastle. Hastings MP 1741-61. Coronation canopy bearer with Collier 1727.

Duke of Newcastle – Thomas Pelham-Holles. 1693-1768. Whig statesman, party manager and fixer. Sussex Land owner. Elder brother of Henry Pelham. Secretary of State for 30 years. Prime Minister 1754-1756 & 1757-1762. Benefactor of John Collier

Andrew Stone 1703–1773. Private secretary to the Duke of Newcastle. Confidant of Pelham family. MP for Hastings 1741 to 1761. Government minister. Royal advisor, tutor secretary and treasurer under George II and George III.

John Greening Steward to Duke of Newcastle initially in charge of the grounds, gardens and trees at Duke's Palladian residence, Claremont, built in 1708 by Sir John Vanbrugh near Esher in Surrey.

William Cranston – Mary Collier's younger brother. John Collier's legal partner based in London. John Collier always refers to William as 'my brother' rather than brother-in-law.

Chapter 15

A Family Man

There's no doubt at all that John Collier was a busy man - one who clearly had a huge capacity for hard work and a mind that could encompass a whole host of disparate subjects. His legal work in London, his estate work for the Pelhams and others in Sussex, his work for the Customs Service both prosecuting cases and surveying the Riding Officers of Kent, his regular work as clerk and, over five years, Mayor to the Hastings Corporation, these should have been enough to keep him pretty well occupied. But there was also his law practice on the South coast, his work as solicitor for the Cinque ports, not to mention his duties as agent for Newcastle as Admiral of Sussex and political fixer for the Whigs.

Yet, amongst all this Collier was a family man too. Father of twenty-four children that we have records for – six by his first wife Elizabeth Elphick, and eighteen by his second Mary Cranston. Tragically only eight of these children survived him, and some of them suffered serious ill health. So parenthood must have been a constant worry – if not a time of almost constant mourning.

We saw in Chapter 3 his reaction to the death of his son John from Smallpox, and throughout his letters there are numerous references to sickness and death. The first comes just one year after his marriage to Mary

My Dearest I received your kind and obliging letter but am extremely con-

cerned at the contents of it viz hearing of
our poor dear girl being so ill. [27 Nov 1718]

Then, just five days later, he receives news from
his 'father'. This was probably his father-in-law the Rev
James Cranston in Hastings rather than his actual father,
Peter Collier in Eastbourne.

My Dearest Life I received by the last post
from my father the melancholy afflicting
news of our poor girl's being dead, on
which account I doe assure you I am under
a very great concerne which is much more
increased by my absence from you, which
deprives me from being a comfort and
support to each other under this tryall ....
My dearest I din not think this fatall news
would have been so shocking to me, the
concern I am under on your account makes
a very great increase and be assured I cant
enjoy a minute's true satisfaction until I
have the pleasure of being with you ...
patience and submission to the divine will
is the greatest comfort and support in
these cases. Ps I write to my father this post
to thank him for his care and constant
visits to you. [2 Dec 1718]

We do not need to, nor will we, intrude further on
John Collier's grief over this death nor those of the other
10 of his children who died in infancy. Instead let us
share his joy and, sometimes, frustration at the progress
of the ones who lived longer and, in the case of the girls,
longer than Collier himself. In chronological order they

were John, born 1720, James 1721, Cordelia 1722, Mary 1725, Jane 1727, Sarah 1739, and Henrietta 1741.

From around 1724 the children's names start to appear in his letters to Mary, often in a slightly admonishing tone:

> *I don't doubt that Jacky is highly delighted with his cork (boat?) but it was certainly not right to permit his going to the seaside* ... [9 February 1724].

Nevertheless Collier was clearly missing his children's development while he was stuck in London:

> *I imagine it is needless to acquaint you that my life is intirely wrapped up in you and my children and 'tis impossible for me to enjoy any real pleasure separated from your company.* [2 February 1724]

However, being in London did enable him to buy gifts for the family that were evidently not so readily available in Hastings:

> *I have bespoke yours and children's shoes and Jacky's coat, hat &c, & have not forgot little Dely's baby (doll).* [6 February 1724]

By 1728 Collier was writing to his eldest son Jacky (John) who, aged 8, was boarding at Mrs Thorpe's school in Battle, cajoling him to be a good boy and to mind his learning. This the lad clearly did because three months later in February 1729 Collier told him he was:

> *very much pleased to find you mind your book so well and you may be sure I will buy*

you anything in reason you can desire for your encouragement.

Curiously, for the boy's edification, Collier enclosed with the letter the dying confessions of 'the five persons hanged at Tyburn last week'. But it seems child rearing in the early Georgian period was rather different than today. That June when Jemmy (James) would have been just seven years old, he was apparently caught drinking alcohol on market day having ventured out on the balcony of the local inn in Battle. Collier told his elder brother Jacky:

> *I think he should have wrote a letter and begged pardon for being so naughty a boy a market day as drinking and getting out of the George balcony – if you expect my favour you must both keep from any dangerous places or plays and never drink anything of strong liquor but what I give you.* [14 June 1729]

Which rather suggests Collier was in the habit of giving his sons 'strong liquor' himself. But it wasn't just drinking alcohol that Collier seemed to condone, but cock-fighting and gambling – though only for modest sums. In February 1732 John wrote to his mother from his school in Battle:

> *This is to let you know I am in good health and hope you are a likewise. I desire you to send me a letter to let me know whether my papa is come home for he has not called here, and if he is, I desire him to send me the 4th and fifth volumes of the Arabian*

Tales I desire you to send me my Greatcoat and boots, both which I want very much. We have had very ill fortune with our cocks, and we haven't had any money had not Miss Nelly lent us some ...

A couple of weeks later Collier wrote to the boys in stern terms:

I hope God Almighty will give you grace to perform your promise of not gaming again at soe high a rate and to abstain from sin and wickedness; for the contrary will lose you all my favours and incurre God's displeasure and you must be miserable in this world and the next. My Blessing to both of you ... your affectionate and indulgent father. [18 March 1732]

Well, indulgent perhaps. Drinking alcohol was alright as long as it was provided by Collier himself, and it seems gambling was also acceptable as long as it was only for modest rates! But the threat of eternal damnation would seem rather to temper the paternal affection!

By August 1732 both boys had started at Westminster school ensuring usual parental pleas for letters and news. Mary Collier wrote to them telling Jemmy about his chickens and his pet squirrel, then in the care of his elder sister:

Dely is as careful of your sqiriell as she can, but tis almost too much for her as it gets lose and runs under the ceiling.

255

His father seems less concerned for the boy's feelings when he informed him a couple of months later:

Your squirrell, last night, unfortunately hung himself by his table, but he was grown so mischievous, soe that I believe you will think it no great losse.

The tone of Collier's letters to his younger son is noticeably cooler than to John, indeed he regularly chastises the former for not writing

We both very much wonder that Jemmy has not once wrote and think him very naughty in not doing it and shall not excuse him without his writing next Saturday. [24 October 1732]

James must have taken the admonishment to heart because a few weeks later he was writing to his father in Hastings at the start of the Christmas holidays which the boys were spending with their uncle in Johnson's Court in London. Mary Collier had just given birth and it seems the 11-year-old Jemmy was gently ribbing his father about the baby:

I am very sorry that in my last letter I made so many mistakes in my spelling, but promise to be more carefull (sic) in the future. I am glad to hear my mamma is safely brought to bed and wish you and her much joy of my new brother, who I should be very glad to see at Westminster School. Though I believe he has not much occasion for it for he is already so great a scholar that he, I don't doubt, as fluently talks Latin, Greek and Hebrew as English ... [19 December 1732]

Subsequent correspondence has been set out in greater detail in Chapter 3, for this was the Christmas that John contracted Smallpox and the heart-wrenching news of his decline and death had to be conveyed to his parents by his unfortunate uncle, William Cranston.

The effect of the death of his eldest and probably favourite son was profound. Even six month later Collier was writing to Mary about his continuing bouts of depression:

some days I have terrible conflicts with dear remembrances of (John) that cut me worse than swords and several times hope and think I have resolutions to repel them but woefully find to the contrary. [14 June 1733]

And descendant Charles Sayer found a loose sheet in Collier's hand in a pocketbook which he believes was a verse on death of John:

Ah my poor son! Ah my Tender child
My unblown flower and new appearing sweets!
If yet your gentle soul flies in the air
And is not fixed in doom perpetual –
Hover about me with your airy wings,
An hear your Father's lamentation!

§§§

Collier's children all began their education at Mrs Thorpe's private school in Battle until the age of 11 or 12. As we have seen the two boys went on to Westminster while the five girls attended Elizabeth's Russell's boarding school in Hampstead.

It is, perhaps, curious that Collier, freeman, jurat, Corporation clerk, and five times mayor of Hastings should not have sent his children to the local grammar school. According to Mainwaring Baines' detailed research, the Hastings school dated from 1607, founded quite possibly by the Rev William Parker, rector of All Saints, and funded by the corporation. As an interesting sideline, within a few years Parker had died and later his great nephew, also called William, became schoolmaster. But by then a certain Samuel Oates had taken over as Rector of All Saints and installed his son, Titus, as his curate. This young man had already embarked on a life of lies by falsely claiming to have obtained a degree from Cambridge. Now in Hastings he set his sights on the post of schoolmaster. That there was already an incumbent worried him not a jot, and he promptly accused William Parker of sodomy with a pupil. At the subsequent trial Parker was acquitted after Oates' evidence was shown to be false.

Titus Oates prudently disappeared from Hastings – only to reappear on the national stage three years later in 1678, accusing the Catholic Church authorities of planning the assassination of the protestant monarch Charles II. The King's Privy Council questioned Oates who made 43 allegations against various members of Catholic religious orders—including 541 Jesuits—and numerous Catholic nobles. His accusations let to the execution of at least fifteen innocent people including Oliver Plunkett, Roman Catholic Archbishop of Armagh, who was hanged, drawn and quartered on 1 July 1681.

After Oates' testimony was again shown to be false, he himself was tried and convicted of perjury - though later being pardoned by the succeeding Catholic monarch James II.

It is improbable that the association, fifty years earlier, between the perjurer Titus Oates and the Hastings Grammar school would have been grounds or reason for Collier's decision to send his children elsewhere. More likely was the social mix of pupils at both the Grammar school and the other school in the town which had been founded shortly after 1708 by James Saunders. This was to *"teach and instruct ye poor children of both parishes and both sexes in spelling and reading English."* It is entirely likely that the Colliers would have wanted a greater proportion of children from the 'middling sort' of families than were to be found at either school locally. All but a very few people in Hastings at the time were engaged in what we would today call blue-collar jobs. A large proportion was from the fishing community, and the remainder from trades of one sort or another (see chapter 1). However it would seem entirely possible that the decision to send his children away to fee-paying boarding schools would not have endeared Collier to some in the town, and may well have contributed to his undoubted unpopularity among a number of his fellow freemen.

The Colliers' association with Mrs Thorpe and her school in Battle seems a curious one. Her name occurs with considerable frequency in the correspondence, but not always in relation to education. It seems the teacher was also a regular companion to Mary Collier, often residing with her in Hastings. Charles Lane Sayer notes that: 'Mrs Thorpe seems usually to have stayed with Mrs collier during Mr Collier's absence in London.' And Richard Saville concludes that 'Intermittent depression

TITUS OATES.

Titus Oates. Onetime curate at All Saints, Hastings. Convicted perjurer

affected Mary Collier, alleviated by conversation with Mrs Thorpe of Battle'. There is certainly no doubt but that this lady spent a good deal of time at the Collier house. In November 1734 John, writing from London tells Mary:

> I am very much surprised by your letter that Mrs Thorpe has left you. Tis much she did not tarry till my return. I really liked her very well and soe indeed I shall anybody that is agreeable to you and unless she intends soon to return again hope you will think of somebody else for I would not have you without a companion.

However she was certainly back at Mary's side a year later as John was extending her his 'humble service' in a letter. Similar salutations were sent by the Collier children on countless occasions when they wrote home from school in London. John Collier even helped her out in a legal capacity when there was a problem over her mother's house even referring the dispute to Sussex landowner and family friend, Lord Ashburnham:

> Pray give my services to Mrs Thorpe and tell her I have met Botting's lawyer about her mother's affair twice to discourse it over, but we come to noe resolution. I have taken the opportunity to inform Lord Ashburnham of its situation and Mr Botting's behavior. I am sure my lord is at no expense on the affair but it came out imagined in good measure. [12 June 1733]

The correspondence also details concern over Mrs Thorpe's health, and contains letters from Miss Thorpe, one of her daughters who was clearly a friend of the younger Collier girls, writing to Mary on decidedly informal terms. Mrs Thorpe was also among the mourners to attend John's funeral at Westminster Abbey in 1732.

So it's clear the Thorpes were close confidants of the Colliers and the only mystery is how Mrs Thorpe managed to run her school in Battle while also spending so much time in Hastings. "*I think it is right to have Mrs Thorpe with you and perhaps her time may be prolonged when she is at Hasting beyond the supposed one month*" wrote John to Mary in June 1741.

But when the Collier girls were in Battle at Mrs Thorpe's establishment it is obvious she was very much in loco parentis. Here she writes to tell Mary about Jane's ears being pierced.

> *I designed letting you know Miss's ears were bored and to desire your order for rings. We took her whilst in the mind, all that knew of it thought she would have but one done. Mr Collier sent word I should buy a paire ... you'll be surprised when you see her for this warm sun which she is in all day has made her nut brown as a maid. She gives her duty and love on condition you send such a hoop as Molly's.* [25 June 1736]

It is interesting to note that at the time Jane was just nine years old, and Molly only two years older.

After leaving Mrs Thorpe's in Battle all the girls went on to a boarding school in Hampstead run by Elizabeth Russell. Richard Saville tells us that by 1741 this establishment in Church Row had 29 boarders, each paying a minimum of £30 a year. The curriculum 'included dancing, French embroidery, bible study, handwriting including the Italian hand for older girls ... tuition on musical instruments including the spinet, visits to nearby sites and religious instruction.' The school was also keen to instil social graces and deportment into its charges. Cordelia arrived there in the summer of 1735, writing home to her mother that: *'I like the school very much and will endeavour to improve myself as much as possible'.* One of the advantages of Hampstead was that it was relatively convenient for visits from the city. A stagecoach plied the route, and if that was not available walking the six miles was not too taxing, even for the 50 year old John who went to visit Dely shortly after she'd started at Miss Russell's:

> *After dinner my brother, Jemmy and I set out for Hampstead and came there before they came from church. Dely is very well and really improved in her looks and behavior. We drank tea and walked two hours on the heath and though we went up in one of the stage coaches we were obliged to walk home. I told Mrs Russell that she should have everything there was occasion for.* [17 June 1735]

Mary – always referred to as Molly – followed her sister in 1741 and clearly impressed Miss Russell who wrote to her mother Mary Collier on 12th June:

> *...I had the pleasure of seeing your agreeable daughter who came last night. I am certain Miss will be an improving*

young lady and comes with an exceeding good will ... I wish Miss may like school as well as Miss Collier [Cordelia] *did though I told her there was nothing to be learned without pains, music and French requires study... I hope, madam, you will be very easy on Misses account. I shall take care to indulge her as much as possible. I am certain her temper will both require and merit it.*

A few months later a family friend and quite possibly a fellow lawyer, John Coppinger wrote from Hampstead to John Collier who was then in Hastings giving news of Molly:

Your daughter is very well and a good neighbour; my girl and she are to be very intimate and take their morning and evening walks together I give you joy at the increase to your family and hope the good lady in the straw and the young one are both well; my wife joins in our complements to you on the occasion and she says, not I, that Mrs Collier is well entitled to a quietus. [5 September 1741]

Coppinger is mentioned in a number of letters as being a dinner companion of John's and of William Cranston's, and he accompanied them on various trips to London's pleasure gardens. The birth he refers to was that of Henrietta usually known as Harriett. There had been a considerable gap in the Collier offspring. In the thirteen years after Jane was born in 1727, six children died either in the same year, or in the year after they

264

were born. It wasn't until 1740 that Mary gave birth to a daughter who survived to adulthood, this being Sarah.

Another aspect of the Collier's family life that we might find strange today is the time they spent apart. We know that John was absent from the family home for three months or more each year while in London or on his tour of the Customs houses of Kent. But the children also seem to have spent protracted periods apart from their parents. We found young John and James spending Christmas with their Uncle and Aunt in London in 1732 rather than travelling back to Hastings to be with their more immediate family. The girls too were often absent in London or Battle for substantial periods. Cordelia's letters show a marked reluctance to leave London in the holidays, and even when she was in Sussex, she spent a good deal of time in Battle rather than Hastings. In 1741, Elizabeth Worge – Mary's step-daughter – writes to her from Battle inviting the 19-year-old Cordelia to a dance. It seems she went, and stayed in the town for a month or more, being joined by her younger sister Molly, and enjoying a number of balls and dances, as she reported to her mother:

> *This morning Mrs Tilden was here who informs us Mr Nickoll is to have a ball but that there is to be no married ladies and part of the company is to be Miss Webster and the two young gentlemen ... so if it goes forward believe we must desire Miss Webster to take us in the coach with her.*
> [January Probably 1741]

Dely and Miss Webster evidently hit it off because shortly afterwards Cordelia is writing from the Webster's family home, Battle Abbey, where she is being

Battle Abbey. 18ᵗʰ Century home of the Webster family who befriended the Collier daughters

pressed to stay. It's evident from subsequent letters that she remained there for some time accompanying her friend to various social events including a ball given by the Fullers.

Honoured Madam, I went to Catsfield a Monday with Miss Webster and did not return till Thursday when Miss Eversfield was so obliging as to bring me home in the chariot ... we had a very agreeable ball and I danced all the time and had one of the Fullers as my partner. [January probably 1741]

A year later it is Mary who is extolling the pleasures of balls in Battle and hospitality from the Websters:

My sister Worge begs ye favour of you to send three or four pickled Herrings tomorrow by Palmer to make Solomun-grundy for ye Ball, which is next Monday, and the Captain talks of having his Ball sometime next week, and if he does, believe it will be a Friday, so hope you will be good as to let us stay till Saturday ... Our ball at the Abbey was very agreeable. We broke up between five and six in the morning and I stayed and lay with my sister Delia which was much more comfortable than mounting the hill after dancing. This evening we are all invited to spend at Miss Smith's, but the gentlemen are gone to Mr Nicholl's to dinner so believe we shan't have their company ... we stayed the

*evening a Tuesday at the Abbey and my
lady was prodigious civil to us.* [Mary Collier
to her mother January 1744]

There's a certain irony that the set in which
Cordelia and Molly were now moving comprised, by and
large, the same Tories who had opposed Collier just a
few years before. We saw in Chapter 9 it was Sir Thomas
Webster who brought the case against Collier and the
Hastings Corporation in the mid 1730s for trying to
restrict the electoral franchise. His son Whistler Webster
even stood as a Tory Candidate. The Eversfields who
supported Whistler, were also local gentry, descended
from Sir Thomas Eversfield. And the Fullers were
prominent - and wealthy – Tory ironmasters of
Brightling. John Fuller had an elder daughter, Elizabeth,
and four surviving sons. The first, John, was born in
1706, the next, Rose, in 1708. So it is more likely that
Dely is referring to one of the younger sons, either
Stephen who was 25 in 1741 or Henry who would have
been 28. Henry went on to marry a cousin, Frances
Fuller, and their son, 'mad' Jack, became an eccentric and
MP who found some fame later in the century.

Curiously Cordelia wrote to her mother about
Henry (known usually as Harry) and his decision to join
the church:

*Harry Fuller has taken orders, so we have
lost him forever now which is a misfortune
for here is none to spare and we often wish
for Gore and Maull again to make up the
dance* [early 1741]

It is interesting to speculate on John Collier's
likely reaction to his daughters' choice of friends. On the
one hand he would surely have been suspicious of the

politics of this Sussex set and doubtless resentful of the trouble they caused over the court challenges. On the other hand he would likely have been but delighted his daughters were mingling with young men of such wealth and social standing. In an era when making a 'good' match was vital they would certainly have appeared entirely suitable as potential sons-in-law.

As we saw, ultimately Dely ended up marrying an impecunious Jacobite, and it's notable that some of the young men she identified as dancing partners in her letters – including Gore and Maull - were soldiers, stationed in Hastings. It was of course one such, James Murray, Cordelia eventually married.

The Collier girls certainly kept their father busy with constant demands for London clothes and materials including a long running saga involving the purchase of Chip hats – a sort of flat bonnet fashionable in the mid 18th century. Hastings, it seems, was a considerable backwater when it came to women's fashion, and James Bossom was forever being pressed into service to transport some new *a la mode* item from the capital to the coast.

While the sisters were enjoying the Sussex social life, James had been making steady progress at Westminster leaving in 1738 and going up to Clare College Cambridge in the same year.

I returned from Cambridge this day where I left Jemmy very well, and I believe extremely well satisfied with his new habitation and am sure he ought to be soe for its not only a delightful situation but I have not been niggardly in settling him as well as any gentleman in England... [John to Mary 27 June 1738]

James – seems to have spent most of his vacations from 'uni' in London attending the theatre and joining trips to pleasure gardens. But he was becoming increasingly interested in politics as this letter home to Mary demonstrates:

> *I received my Father's letter on Tuesday, giving me particular account of the proceedings of the late election in Sussex, the contents of which I communicated to Lord Ashburnham, who expressed great satisfaction therewith. I intended to have wrote yesterday but had that day my infrequent distemper attend me viz a violent headache which obliged me to defer till this. The university, both in combinations and private rooms affords no other topic of conversation but politics...* [21 January 1742]

There is a clear hint in this letter that Jemmy's health was far from robust, possibly as a long-term result of the smallpox he contracted after his brother's death ten years earlier.

In the Summer of 1742 Jemmy came down from Cambridge planning to train as a lawyer and entered the Middle Temple. He first sought suitable accommodation:

> *I went yesterday morning accompanied by my uncle to visit two setts of chambers ... those in Fig Tree Court are very pleasant chambers pleasantly situated and lately built... this sett I must confess please me extremely.* [26 October 1742]

The trouble was that they were rather more expensive than another set in King's Bench Walk and uncle William Cranston had to persuade John Collier they were worth the extra:

> *I don't find there is a possibility of getting chambers fit to put a head in under £30 so I must confess the £36 chambers are better by more than double the difference of the 30 guinea ones.*

Collier evidently accepted his brother-in-law's arguments for, by the 18th December, James was writing to his father from Fig Tree Court in the Temple obviously excited about his new digs:

> *I lay in chambers for the first time and am extremely well satisfied as to the bed and when I am entirely well settled will give you a particular account of the measure and furniture of the rooms.*

But it wasn't just the cost of accommodation that John Collier had to bear, but an allowance for James as well. And once again William Cranston ended up acting as advocate for his nephew. Collier obviously raised the subject – along with a number of other admonitions to his son – in a letter we don't have. But it was clearly quite critical, and James' reply is defensive, apologizing for not having taken is father's advice over studying dancing, French and writing. But it's on the subject of money that they clearly most disagreed:

> *I am sorry to find the proposed allowance does not meet with your approbation and*

was in the hopes that, as it did not exceed what I have hitherto expended, you would have been so good as to have agreed to it. For upon reflection I can't see but that I must be as much expense here as at Cambridge ... and the study which I am engaged in will unavoidably oblige me to buy many books and those of the law are none of the cheapest. [1 January 1743]

By the same post Cranston wrote to Collier supporting James' plea. It's a particularly interesting letter as it demonstrates the circles in which Collier evidently wanted his son to mix – while apparently denying him the means so to do:

That you have brought him up hitherto as a gentleman is apparent to all the world and that the expense of it has been paid with cheerfulness, that I am witness to... He is already in intimacy and friendship with Lord Ashburnham, Shadwell, Randoll ... others as they offer will be taken in. But this is naturally a work of time ... how does it or can it appear that these sort of acquaintance will cost him less to keep company with than those he is already engaged with? ...(they) have their estates in their own hands as well as others who ... have very large allowances... for some of em have ten times such a sum to spend yet they will take it for granted whenever he is with them that he is enabled to pay his quota. ... Young people are young people still and nothing but time can make them see the folly of their present pursuits. As you have hitherto for these four years past allowed him as much or more than he now wants, it will be a difficult thing to convince him that you are not able in circumstances still to continue it or that you had then expended upon him more than you could afford.... I am fully convinced by numberless examples that more young people have been ruined by too narrow, rather than too liberal an allowance.

Cranston tactfully says he can't know how much Collier can afford. But in fact he did have a pretty good idea of his wealth. It seems he kept accounts for Collier, collected all the fees for their joint legal work in London, and then forwarded Collier's share to him if he was in Hastings.

One wonders is there, perhaps, in Collier's attitude a hint that he never got over the fact that Jackie was less favoured in his eyes than John? And might there be some lingering resentment that it was Jackie, not John, who was alive and carrying on the family name? Such resentment would seem to go against his general behaviour, but his attitude over his support for Jackie does appear uncharacteristic.

As it turned out it seems that Jackie got the higher allowance he sought and posterity was the beneficiary. For between then and his untimely death just four years later, Jackie wrote some of the most literate and illuminating letters in the whole of the Collier collection, often charting and analysing political events, and reporting in detail on proceedings in parliament. Perhaps as a concession to his father he was also sworn in as a Jurat in Hastings and, in 1745 followed in his footsteps to serve as mayor of the town. It was to be his only term of office.

§§§

Who's Who Chapter 15, A Family Man

Duke of Newcastle – Thomas Pelham-Holles. 1693-1768. Whig statesman, party manager and fixer. Sussex Land owner. Elder brother of Henry Pelham. Secretary of State for 30 years . Prime Minister 1754-1756 & 1757-1762. Benefactor of John Collier

Elizabeth Elphick. Collier's first wife. Died 1714

Mary Cranston - 1696-1768, second wife to John Collier. Elder sister of William Cranston, Collier's London partner

Rev James. Cranston. Mary's father Hastings vicar.

William Cranston – Mary Collier's younger brother. John Collier's legal partner based in London. John Collier always refers to William as 'my brother' rather than brother-in-law.

Collier's children with Mary (who survived beyond the age of 10)
John (Jacky), 1720-32
James, (Jemmy)172 -47,
Cordelia (Dely)1722-1779
Mary (Molly)1725-83,
Jane (Jenny) b 1727-1802,
Sarah b 1740-1822
Henrietta (Harriet) b 1741-1794.

Mrs Thorpe (not related to Mayor William Thorpe) Proprietor of school in Battle attended by Collier children. Companion to Mary Collier. Friend of the family.

Elizabeth Russell – Proprietor of private boarding school in Church Row Hampstead, attended by the

Collier daughters. She was a mourner at the funeral of John (Jackie) Collier in 1732

Charles Lane Sayer – *descendent- great great grandson - of John Collier, transcriber and editor of The Correspondence of John Collier and his Family pub. 1907*

J Manwaring Baines. *Hastings Historian. Author of Historic Hastings a Tapestry of Life.*

Richard Saville. *Historian. Author of 'The Letters of John Collier of Hastings 1731-1746'*

William Parker (1) Rector of All Saints in the early 17th Century and believed founder of the Hastings Grammar School

William Parker (2) great nephew - Schoolmaster Hastings Grammar, falsely accused by Titus Oates of sodomy with a pupil

Samuel Oates Rector of All Saints 1660 to 1674 father of Titus

Titus Oates, (1649 – 1705) perjurer, curate of All Saints, Hastings, falsely accused William Parker of sodomy and, later, fabricated a conspiracy asserting a Papist plot to kill Charles II.

James Saunders, founder of second Hastings School 1708

2nd Earl of Ashburnham, John. 1724-1812. Inherited father's title and estates. Was a friend and intimate of James Collier.

John Coppinger, resident of Hampstead, family friend and probably fellow lawyer.

Elizabeth Worge (nee Collier). b 1707. Eldest daughter of John Collier and Elizabeth Elphick. Married George Worge, Battle solicitor and friend and associate of Collier's

Sir Thomas Webster clothing manufacturer, elected MP Colchester 1705 and 1711. Subsequently expelled from Parliament on both occasions. Financed legal action against Hastings Corporation

Whistler Webster, son of Sir Thomas. Unsucessful Tory candidate for Hastings in 1734 election

Miss Webster - probably daughter to Sir Thomas and sister to Whistler. Friend of Cordelia's

Sir Thomas Eversfield Royalist MP for Hastings from 1640-44

John Fuller 1680-1745) Brightling Ironmaster. Unsuccessful Tory Candidate for Sussex in 1734 election. Fuller's children are mentioned in various Collier letters. Among them may be elder daughter Elizabeth, sons John b 1706, Rose b 1708, Henry b 1713 and Stephen b 1716. (Henry married a cousin, Frances Fuller, and their son, 'mad' Jack, became a famous eccentric and MP later in the century.

James Bossom, 1688-1764. Boat owner and carrier between Hastings and London. Freeman and Jurat of Hastings. Sometime friend of Collier's.

Shadwell, possibly son of Sir John Shadwell (1671–1747), famouus Royal physician, and grandson of Thomas Shadwell (1642–1692), dramatist and poet-laureate

Chapter 16

Life Cycle

Honoured Sir .... We are to sup at my Brothers chambers with the family of ye Coles a Monday night ... we was at Ranleigh last night ...my brother and he (Mr Green) walked in the park with us the other night and afterwards came a supped here ... [16 May 1747]

This letter to her father from the 20-year-old Jane Collier is the last reference to her brother James in the Collier correspondence before his death on 30 May 1747. It happened in his chambers in Fig Tree Court as evidenced by a receipt from the Temple authorities for *"the dues for carrying James Collier Esq., who died in ye Temple and carried out to be buried elsewhere."*

There is a gap in the Collier correspondence around this date, and it was left to Charles Lane Sayer to piece together the events from various fragments and bills among his ancestor's papers:

He was buried, as his brother John had been (and by night, as it would seem) in the north cloister of Westminster Abbey. The bill for the funeral, including the Temple dues, (£2 2s.) and the fees for the Abbey (£12 17s. 2d.) amounted to £88 16s. 2d. Among the items are "10 pages in

Mourning with Velvet Caps and truncheons to attend the hearse and bear the body," and *"38 Men in Mourning with Branch-lights," also "A hearse and six Horses & 5 Mourning Coaches and pairs of horses,"* and *"A large Roome hung in deep Mourning and the Passage & the floor covered. The bill is headed "Funeral of James Collier Esq., June 6th 1747."*
[Note from Correspondence of Mr John Collier, ed. Charles Lane Sayer 1907]

It was clearly an extremely elaborate – not to say expensive – funeral. There is no confirmation of what the 26 year old had died from – though he had been ill the previous year with an unexplained disorder. Cranston had written in October 1746 that *'recovery from each ffitt was a great mercy ... but such terrible shocks can't but leave their traces.'*

There is no recorded reaction to his death from the immediate family. But it's clear losing the second of his two sons hit John hard. Around the end of June he told a correspondent *"I have been for some time indisposed and see as little company as possible."* And later, in September, to the same writer, he mentions a lowness of spirits: *"I have been at times very much indisposed the last three or four months and sometimes hardly capable of transacting any business."*

The family was in mourning throughout the remainder of 1747, wearing hats and clothes provided by a Mrs Selby who wrote to Cordelia shortly after Jackie's death:

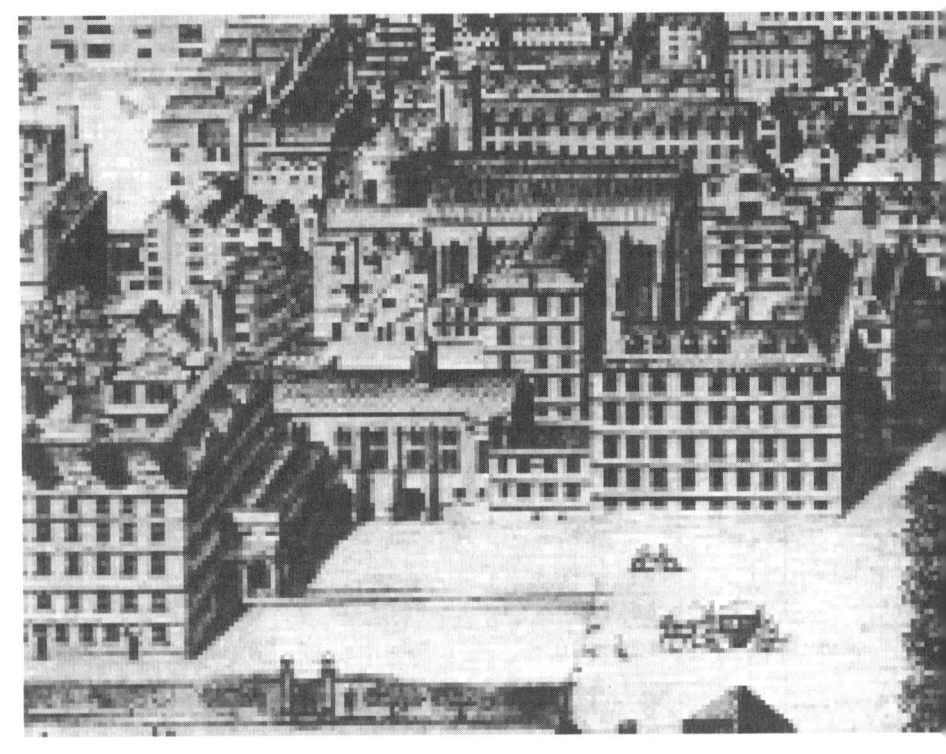

The Inner Temple in the 18th Century.
James Collier's chambers in Fig Tree Court were in th buildings to the left

Madam I hop the things I have bought will bee to your satisfaction. They are of the best of the sort, for I think indifferent silks in mourning soon grows very shaby. I have bought Mrs Collier the best crape I could git & have taken the liberty to bespake her a mob (hat) & rufells & hankerchief .... As for you young Ladys have had hoods made which I hope you will like.

It raises an interesting window on 18th Century death rituals. The following Christmas, seven months after the death, Cranston writes to Collier in stern tones about his perceived breach of etiquette for remaining in black for too long:

Your Mourning should have been half a year vizt. 3 months deep & 3 months slight, that the Mourning a whole year is not customary in your case & as you have not gone into second Mourning at all, it is now too late to do it, but that you now go into Colours. [Cranston to Collier 24 December 1747]

Around the same time he wrote a more sympathetic note to his brother-in-law:

'I am sorry to hear that you think of drooping again - rouse up all your spirits and be but determined to think the best of everything and I dare say the winter may be happily and cheerfully got through ... Come to town with my sister etc ... some coffeehouse chatt - a play - an opera - a

levee - a cheerful bottle at Fletchers - the
House of Commons - Lords - cum multis
aliis etc would greatly contribute and
infallibly do the business - pray consider
yourself and if that won't do, consider your
family - your daughters'

With the loss of his last son Collier perhaps looked for potential sons-in-law to carry on the family 'firm'. And he didn't have to look much further than Edward Milward who seems to have found favour with the patriarch – even if not entirely with his wife and some other members of his family.

The Milwards were an old Hastings clan – 17th Century members had held mayoral office in 1686 and 1699. Most generations seem to have chosen the Christian name Edward and so to differentiate we will call them Edward 1 (1682-1749), Milward Senior - Collier's son-in-law (1723-1811) and Milward Junior – Collier's grandson - (1765 –1833).

Edward 1 was a contemporary and colleague of John; a freeman, jurat and, in 1721, mayor. His son, Edward senior, clearly decided that his personal advancement lay with the Collier family and set about trying to marry into it. Accordingly he first set his sights on the third daughter, Jane, and in 1750 when she was 22, received Collier's permission to court her. It did not go well. Indeed he felt impelled to appeal to his hoped-to-be father-in-law for help:

I think myself duty bound ... to acquaint
you with my ill success ... which really is
entirely the reverse from what I had cause
to expect

Edward Milward Senior, Suitor to Jane and Mary

Edward Milward Jnr, Collier's Grandson

*from her at first ... Miss Jenny's behaviour
... has been one day very civil & the next day
the reverse (&) is the only reason why I
have not so frequently made use of your
house as I should otherwise have done – for
she has often seemed displeased when she
has known of my intention of coming there
... she was wavering in the affair since I
obtained your leave and acquainted her
thereof – and as the more I endeavoured to
oblige her, the more she seemed at a
distance ... I really do love her too well
which she is very sensible of...* [5 June 1750]

It seems the young Edward had never heard of
playing hard to get, and perhaps the ardour of his
courtship was rather overwhelming – it would certainly
seem so from the tone of the above letter which
continued in very much the same vein for a number of
paragraphs.

Collier appears to have liked the Milward enough,
and seems to have promised him a decent sum to take
Jane off his hands!

*I can't conceive why (your conduct) should
be disagreeable to her and I hope what I
said on the occasion convinces you of my
good opinion ... as she is of a proper age it
will be very agreeable to me to see her
disposed of in my lifetime and you will not
find me wanting in parting with a suitable
fortune for that purpose.* [June 6 1750]

A clue to Jenny's reluctance may have come from her elder sister Molly who had written to her father in November the previous year:

We have no news stirring at present, only that Mr Milward keeps open house and laughs and haloos so loud that they can hear him down to ye Swan.

There's a delicious irony in this apparent criticism in that, after Edward Milward had finally given up on the seemingly fickle Jane, he turned his attentions to her elder sister. With considerably more success. Molly and he were married four years later in 1754. Milward had already served his first term as Hastings Mayor in 1750, an office he was to occupy every alternate year from 1753 to 1801. And for the last 16 years it was his son, Edward Jnr, Collier's grandson, with whom he shared the office. Milward also inherited other posts of John Collier's, including that of Surveyor General of the Customs for Kent. In proposing him for the job Collier was fulsome in his praise for his son-in-law describing him as:

an active person about 30, very capable of performing the duty in all respects, and I truly believe with honour and reputation, and has an Estate, and on which he lives in a prudent, respectable manner. He was bred to the Law, but not pursued it.

Jane Collier (top) and Mary (Molly) Collier.
Both were courted by Edward Milward

Mary Collier seems not to have been so convinced as to Milward's character. In 1764, after her husband's death, she wrote to her brother John Cranston:

> *Mr. Milward is set off this day for London - the way he goes on here is quite amazing to all the world, neither house nor land within ten mile of this place that he will not purchase if it's possible, by offering more than people can withstand.*

There was even a protracted battle over who would inherit and occupy the Collier 'mansion' which was finally won by Edward Milward and Molly.

However the marriage seems to have been successful producing four daughters and one son Edward Jnr who seems, if possible, to have been even more rapacious than his father.

So far we have seen two of Collier's daughters married off; Dely and Molly. The remaining three Jenny, Sarah and Harriett didn't marry until after his death and so are a little tangential to our tale. But for completeness' sake it's worth noting that the flighty Jane, after rejecting Milward, eventually fell for an engineer named William Green who was working in Hastings building a gun battery. The match was opposed by her mother as he seemed impecunious and so she eloped with him, leaving a note for Mary on the table:

> *...tho' I follow my own inclinations yet it is with much regret I leave my friends ... there can be no particular reason alleged against ye person I've made choice of, only that it is not to my advantage in not*

marrying an estate. It has been and is now a great trouble to me that I could not have your approbation & that I have acted thus without it must be imputed to my despair of ever obtaining it. I ask your pardon in acting contrary to your sentiments and am in all other respects your most dutiful daughter. [Jane to Mary 'Sunday night at 11 o Clock' – probably 1761]

According to the recollections of Jane's niece, Mary Sayer, the couple arrived in London planning to wed immediately only to find they had to wait a month for the license. Jane ended up staying with her uncle, the ever-obliging William Cranston, until the ceremony. Heather Warne notes that afterwards the Greens lived in Lewes and paid frequent visits to Brighton where they 'seem to have enjoyed a gay social life.' Mrs Green had a number of miscarriages and died childless, leaving the greater part of her property to be divided between the children of Mary and Henry and her sister Sarah.

Sarah was married in 1763 to a lawyer of Lincoln's Inn, Henry Sayer and lived in Red Lion Square producing a number of children including the Rev Edward Lane Sayer. It was his third son Charles Lane Sayer who fixed the family for posterity by transcribing, editing and publishing, in 1907, the Correspondence of John Collier and his Family.

The youngest Collier daughter Henrietta also married, in 1771, a lawyer, Henry Jackson of the Middle Temple, and they settled in Hastings. Jackson, though, was apparently unfaithful and incurred the wrath of Edward Milward who is reported to have given him a black eye following a fracas in the town hall.

John Collier would doubtless have been delighted to know that all five of his surviving daughters did marry, and that two at least produced heirs to carry on the family line even if not the Collier name. Having lost so many children in infancy and his two surviving sons in boyhood and adulthood, Collier was naturally extremely fearful of illness. And of all the illness he feared, Smallpox was clearly the most terrifying.

Here we need to take a little diversion and introduce ourselves to the formidable Lady Mary Wortley Montague. She was a celebrated beauty and courtier who had been disfigured by Smallpox in 1715. Later she moved to Constantinople when her husband was appointed ambassador and was amazed at what she found. People there had been deliberately infected with Smallpox in a procedure known as variolation that dated back to the 10th century in China and India. It used live smallpox virus in the pus taken from a smallpox blister in a mild case of the disease and introduced it into scratched skin of a previously uninfected person to promote immunity to the disease

Writing home to a friend she described how children were 'engrafted' with diseased matter inserted into a wound in the arm. After a week they developed a fever which lasted up to 72 hours and pustules which didn't leave a permanent mark. Within a fortnight they were quite recovered and immune to future bouts of the disease. She had her young son inoculated safely and, in 1721 after her return to England and in the midst of a widespread outbreak of the disease her three-year-old daughter was publicly inoculated. Opinion as to the efficacy and safety of the procedure was sharply divided, and even after Lady Montague persuaded the authorities to carry out a test on condemned prisoners in Newgate – in which all survived - many remained vehemently opposed to the idea. But the idea received considerable traction when Caroline, Princess of Wales, became convinced of its value and had two of her daughters Amelia and Caroline successfully inoculated in April 1722.

Despite the successes demonstrated by Lady Wortley Montague, the procedure was, generally, far from safe and mortality rates were high. There was a severe outbreak of Smallpox in Hastings in 1729, and historian Thomas Brandon Brett contends that Parish records in Ore showed that, in just two months, eleven people died of the disease in the 'natural' way, but as many as 61 perished after inoculation. Over the town as a whole he says 705 people contracted disease, 91 died 'nearly half of which (deaths) were caused by the new-fangled system of inoculation', though it has not been possible to verify those figures.

By contrast James Jurin, secretary to The Royal Society and a British pioneer of inoculation, advertised in the society's journal asking for practitioners' experiences of variolation. From the replies he calculated that the risk of dying from the procedure alone was 1 in 50. By contrast the risk of death from the disease itself was 1 in 7 or 8. He published the results in various papers in t the mid 1730s, thus adding to the growing debate.

So the dilemma for people was whether to take the undoubted risk of subjecting themselves to the disease through inoculation, or gamble that they might not contract it at all in the 'natural' way but that, if they did, it was much more likely to prove fatal.

In 1750 John and Mary Collier decided – doubtless after much heart-searching – that the risk was worth it and that the eldest two of their four unwed daughters should undergo treatment. Interestingly Dely, who was by then married to Major Murray had

Lady Mary Wortley Montague

become ill with Smallpox while in Ireland where they were stationed. They deliberately neglected to impart the news until she was recovering so as not to worry her parents. It makes Murray's letter to Collier in January 1750 all the more interesting:

I am very glad the young ladies have taken up resolution of being inoculated, as I am confident there is little or no danger attending to it, & I wish Mrs Collier had agreed to Miss Sally and Hariot's undergoing the same operation, for I believe the younger the better. In this place above a hundred have been inoculated since we came & I don't hear of one that has died.

In fact the plan was for both Sally and Hariot to undergo the treatment if it had proved successful for Molly and Jenny. The Colliers were lucky that one of the pioneers of variolation was a friend of theirs who lived in Rye and ran a sanatorium in a private house, Farthings, in Northiam. Dr Thomas Frewen was born in 1704 and studied medicine at Utrecht and in Leiden under the famous Herman Boerhaave – such an eminent a physician that he was dubbed the 'Dutch Hippocrates'.

However Frewin publicly disputed one of Boerhaave's theories - that Smallpox could be cured by the taking of an antidote - and published papers demonstrating the effectiveness of inoculation. His sanatorium, though, was none too popular with the villagers of Northiam. The rector, churchwardens and overseers of the parish demanded he cease conducting inoculations there and, when he refused, brought a prosecution alleging he was of *'wicked mind and disposition and being greedy of unlawful gain and having no regard for the health and safety of people'.* His hospital was described as having been converted from a dwelling house to a pest house.

Nonetheless it was to this house that Mary and Jenny arrived in January 1750:

> *Jeny and I are very well and in good spirit hitherto and must say that we have spent our time so agreeably since we have been here that we have not had time to think of anything bad for we have not yet been a quarter of an hour without company since we came.* [letter to Mary Collier from Northiam 3 February 1750]

After being infected the girls had to remain indoors for the disease to manifest. And very boring it was too, according to their letters *'We often fancy ourselves in a nunnery as we don't dare go out of ye gates,'* wrote Mary, and on another occasion they complained the only distraction was: *'Cards, cards, nothing but cards'*, though Jane did report winning 20/- on one occasion.

Eventually the treatment was successfully completed and they left Northiam, to be replaced by 10 year old Sally and the 8 year old Harriett along with their Mother Mary who was to stay with them throughout the period of their treatment. By May 1750 Sarah (Sally) was writing to her father from Farthings:

> *Honoured Sir, I do myself the pleasure to tell you that Hariot and I are both as well as ever we were in our lives & I believe that by the time we come home you will not be able to see we have had the Small-pox.*

So John Collier was 'lucky' in providing precautionary treatment for these four of his daughters, just as he had been desperately unlucky in the death of his two sons who survived infancy ... and the passing of the thirteen or fourteen children who did not. There were, of course, many other medical concerns and crises to worry him. Dely appears to have contracted consumption at some stage which might explain her death at the comparatively young age of 57. There was also a serious scare over Sally's eyesight in 1756, although the problem seems to have recovered after a consultation with Dr Frewen. But three years later when she was 19, it reoccurred and her mother contacted an eminent London surgeon, Mr Sharpe, and asked her brother William Cranston to go and see him. He wrote back to her in Hastings:

> *I read your letter to him in which you mention the Application of Bleeding, blistering and purging – these remedies in the common disorders of the eyes he says are very proper, and how much this case may exceed others 'tis impossible for him to judge without seeing her ... her being in Town is infinitely the best, nay, the only way of getting the best help and assistance for there is none other, for these Great Ones will not stir & especially when you mention Sussex Roads.*

Ultimately, after some cajoling, Mary sent Sally up to London to see a consultant, Mr Girl of Lincoln's Inn, who had previously recommended that if the problem was *'matter formed in the pupil of the eye (it) ought instantly to be let out by the point of a Lancett'*. The correspond-dence doesn't record whether he conducted this or another procedure, but there's no doubt that her parents were on tenterhooks about the outcome

> *The agonies I go through every post night are not to be described. I am sensible that it must give a great deal of trouble in your little house ... Poor Sally, my heart aches for her, but I hope it will please God to send her home in a better condition. You are desired to let them have any money they want.* [Mary Collier to William Cranston 8 May 1759]

The operation appears to have been a success for by October Cranston was writing to Mary in Sussex to say:

> *It gives me great pleasure to hear by my sister that Mrs Murray and Sally got safe to Hastings and that the latter's eyes appear to be better than was expected.*

By this point John Collier was far from well himself. For much of his life he'd been afflicted with the gout and at some later stage appears to have suffered a stroke which, at that point, rendered him unable to write. We will deal with the melancholy task of recording his death shortly, but for now let's leave him and Mary welcoming home Sally, her eyes recovering, and Dely whose husband General Murray is now in Canada distinguishing himself in the battle for Quebec.

§§§

James Collier 1721-1747 (Jemmy) Colliers' second son. Lawyer. Hastings Mayor.

Cordelia Collier (Dely) Eldest daughter 1722-1779 Married (General) James Murray

Mary Collier 1725-83 (Molly) Married Edward Milward Snr.

Jane Collier (Jenny) b 1727. Rejected advances of Milward Snr, eloped and married William Green in 1761

Sarah Collier b1740. Married lawyer Henry Sayer 1763

Henrietta Collier (Harriet) b 1741. Married Lawyer Henry Jackson

Mary Sayer: *Daughter of Sarah Collier, (niece to other Collier's children) Great Aunt to Charles Lane Sayer*

Charles Lane Sayer. *Transcriber and editor of The Correspondence of John Collier, pub. 1907*

William Cranston Mary Collier's younger brother. John Collier's London partner

Edward Mllward (1) 1682-1749. Hastings Freeman, Jurat and Mayor 1721.

Edward Milward (Snr) 1723-1811. Collier's son-in-law via marriage to his daughter Mary 1754. 26 times Mayor of Hastings

Edward Milward (Jnr) 1765 – 1833. Grandson to John Collier. 20 times Mayor of Hastings

William Green - Engineer. Husband of Jane Collier

Heather Warne *catalogued the Collier Archive in 1966*

Lady Mary Wortley Montague introduced smallpox inoculation to England

Thomas Brandon Brett *1816-1906. Hastings journalist and historian.*

James Jurin secretary to The Royal Society and a British pioneer of inoculation

Dr Thomas Frewen b 1704. Rye doctor and friend of Colliers. Pioneer of Smallpox inoculation in Sussex. Treated the 4 Collier daughters in 1750

Chapter 17

Home in Hastings

When John Collier was at home in Hastings there was certainly plenty to occupy his time both domestically and professionally. For the latter there were his duties as Town Clerk, an office he held continuously from 1706 to 1749 except for the five years when he was mayor. He had been running a law practice in Hastings since at least 1712 when he took on his first recorded apprentice – John Thompson of Winchelsea. He added another, Anthony Ellesdon of Lydd, two years later and, in 1717, a third joined the practice, Thomas Godley. Henry Dodson arrived as a seven-year apprentice in January 1725, paying £140. Richard Patrick was Collier's long-serving clerk who, in 1747, also became an apprentice attorney. So this is, then, a fairly sizable law firm – doubtless with its own premises - which Collier has to oversee. Part of their regular work involved preparing prosecution cases against smugglers. He remained clerk to the Commissioners of Sewers for various places on the Pevensey levels throughout his working life, clerk of the militia, joint solicitor for the Cinque Ports and Commissioner for the East Sussex land tax. Then, after 1733, his position as Surveyor-General of Kent Riding Officers came with another office in Hastings, and would have required a good deal of his attention. There was also his role as Newcastle's local election agent, as well as acting as his deputy as Vice Admiral for Sussex. Plus he was agent for several local landowners in Sussex.

Because most of his surviving letters to Mary were written while he was in London, there are not that many references to his professional life in Hastings. William Cranston his most regular correspondent was writing from the capital to Collier in Hastings, but naturally most of the content is about cases they were working on in London rather than in Sussex.

It is, therefore, hard to know precisely what Collier's daily life would have been like but we can surmise that in Sussex, while he would have spent long hours fulfilling his array of responsibilities, he would also have had time to socialise. There are references to some sort of club or regular gatherings at the Swann with any luminaries that happened to be around such as Colonel Pelham. One letter from Collier in Hastings to Mary, apparently visiting her brother William Cranston in London, is more than usually revealing, outlining aspects of his daily life:

> *We have been this whole day a bottling out the wine ... Saturday night after writing my letters I sallied to the end of the walk, all forlorn, and the doctor's house, window shutters all up close, his maid and Misse Nanny being at Battell. I saw Mr Sansum at his door, and went along and sent cross for Mr Cant and took them home to supper and we set till 12 a'clock in which time Mr Cant was wondrous wise. Sunday Mr Mayor and Mr Hill invited the jurats in, though few went. I saw there Mr Hill's sister and invited her and Mrs Wicking to come up yesterday afternoon and drink tea. Molly desired me to send for her aunt Cruttenden to be here when they come, and Mr Mayor and Hill came with them ...together they tarried (for) supper,*

North Hastings in the later part of the 18th Century from a painting by Samuel Hieronymus Grimm

which was two little chicken, prawns and pease, an elegant supper, and went away a little after ten...Molly was down at her aunt's (in Battle) ... and as there is a puppet show in town, fancy she tarries to go thither, not being returned ... Just as I was putting up my letters Mr Cant and his wife and son came in to hire Mr Mead's house and are to enter upon it at Michaelmas. (11 March 1736)

This seemingly trivial account of Collier's life in Hastings without Mary is, interesting just because of its mundanity. It is clear that there was little intellectual stimulation to be had in the town, save for the 'wondrous wise' Samuel Cant. He was to become, in 1738, the new schoolmaster who, Richard Saville believes, was encouraged to move to Hastings by Edward Milward. Cant was a surveyor and cartographer, indeed he drew the 1750 map of Collier's estate - *A Survey Measurement and Representation of the Home Estate of John Collier Esquire situate and being in the Parishes of Saint Clement All Saints and St Mary in the Castle appertaining and adjoining to the Town and Port of Hastings ... with an Iconographical Plan of the said Town'*, and also the invaluable map of the town in 1746. Again according to Saville he was a collector of 'instruments, globes and books'. His appointment followed the death of the previous schoolmaster, Stephen Wicking, in 1743 and it is probably his widow, Elizabeth, whom Collier invites to tea.

The regular references to relatives throughout all the correspondence suggests their comparatively greater importance in 18th century social life. Collier's business partner is his brother-in-law. The children are forever visiting or staying with the Worges in Battle – Mrs Worge being Collier's daughter Elizabeth from his first marriage. Molly's 'aunt' Cruttenden was, in fact, Collier's sister Sarah, and she and her husband Samuel lived in a cottage next to the Collier residence in Hastings.

As time went on Collier acquired more and more property in and around the town. Some of it was let, but some of the land was worked. There are references to harvesting and mowing - *'I hope you will have fine weather for making the hay'* (June 1735) – albeit under Mary's direction as he himself was often in London.

His garden also occupied Collier's attention whether he was at home or not. In February 1737 he wrote to Mary, worrying about the coming season:

> *I believe it will be best to have the old cherry trees in the long walk quite taken away, for they have bore but little a great many years. I should be glad to know how the spring comes on and whether the pease are come up and if the birds wake you in the morning with their cheerfulness ... I hope Morris takes care to have everything proper for the season of the year planted and set in gardens. I shall send him some matts and if he wants anything else you must write word.*

Running the house also required staff and, it seems, servants were often a problem. One William Ayrton is mentioned in correspondence in 1751 when Collier accuses him of *'impudent and undutiful behaviour'* and orders him to leave Bath where John was recuperating, and to wait for him in London. William Cranston refers to the incident in a letter on 12th November:

> *I'm troubled also for William's villainous Behaviour which would be nothing was you well but in your present situation is terrible. I hope with the assistance of your coachman, with some little aid called in, you'll be able to manage so as never to lett the other fellow upon any Terms come under your roof with you again.*

Tantalisingly we never discover just what it was that Ayreton did to cause such displeasure.

Drink seems to have been a fairly constant problem among servants of various members of the family. Collier directed Cranston's 'man' to deliver a capon to a friend, but it never arrived:

> *The fellow went out at 11 a clock, but not coming home to dinner and being drunk the day before so that he was turned out from waiting at table we imagined he was got at it again, tho he had had a reprimand.* (John to Mary 16 November 1734)

The Murrays, on their way to Ireland June 1749 had the double problem of a drunk manservant and a maid in love with him, as Cordelia told to her mother from Chester:

> *I believe you will be surprised when I tell you Molly left me at this place and indeed can't help saying she is an ungrateful creature as ever was. I can't account for it*

303

in any way but her love for Tom, which I think she showed very strongly all the way down ... as for him there was no bearing with it any longer for he was drunk every day ... so upon Mr Murray discharging him yesterday morning Molly told me she did like to go if he was turned off ... & this morning ye gentleman & lady set out for London together without asking leave of me tho' I gave her half a guinea over her wages. This, to be sure, puts us at some inconvenience just at this time...

Finding good help in the first place seems to have been a regular issue. Cranston recommended a manservant to Collier in 1750 and negotiated a wage of £8 per annum. But at the last minute the man turned down the offer saying his father was ill and he was obliged to go to Yorkshire. A story Cranston clearly disbelieved:

I take it to be all a sham. He has got some other place that he likes better and this is the way they all act, both men and women, having had experience of both sexes before in the same way. I am heartily provoked and vexed at it, but there's no remedy. [23 August 1750]

There seems to have been a good deal of discussion among employers as to the merits of various servants and, in some cases, recommendations. In 1739 Mary Markwick, sister to Sir Charles Eversfield, wrote to Mary Collier from her home at Catsfield Place near Battle:

In your obliging letter you mentioned a want of servants ... my head maid I can recommend as a neat workwoman, good natured and willing to do anything she is bid. She is but 19 years of age and never was out before I took her. I have a pretty large family and want one at the head in some degree to manage the rest and likewise to understand a kitchen which are the reasons I part with her. [6 February 1739]

But it didn't work out. Cordelia, who was staying at Catsfield place, wrote to her mother the following week to say Mrs Marquick (sic) was *'very sorry that the maid wont do for she can't recommend any of her others.'*

In turn, Mary Collier was happy to recommend her servants to other families when they were looking for new staff. Though such arrangements could sometimes result in misunderstandings and disappointment. Lady Margaret Ashburnham wrote to Mary from Broomham in March 1739:

I am mighty sorry to find ... you dislike some blunder made between Lucy Stevens and me about a servant in your family which makes me give you this trouble to repeat what passed on this occasion. Lucy, knowing I wanted a cook, sent me word there was a servant going from you ... that yours was a good cook and could do a great deal of work, but she was going to Newcastle from whence she came .... (but) she was willing to come to me if I could stay until she came back from Newcastle ... last week she desired Lucy would let me know I must not depend on her, for she could not come to me, which was some disappointment.

We do not know exactly how many servants the Colliers maintained, and definitive information about numbers for such a household is sketchy for the first half of the 18th Century. However it seems that a family of their status would have had between 6 and 8 domestic staff living in, including a footman, household maid, laundry or scullery maid, cook, and nursery maid. There would also have been at least one groom to look after the horses – plus latterly the intemperate coachman - and probably several gardeners, so it's no great surprise that organising, finding and keeping, domestic servants occupied a considerable amount of time. One gardener was mentioned in Collier's will. Stephen Morris was originally left £20 but that sum was reduced by half in a subsequent codicil. We don't know what Master Morris had done to incur Collier's displeasure and make him reduce his bequest.

Servants could be the source of embarrassment if they behaved inappropriately. George Worge, Collier's son-in-law from his first marriage and a fellow solicitor and family friend, complained bitterly about the actions of Collier's coachman after he had acquired the new vehicle.

Your coachman swore and Damned in a most Insolent Outrageous manner, because there was not four stalls for your coach horses, & insisted upon one of my horses (that are always kept in) to be turned out. This not being Complied with by my servant & two of your horses being obliged to stand in one stall was the occasions of his Intemperance. My man opened the Oat chest ... but he swore he would not give them an oat & desired my servant to tell me that when I came to your house my horses should not have either hay or oats.

Horses are often referred to in the correspondence, usually with Collier arranging for them to be sent to, or taken back from, London or Sevenoaks for his thrice annual commute.

I desire you will send Nick with the horses a Munday, soe as to be in town a Tuesday. He may bring my mare and ride the black horse and let him come on very softly.

Arranging transport for women was a trickier affair. It seems they were permitted to ride 'double', usually with a male chaperone, or travel in a coach – though given the state of the local roads this was often very difficult. In November 1730 Mrs Worge invites Mary Collier to make the journey to visit her in Battle 'which you may very safely do if you ride double'. Interestingly there is little mention of the adult Collier women ever riding singly on a horse or having horses of their own, and Cordelia was discouraged from riding a pony when she was 15:

I hope if you went to Battell you had Barnse's horse and you did not let Dely ride pony, for I think it is by no means a proper horse.

Cordelia was advised, in 1743, to "ride out" by Dr Richard Russell of Lewes to improve her health, though it's uncertain whether he meant on horseback or by coach.

Horses were certainly essential for travelling any sort of distance and so were a valuable commodity. In May 1744 a lonely Collier in Hastings tells Mary in London about the mayor's misfortune:

> *I live as merrily as I can with the little girls though I think it sometimes very dolorous. The mayor has had his mare stolen which he had from me and sent out advertisements and I have wrote for him about her to the custom officers in Kent who well know the mare and Mr Carswell lost a saddle and bridle the same night. ...My sister Sally and Miss Cruttenden came up this afternoon and are now here. I have been in the parlour to drink tea and find my sisters not here.*

Horses were not the only animals in danger of being stolen. It seems that Collier bred rabbits for the pot on land he owned at Coney Banks - part of the West Hill. In 1751 Richard Patrick writes to him to say that a man had been detained and accused of 'wiring' rabbits on his land. No actual animals were found, but the lines and wires in his possession earned him a £5 fine. Unable to pay he was sentenced to three months in the House of Correction from which he later escaped.

There certainly doesn't seem to have been a surfeit of entertainment in Hastings in the 1740s or 50s. There is a reference to a play in the Court Hall in 1737 and players coming to town in January 1747 with a suggestion from William Cranston that Collier would *'attend 'em 3 or 4 times a week'*. Mary Collier noted in 1750 that the *'Fair Penitent'* by Nicholas Rowe was to be acted in the town. It seems the Corporation refused to license a theatre and the only playhouse around this time was at the Hare and Hounds public house in Ore - outside the town's boundary. According to JM Baines it wasn't until 1825 that a license was granted to Mr Frederick Brooke to build a theatre in what was then Great Bourne Street. The building still stands (on The Bourne – the A259) and became the Wesleyan Chapel.

Apart from intermittent theatrical productions, much entertainment in Hastings revolved around the three fairs: Whitsun, Rock and Winter (see JM Baines *Historic Hastings* p 250). Cordelia refers to the two-day Rock fair in a letter of July 1734: *"Pray tell my sisters I am glad they have such fine weather to go to Rock fair"*. In some ways Hastings fairs had to substitute for a regular market, which the town lacked, possibly because it was a maritime rather than agricultural hub.

Evenings out, therefore, were pretty much confined to visiting one of the various Inns or Public Houses in the town. Foremost among these was undoubtedly the Swan. It had been in existence since at least the first half of the 16th century, and received a major boost during John Collier's time when it became Hastings' main coaching inn. At this period it was also the venue for all civic functions and dinners and many political events as well as public auctions. Entertainments as diverse as cockfighting and balls were held there. Molly Collier, writing to her mother Mary in 1749 said:

We were at ye Swan yesterday to keep ye birthday but can't say there was a brilliant sett of company. Tho' we had a ball, and Mr Polhill and Mr Bayley were some of ye Head of ye Dancers. I danc'd with little George Coulton, who was as well as anybody. [31 October 1749]

The Swan was evidently Collier's 'local' though he was not always enamoured of the conversation to be had there:

Sir W A (William Ashburnham) and Mr Frewen came to town about 12 ... and I was sent for from the Swan about 4 and found them strongly engaged in low, obscene, discourse and nothing diverted it during my stay about an hour [May 1742]

Then in 1758, just two years before his death, John Collier became the Swan's owner. At that stage in his life he would have had little interest in running the inn, and it's probable he acquired it in settlement of a debt, or foreclosure of a mortgage he had advanced on the building. In any event ownership passed to Mary on his death, and then, on her demise, to their daughter Henrietta. Later it was acquired by her brother-in-law James Murray.

There were other events in Hastings that were then classed as 'entertainment' though we now might beg to differ with the definition. Earlier in the 1742 letter quoted above Collier had referred to a public whipping:

Dame Arthur was about one a clock Whipp'd at the Carts Tayll round the Town and had some strokes at every lanes End, but I find its thought she had not half enough, but I

*inclined to mercy and compassion, &
considered the long time of her confinement
in the Cold weather.*

The town records show that the widow Elizabeth Arthur's crime had been receiving and selling three stolen pullets or young hens. According to Baines, Hastings had a whipping post near the Court Hall, but to ensure more room for spectators the sentence was often carried out at the 'cart's tail', with it stopping at specified places for more lashes to be administered by the Common Cryer who received one shilling for his work.

A decade earlier Collier had written to his sons at Westminster school about another curious punishment that seems to have been prevalent in Hastings and elsewhere at the time:

*Mr John Hall beat his wife and Skimington
was rode which would have pleased you to
see, though you see much finer things every
day.*

Skimmington was a folk custom in which a mock parade was staged through the streets as punishment for domestic violence or infidelity. According to John Brand in his Dictionary of Faiths and Folklore *"to ride Skimmington is a ludicrous cavalcade of a man beaten by his wife. It consists of a man riding behind a woman with his face to the horse's tail holding a distaff in his hand at which he seems to work, the woman all the time beating him with a ladle ... they are accompanied by what is called 'rough music', that is frying pans, bull's horns, marrow bones and cleavers."* A distaff was a stick holding a bunch

Detail from Hudibras Encounters the
Skimmington
a print by William Hogarth of 1726

of fibres of flax or wool for spinning – then a woman's job, hence the 'distaff' or female side of the family.

Great sources of excitement in 18th century Hastings were provided by the sea – often in the form of shipwrecks. The most renowned of these must surely be the destruction of the Amsterdam in January 1749. Collier first learned of it from his Brother-in-Law, Thomas Smith, who was house sitting for the family at the time:

> *There is a large Dutch Ship a shore about half a mile to the East of Bullverhithe ... her name is the Amsterdam, bound to Batavia in the East Indies, burden about 600 or 700 tons, 333 men, 45 guns ... having on board 28 chests of silver ... but what value in each chest is unknown.* [17 January 1749]

The Amsterdam was on her maiden voyage which had been beset by disasters. It took her three attempts, spread out over seven weeks, even to leave her home port of Texel in the Netherlands because of adverse winds. Once in the Channel the winds turned into a full-blown gale described by one unnamed writer "as violent a storm of wind as has been known in the memory of man". It scattered the six East Indiamen along the English coast. Unable to tack down the Channel the Amsterdam lay for days off Beachy Head. An epidemic illness broke out among the crew, killing more than fifty in 10 days. It's believed a number of the sailors mutinied. Finally her rudder broke off and she was driven ashore where she foundered and eventually settled fast in the mud.

George Worge also wrote to Collier on January 17 telling him he'd been to visit the wreck:

Yesterday I rode down to see her and from one of the officers who spoke a little English I had this account ... (there were) three hundred men about half of which had been lost by sickness and washed overboard & loaded with money ... she stands in a good place & in appearance quite whole & may do so for some months but no possibility of getting her off. I believe they will save everything that is worth saving, to the great disappointment of the wreckers who come from all parts of the country for plunder, there was yesterday when I was there more than a thousand of these wretches with long poles and hooks at the end. But all the soldiers on the coast are there and behave well at present.

Worge went on to say that while 27 of the 28 chests of silver were recovered, the final one was emptied by persons unknown and its contents, valued at £60,000, vanished.

John Collier was recuperating in Bath while all this excitement was taking place back at home in Sussex, and his assistant in his law practice, Richard Patrick told him he had become, by default, the town's coroner:

The ship is not on shore in the Liberty of Hasting, and the soldiers have shot a man indiscreetly at the Wreck and Mr Tilden, as coroner for the Rape of Hasting, has been applied to upon the affair to

Dutch East Indiaman, the Amsterdam

summons a jury to view the body and to enquire into the death of this person, but as Mr Tilden is laid up with a fit of the Gout he desired me to act as his deputy upon which I went over to Battell to him and consulted him ... likewise Mr Worge, who both joined in the opinion with me that the death of this person was not to be enquired into by the coroner and jury, by reason he was killed at sea ... below high water mark. [24 January]

Not one to want to miss out on the action, and anyway an extremely safe distance from the muskets of the soldiers guarding the Amsterdam, Collier seems to have instructed Patrick to seize part of the ship's fittings, a request to which his assistant acceded:

I received your last (letter) without a date and will take care to Seize the best Anchor and Cable belonging to the Dutch ship stranded near Bulverhith.

In fact Collier was acting on behalf of the Duke of Newcastle, though in his notes Charles Lane Sayer questions the legitimacy of such a move:

It will be observed that the anchor and cable were seized on behalf of the Duke of Newcastle but in what right does not appear. Bulverhythe is in the manor of Pebsham and the Lord of the Manor in 1748 was Mr Thomas Pelham. MP for Lewes and a kinsman of the Duke ... the

Duke was Vice Admiral of the coast of Sussex and it seems to me possible that he claimed the anchor ... over-riding the right of the lord.

Even if the lord of the manor, or a coastal vice-admiral, had a legal right to salvage, to the modern eye, it doesn't seem that they were acting very differently from the 'thousands' of ordinary people who had come in a hope of sharing the plunder – at least one of whom was shot and killed for his pains.

As a footnote, Richard Patrick established that the missing chest of silver had been *'broke open the night the ship came to shore by some of our Town gentlemen'* and a great number of wedges of silver weighing about 5 lb each dispersed around the town. The authorities offered *'forty shillings per wedge and no questions asked, otherwise in case they were found guilty they would be severely punished.'* However Mr Patrick was not in the least confident that many would take up the offer.

Even though Collier was 150 miles from the wreck it was his correspondence that has provided historians with the best first-hand accounts of events in the days following the Amsterdam's beaching. Peter Marsden, the marine archaeologist who was closely involved with the excavation of the site in the late 1960s wrote in his book 'The Wreck of the Amsterdam':

It is thanks to a man who never actually saw any of the historic events connected with the Amsterdam that we know so much about her shipwreck. It is a stroke of luck the more to be appreciated in that the newspapers of the time, and even the

records of the Hastings town council...have
no mention of the affair at all.

As a man of books with a keen interest in history, Collier would doubtless have appreciated Marsden's comments, even if he would also have been amazed at the idea his letters would have been so helpful – indeed were still being read - more than two centuries after his death.

Collier's library perhaps provides us with another clue as to his leisure activities when he was at home in Hastings – he certainly read a lot (see chapter 2). There was also music in the house, though no evidence that Collier himself played an instrument. But in 1736 he discussed the purchase of a brand-new Spinet for 8 Guineas but determined to look for a second hand one ... *"if I can and save half the money, but if I can't get a good one will have this – in for a hundred in for a Thousand ..."*

It's a curious irony that John constantly hankered to be in Hastings whenever he was away from the town – yet found it 'dolorous' if he was there for any length of stay without Mary. And there seems to have been more friction between them when Collier was in Hastings and Mary in London:

> *I think at present we are in an odd situation by the distance between us and therefore something out of the way, but hope that all that will centre to our mutual pleasure.* [8 May 1742]

Mary, on the other hand, was much less enamoured of Hastings, and evidently often expressed a preference for living in neighbouring Battle or Rye. An idea that failed to find favour with her husband:

I am sorry you think Hasting so desolate a place, & your so often repeating it makes one imagine you are unfortunate in being there.   For my part I should with satisfaction spend the remainder of my days there without seeing any other, & I can't agree with you in the politeness of the two neighbouring towns. [29 November 1737].

§§§§§

Collier's Apprentices:

John Thompson of Winchelsea.

Anthony Ellesdon of Lydd,

Thomas Godley.

Henry Dodson.

Richard Patrick 1710(or11)- 1763. Legal clerk then, in 1747, apprentice attorney to Collier and later manager of his estates. Hastings Town Clerk 1741 & 1750-62. m 1746 Elizabeth Carswell.

William Cranston – Mary Collier's younger brother, John Collier's legal partner, based in London

Samuel Cant - Schoolmaster and cartographer

Molly Collier Second daughter of John and Mary. Married Edward Milward Snr.

Sarah Cruttenden (nee Collier) b1693. John's younger sister.

Samuel Cruttenden - her husband. They lived in a cottage next to the Colliers.

Stephen Wicking - former schoolmaster

Elizabeth Wicking - his widow. Married Thomas Godley 1744

Richard Saville. Historian. Editor of 'The Letters of John Collier of Hastings 1731-1746'

Edward Milward (1) 1682-1749. Hastings Freeman, Jurat and Mayor 1721

Elizabeth Worge – Collier's daughter from his first marriage

George Worge. Collier's son-in-law (as husband to Elizabeth Collier – daughter from first marriage). Solicitor in Battle. Confident and friend.

William Ayrton - Collier servant

Cordelia Murray nee Collier (Dely) - eldest daughter 1722-1779. Married (General) James Murray.

James Murray 1721-1794. John Collier's son-in-law, m. Cordelia 1748. Successful army career, Captain 1742, Major 1745, Lt Col 1751, Major General 1762. Served with General Wolfe in Canada. Governor Quebec 1760-68, Deputy Governor Minorca 1774-84. Owner Beauport Park Hastings

Sir Charles Eversfield 1682-1749.   Local MP and landowner.

Mary Markwick, sister to Sir Charles Eversfield

Dr Richard Russell 1687-1759. Physician of Lewes consulted by John Collier over the health of daughters Mary and Cordelia

J Manwaring Baines. Hastings Historian.   Author of Historic Hastings a Tapestry of Life.

Sir William Ashburnham 1678-1755 (2nd Baronet of Broomham). Hastings MP 1710-1713 and 1722-1734. Fellow coronation canopy bearer with Collier 1727

Lady Margaret Ashburnham. Wife to Sir William

Dr Thomas Frewen 1704-1791. Rye doctor and friend of Colliers. Pioneer of Smallpox inoculation in Sussex Successfully treated four Collier daughters in 1750

Elizabeth (Dame) Arthur. Hastings resident. Publicly

whipped for stealing 3 pullets

John Brand *1744-1806 editor Dictionary of Faiths and Folklore (Published 1905)*

Thomas Smith, Collier's brother-in-law.

Mary Smith – nee Collier, John's youngest sister.

Mr Tilden – Hastings coroner in 1749

Charles Lane Sayer – *1845-1927. Barrister. Great-great grandson of John Collier, transcriber and editor of The Correspondence of John Collier and his Family pub. 1907*

Peter Marsden, *Marine Archaeologist Museum of London. Head of first excavation of Amsterdam 1969-70. His book, The Wreck of the Amsterdam 1985 covers both his and a subsequent excavation.*

Chapter 18

NEAR ETERNITY

From time to time, while looking at John Collier's life, it has been necessary, or at least instructive, to trespass along some parallel byways. Usually this is to enhance our understanding of the man and his circumstances, but just occasionally it is for the sheer fun of historical enquiry or intellectual curiosity. So when, as we will do in this chapter, we examine Collier's wealth and finances, we could just note that he often seemed to be owed money by the Duke of Newcastle. But in chapter 6 we saw Newcastle first meeting Collier in the Swan in Hastings in 1715 and observed that the Duke had become 'one of the richest men in England' on inheriting his father's estate. Why, then, did Collier find it so hard to get money out of him? We have to investigate further. Collier received this letter from the Duke's agent James Waller in May 1740:

> *My Lord the Duke of Newcastle has commanded me to acquaint you that you may draw upon me for one hundred and sixty-eight pounds 17s, part of the £318 17s, the amount of your bill about the corporation suit. At the same time I cannot help telling you that the making this payment is very inconvenient to his grace's affairs and I wish you would let it be deferred...*

In fact it wasn't just £318 that Collier was owed, but a full £1000 plus interest. The Duke had agreed to foot the bill for the court case in the early 1730s in which Hastings Corporation defended its decision to deprive sons of freemen the right of freedom of the town and with it the ability to vote. As we saw in chapter 9, the corporation lost that and subsequent cases, and the solicitor who acted for the corporation, Anthony Trumble (who had also been an agent for the Newcastle) ended up being £1000 out of pocket in fees and expenses. Trumble died in 1733 and when the Duke failed to pay his executors, Collier advanced the money which it appears he himself borrowed at commercial interest rates against a bond lodged with Newcastle's trustees - and for years afterwards tried to get the money repaid:

> *I humbly beg your grace will please to consider the time I have been out of the money and the disappointments it has made me, and please to order immediate payment. By the usage I have had I am constrained to apply to your grace in this affair though with the greatest reluctance and humbly hope for your forgiveness . I humbly wait for your grace's order to the trustees about the three notes for £1000 which I advanced on the account of Trumble's executorship on my own credit.*
> [Collier to the Duke of Newcastle 13 October 1739]

So just what was going on? According to biographer Ray A. Kelch in his book 'Newcastle, a Duke without Money', Pelham-Holles was, theoretically, not without means:

> *The Duke of Newcastle possessed by inheritance one of the great estates of the*

realm, an estate unencumbered by debt and charged with only modest provisions for his brother and sister. He held land in freehold and leasehold tenure in eleven countries of the kingdom. His most extensive estates lay in Lincolnshire, Nottinghamshire, Sussex and Yorkshire, with smaller holdings in Middlesex, Dorsetshire and Wiltshire ... besides these lands he held the very profitable Clare Market estate in London which lay to the south of Newcastle House and Lincoln's Inn Fields.

His estates provided an income of around £27,000 a year, equivalent to rather over £3 million today, but he also obtained remuneration for the various public offices he held, including Lord Chamberlain (1717), Secretary of State (1724), First Lord of the Treasury (1754) and Lord Privy Seal (1765). These provided, certainly from 1724, an average addition to his personal income of around £5,000 a year.

One of the problems Newcastle faced was the cost of collecting the rents from his estates. Take the 'Manor and Royalty' of Hastings for instance. In 1714 it contained 667 tenants spread over 37 parishes, paying a total of just £21 18s 2d a year. The rent collector, a Mr Austen, charged £30 a year for his services. Thus, unless fines were imposed on sufficient tenants for late payment of rent, the cost of collecting the Duke's money actually exceeded the income itself.

And the Duke of Newcastle was not a frugal man. In order to maintain his social position almost as soon as he came into his inheritance he was borrowing money on the strength of it. In the two years from 1715 he mortgaged his Sussex estates for £16,000 and ran up an overdraft at his bank of £5,000.

There was one saving grace – he was a bachelor, and could expect a hefty settlement upon his marriage. His intended was Henrietta Godolphin – granddaughter of the Duke of Marlborough, John Churchill. After some unseemly haggling - £30,000 was sought but just £20,000 agreed on - they were married on 2nd April 1717, and Newcastle was able to release his Sussex estates from the mortgage. The problem was that instead of just the lavish expenses of the Duke, there was now the Duchess to consider. Plus Newcastle was reluctant, indeed refused, to give up any of his five extensive homes. In Sussex there was the old Elizabethan manor house at Halland, plus a hunting 'lodge' at Bishopstone, not far from Lewes. In London there was the substantial Powis, renamed Newcastle House, in Lincoln's Inn Fields. And there was Nottingham Castle, rebuilt as a 'ducal palace' by the Newcastle family in 1674 after the original 'Robin Hood' castle was blown up during the civil war. But what the young man clearly lacked was somewhere closer to London and the court. Fortunately Sir John Vanbrugh had just the pad close to Hampton Court in Surrey, which he sold to Newcastle around 1716. The young duke immediately set in train a series of costly building works both here at Claremont but also at Newcastle House in London and at Nottingham Castle. Thus his debts mounted, reaching an alarming £88,000 in 1721. Something had to be done, so he commissioned an accountant to establish his financial position. The results made for sober reading. Over two years Newcastle's income was £30,597 while his expenditure, including servicing his debts, amounted to £30,218, leaving a balance of just £379 to the good.

What this accounting exercise did not consider, however, was the money he was spending to maintain the Whigs in office. Ray Kelch estimates that Newcastle paid out an absolute minimum of £3,688 over the course of the 1715 general election. It would hardly have been less in 1722, and one agent in Nottingham alone put in a bill for £820 relating to election expenses. We have already seen that little money was spared in entertaining electors – or financing legal defences when his supporters were accused of gerrymandering or trying to fix seats.

Nonetheless, it seems these sums were relatively minor compared to the expenditure on the Duke's various properties. In 1737, six years before he became Prime Minister, Henry Pelham wrote a heartfelt letter to his brother the Duke, castigating him for his financial incontinence:

> *What goes to my heart is ...that you continue to deceive yourself and that you can think it possible that others can be deceived also ... for this is what you must know, that you have spent more than your income, this is you say occasioned by repairs at Lewes ... but what ruins you is that at the same time near five thousand pounds laid out at Newcastle House, continued expenses from additions at Claremont, hounds and other vast ones at Bishopstone, and now new buildings and alterations going on there.... it is impossible but you will immediately put your affairs and expenses in such a way as you mat satisfy your honest creditors...*

The experience of honest creditors like John Collier show that Newcastle singularly failed to take his brother's advice - though the Duke was clearly embarrassed by his inability to pay his debts. On 25th October 1739 he wrote personally to Collier:

> *I will take it as a favour if you can stay (repayment) some little time longer ... and when I know how long you can stay with conveniency to yourself I will endeavour to make you easy as soon and as punctualey as is possible.*

To which Collier replied five days later:

> *As your grace is pleased to mention my staying some little time longer ... I am humbly thankful for your grace's intentions of speaking to the trustees that I may be paid the £1000 in the trust being money I took up at interest to discharge Mr Trumble's creditors on having your grace's drafts for the same ... I humbly hope to be repaid the interest and beg your grace will please direct that I may receive £400 of the debt before Christmas...*

But Collier was all too well aware that he owed much of his success, standing and income - to the Duke's patronage, and sought to soften the tone of his demand:

> *For the honour and happiness I have had of your grace's friendship, if I may presume to make use of the word, and the obligations I am under for the many favours your*

grace hath conferred on me, I shall never cease to be with the greatest gratitude and respect. My Lord, your grace's most obedient and humble servant. [30 October 1739]

Perhaps Newcastle traded on this obligation. Or perhaps his financial position was so grave that he really couldn't repay the money. Or possibly his priorities were rather different. Collier applied again for the money the following January – after the Christmas deadline – only to get this disappointing, if commendably honest, reply from the Duke's agent James Waller:

I do assure you if it was in my power you should not have the trouble of asking twice for the money that remains due to you from my lord the Duke of Newcastle. I was in hopes to have got some part of it at least for you out of this quarter's income, and when my lord duke, before he went into Sussex, was distributing the money to come in, I mentioned this debt to you. But so much was wanted for his journey, and my lady duchess' journey into Derbyshire, and for Lewes and other extraordinary occasions, that the whole is quite exhausted, and nothing left for housekeeping necessarys which are greatly in arrear. [15 January 1741]

According to Charles Lane Sayer, Collier was still pressing for payment seventeen years later and indeed, *"it seems to have been still unpaid at Mr Collier's death."*

Newcastle House in Lincoln's Inn Fields

The question arises whether this, or any of the other smaller sums owed by Newcastle would have massively affected Collier's overall financial position? There seems little doubt that by Hastings' standards he was a wealthy man. We've seen the many and varied sources of his income; we know he was able to send his sons to an expensive public school and his daughters to a private academy. He maintained a sizeable house with servants, had stables and horses and grooms and, latterly, his own coach. We know that he was able to advance considerable sums to ensure his son-in-law's smooth rise up through the ranks of the army, and that he acquired, during his lifetime, fairly extensive land-holdings. In Hastings itself he owned the Old Hastings house, with the grounds and orchards that now form the modern estate on Torfield close. He also owned Torfield House – immediately adjacent to his home which was originally a 16th century timber framed building but was rebuilt in the Georgian style towards the end of Collier's life.

Samuel Cant's 1749/50 Map of the Collier Estate shows widespread holdings in and around Hastings. According to Henry Cousins, author of Hastings Of Bygone Days ...

> *By this plan, made in 1750, it would seem he had, during the half century, acquired a very large proportion of the lands in and surrounding the Bourne and the Priory Valleys, the East and West Hills, Halton, Ore and Fairlight; besides much house property in the old town.*

Heather Warne concludes that:

> *The deed of partition of 1766 reveals that John Collier owned extensive land in Sussex, Surrey and Kent to the value of £30,866 5s 2d, and the abstract of title to the estate of 1761 indicates that he purchased the greater part of it in his lifetime'.*

£30,000 in 1760 is, according to the Office for National Statistics, roughly equivalent to £6 million today. A pretty extraordinary estate for the son of an innkeeper who started with no capital that we know of. So just how had he got it?

Richard Saville's analysis of Collier's accounts for his London legal work with William Cranston for the year 1727 show totals reaching 'on occasion' a very considerable £500 a month. That's around £100,000 in today's figures or getting on for £1m a year. Clearly the law was as profitable a business in the Georgian era as it is today! Along with the gross rents from his land – around £650 a year in the 1730s [£130,000 today] rising to £1077 just before his death [£220,000 today] - and the income from his sinecures and estate agency work, he was doing extremely well. But there was another income stream to take into account. And this one also provided him with the ready capital to snap up any local property that came onto the market at a favourable price. It seems, according to his great granddaughter, Mary Sayer, that Collier also acted as Hastings' only banker:

> *There being at that time no banks, all the people round who had money brought it to him to take care of, being quite sure of*

having it again when they required it, this however gave him command of much ready money and allowed him to purchase any land in the neighbourhood cheap whenever any was to be sold.

Richard Saville records that:

Collier acted as banker to the corporation and in 1742 held £300 of Hastings' money on which he paid 3% interest.

Bankers, of course, not only hold their client's deposits, but also lend money and charge interest. Collier noted in February: 1727: *'Mr Nairn has now come to me to borrow some money'.* And almost two decades later he advanced £400 to a Customs House official who was also a friend of the family in London:

Just at this time I have a pressing occasion to borrow four hundred pounds and shall want it only three months when it shall be punctually repaid, with thanks and interest and if you will be so kind as to supply me with it I shall forever acknowledge the favour and endeavour by every way in the World to make a grateful return of it. [Mr Freemantle to Collier 24 April 1746].

Charles Lane Sayer points out that:

Either this or a subsequent debt remained owing from Mr Freemantle on Mr Collier's death, and the latter's executors had to take measures for recovering it.

The same Mr Freemantle appears in the correspondence in another guise in 1750 when he's complaining to Collier that The Duke of Newcastle is tardy in repaying him money he's owed. Extraordinarily, Newcastle seems to be offering him a government job or sinecure if he waves the debt:

> *His Grace the Duke of Newcastle acknowledged my pretentions to be well grounded but there was no fund out of which to gratify me in money, and therefore Mr Stone advised me to look out for some sine cure in the plantations (of which there are many in his Grace's gift). Accordingly, some time after, I waited on Mr Stone with an account of such a vacancy of which I had procured such early intelligence.* [Freemantle to Collier 29 November 1750]

Unfortunately Mr Stone, Newcastle's secretary, told him that it was already given away and suggested he looked out for another.

Collier had also loaned money to his church, St Clements - £300 in total - and had charged interest at 3%, clearly ignoring the injunction in Exodus chapter 22: *'If thou lend money to any of My people, even to the poor with thee, thou shalt not be to him as a creditor; neither shall ye lay upon him interest.'*

It was not uncommon for Collier to lend money to relatives, and even the faithful William Cranston borrowed from him at one point:

> *I send you a copy of the account between us, out of the balance of which if you could*

permit me to make use of £150 I should be extremely obliged to you and I must be very disappointed if I don't replace it between this and Lady Day next. I have charged the while 10 tickets to you [27 Oct 1741]

The tickets referred to were £5 tickets in 5th Westminster Bridge Lottery. State lotteries had been established by the Bank of England at the end of the 17th century. By the mid-1700s, as well as generating money for 'good causes' and public projects such as the building of Westminster Bridge, the money raised enabled Britain to wage war. Punters were told they would always get their stake back and usually one in five tickets won a prize. From an early age Collier seems to have been caught up in lottery fever:

The lottery will be finished a Thursday and as all the great prizes are drawn the show is almost over, but such is the extravagance of people that this morning they gave £17 a ticket for those un-drawn. I had one of my five in the morning but don't know what has happened to it, but there is 9 to one whether it's a prize of £20. A Friday morning 3 of my tickets were undrawn and they then sold for 18 guineas apiece but that day all the great prizes were drawn and one of mine a blank. A Saturday I had a £20 prize which brings me to near equall; that I can't lose above 50s [Collier to Mary November 1731]

From Canaletto's 1746 painting 'Westminster Bridge with the Lord Mayor's Procession on the Thames'

Richard Saville calculates that, over the course of all his years, Collier seldom did better than to break even on his lottery gambles.

Before we leave the question of finances, it is worth noting one peculiarity. With no official bank in Hastings, there was nowhere for anyone, including Collier, to deposit cash. Accordingly he devised unusual places to secrete it:

> *I find I am kept in suspense about some money & that I may be prolonged in town about that; desire next post you will send me the 3 bank notes in the book I showed you.* [Collier to Mary 21 November 1730]

> *...as I best remember in the lowest books in my Study in the middle portion there is a book with white leaves ...behind him is some money, and you will take what you please.* [Collier to Mary November 1737]

> *on the upper shelf of the bookcase in the Tea Room at the right side of it behind the books, there are rolled up in a paper 100 Guineas, out of which you'll ... take what you otherwise want.* [Collier to Mary November 1740]

One can only presume that the servants seldom dusted the books-shelves and were not, themselves, great readers!

There are some less charitable views of how Collier acquired his wealth. Certainly he profited from promoting the Whig cause for the Duke of Newcastle. But one near contemporary writer suggests there was rather more to it than that. Thomas Oldfield was a zealous parliamentary reformer and, in 1792, published *'An Entire and Complete History, Political and Personal, of the Boroughs of Great Britain, together with the Cinque Ports'.* Of Hastings he alleges:

> *The appointment of the representatives for parliament in this town was wholly in the Treasury; the number of voters was usually about twenty, the whole of whom had places under or were otherwise provided for by government. The management and conduct of this faithful and well disciplined corps of treasury auxiliaries was, for a long series of years, vested in Mr Collier who, in this situation acquired a very princely fortune whereby he was enabled to provide for five co-heiresses, his daughters, in a very handsome manner.*

Oldfield is certainly wrong about the number of voters in Hastings – at least in Collier's time – and about the claim that they all had government jobs. But his accusation that it was a 'Treasury' borough is indisputable, though just how much Collier profited from his management of it remains open to dispute.

A more serious allegation against Collier is raised by the respected local historian Steve Peak in his online Hastings Chronicle:

> *Local legend has it that Collier and Milward ... received large incomes from their liaison with the chief smugglers over several decades as did other customs officers around the coast.*

As far as Collier is concerned there seems to be no historical evidence at all for any such 'legend'. Indeed he spent a very great part of his legal career involved in the prosecution of smugglers, and seems to have been rigorous in his work as a Surveyor of Riding Officers – often chastising them if they were lax in their duty to combat smugglers.

Throughout the Collier correspondence there is little that shows John's business dealings in a questionable light and hardly anything that puts him at odds with his fellow. But there is a strange exception to this in May 1750. A Mr Chapman writes in extremely angry terms and alludes to Collier's health, suggesting he may not be much longer for this world! Charles Lane Sayer believes the row was about some land Collier had sold to Chapman, but then allowed felled timber on the site to be collected by a tenant – something clearly greatly resented by the new owner:

> *I write this to endeavour to make you sensible of your error and I wish for your sake that you may rectify it before it is too late; for I find you appear to be near Eternity; where riches profit not; nay where riches gotten ungenerously by overcharging will be so far from profiting not, that they will inexpressibly torture.*

Whatever the rights or wrongs of the dispute - which is not resolved in the correspondence - it is true that by 1750 Collier was already suffering serious ill health and his final decade was indeed to be something of a torture.

§§§

On 20th October 1748 the Prime Minister, Henry Pelham, wrote to John Collier to express concern about the state of his health:

Dear Sir, I have been exceedingly concerned att the report we have here of your having been very ill ... I should be glad if you would order your clerk to send me word of how you are. I hope the worst is over, and that I shall soon hear that you have proceeded upon business as usual, for no one can wish you better than your sincere friend and humble servant H. Pelham.

The previous month, just a few weeks short of his 63rd birthday, Collier had suffered *'a sort of Appoplectick fit'*. The symptoms strongly suggest it was a stroke for, in his reply to Prime Minister Pelham, he speaks about it having left him partly-paralysed:

[It] deprived me of the use of my left side and which in great measure continues and very much renders me incapable of business, though I have reason to think I am something recovered & go out daily to take the air in a chaise, but this is my first performance in Writing.

It seems that the stroke not only affected Collier's physical wellbeing, but his mental health too:

Your account of your father's low spiritedness ... gives me great concern and the more so as I see no remedy for that, for

*Doctors may be sent for to Eternity, but to
no purpose in disorders of that sort.* [Cranston
to his niece, probably Cordelia 8 October 1748]

In fact Collier had been unwell for some years –
and had been running his business affairs down since the
mid-1740s. The first to go was his involvement in
prosecutions for the customs board:

> *As I advance in years and often attacked by
> the gout and other disorders and having
> for some years quitted Westminster Hall
> and the assizes and sessions, except
> attending crown business at assizes etc
> and ... I do not think of being concerned for
> the future in any prosecutions.* [11 Dec 1744
> Collier to Henry Simon, Board of Customs]

He started telling Pelham about his declining health the
following year

> *Having for about a year past been followed
> pretty strong by the Gout and an increase
> in my paralytic disorders etc., that I have
> quitted great part of business as being too
> fatiguing for my state of health and
> increase in years.* [26 September 1745 to Henry
> Pelham]

And Pelham was among the first to hear about a
worsening in Collier's condition in the last days of 1746

> *I hope to be in London in May if my health
> permits. The Gout and other complicated
> disorders have been on me from after
> Christmas for the remainder of the winter.*
> [Collier to Pelham March 1747]

341

By the autumn of 1747 it was severely affecting his ability to perform his duties as Surveyor of Customs, as he explained to Mr Freemantle to whom he wrote reminding him that the loan of £400 had yet to be repaid:

I have been at times very much indisposed during the last three or four months and sometimes hardly capable of transacting any business. I was advised [to go] to Bath and designed setting out about the 12th of this month, but was then so ill that I was apprehensive I should not be able to perform the journey ... It's a gouty paralytic complicated disorder with lowness of spirits. I fully intended to have made a Survey in August or this month but was not well enough to undertake it. If I live to the spring I hope I shall be able to perform it or must give over the place. [September 1747. Collier to Freemantle]

In fact Collier didn't finally give up that job until 1756, as he explained then in his resignation letter to the Commissioners

It was my misfortune and great concern that my situation as to lameness renders it at this Juncture Impossible for me personally to obey the Commands of their Lordships & the Hon Board in making my survey of the coast by the fatal stroke and paralitic Disorder in my left foot which has greatly increased the inclement winter with intense pain by not having a due circulation of the blood in my toes that the surgeons were in some apprehension mortification might ensue. [Collier to Mr Wood, sec to Commissioners of Customs, 13 April 1756]

Collier began making regular trips to take the waters and receive treatment at Bath – '*As I had great relief from those salutary waters I have twice visited the place and design it this autumn*' - though the arduous journey can hardly have been a pleasant one or have done much for his condition. And although there were small improvements from time to time, it's clear that, overall, the condition worsened. In April 1758 he told Milward Rowe, a long-time correspondent in Andrew Stone's office:

> *I have been greatly indisposed & in a melancholy situation for 3 or 4 months with gout rheumatism & gravel & a whole direful train of maladies, and indeed incapable of business.*

Then in January 1759 there was another crisis which, according to William Cranston, took Collier to death's door:

> *After your two former letters and one from Mrs Murray last Thursday I gave Mr Collier intirely over for gone, so that the account of him given by yours today quite surprised me though most agreeably and I really now have strong hopes of him. He must be quite Heart of Oak to buffett with death in the manner he has lately done.* [Cranston to Milward 6 Jan 1759]

A couple of days later William Cranston wrote to his sister Mary Collier:

*The accounts received of Mr Collier's illness
gave me not the least glimpse ever to hope
for a recovery and to think what a person
at his time of life has gone through and yet
to be in the land of the living is amazing...*

From observations elsewhere in that letter it is clear that Collier had attempted to put his affairs in order the previous summer and had asked Cranston to help with his accounts. He had also appointed Richard Patrick to be his "Manager in Chief" to collect rents and arrears from his tenants.

But Collier hung on and, by May 1759, he had sufficiently recovered to discuss his affairs personally with Richard Patrick, and to ask Mary to insist that Cranston *'accepts 40 guineas'* for his help and to tell him that his, Collier's, *'memory is quite gone, and if he could hold a pen he would not be able to indite (write) a letter.'*

Indeed from that date there is no record Collier himself writing further letters, and it was left to Mary to conduct his correspondence for him. Nonetheless he survived for another 18 months and celebrated – or at least marked – his 75th birthday on 1 November 1760. But it was to be his last, for on 9th December 1760 he died, leaving instructions in his will that he was to be privately interred in or near the church of St Clement, Hastings, with little funeral pomp at 12 o'clock at night, with the burial service of the Church of England. He gave to the poor of the town the perhaps not overgenerous sum of £10 to be distributed among them by his wife at her discretion, on the Saturday next after his funeral, and he directed that £100 should laid out in erecting a monument in St Clement parish church.

This was duly done. It is still there and reads:

Sacred to the memory of John Collier Esquire who, though not a native, yet was an inhabitant of this corporation for upwards of 50 years, many of which he was town clerk, and likewise, several times mayor thereof. He had the honour of being one of the canopy-bearers at the coronation of their Majesties King George the Second and his royal consort Queen Caroline. He was bred to the practice of the law, by which with his superior abilities and great application, he acquired an ample fortune, with a fair character, and at the same time eminently displayed his benevolence and hospitality. Though possessed of these and many other moral virtues, yet he thought the duties of religion indispensible; and therefore constantly attended the divine service. He was an active and humane magistrate, and indulgent husband, a tender parent, a kind master, and, respecting the community, a worthy member of it. Thus happily endowed whist living, he died lamented on the 9th day of December 1760, in the 76th year of his age, leaving behind him a widow and six daughters.

§§§

Duke of Newcastle – Thomas Pelham-Holles.
1693-1768. Whig statesman, party manager and fixer. Sussex Land owner. Elder brother of Henry Pelham. Secretary of State for 30 years. Prime Minister 1754-1756 & 1757-1762. Benefactor of John Collier

James Waller, agent, accountant and auditor to Duke of Newcastle aprox 1735-1759 with a salary of around £200 a year

Anthony Trumble. Sussex lawyer and coroner. Agent and steward to Duke of Newcastle. Died 1733 owed £1000 by the Duke for work and expenses defending the law suit of Henry Moore and other putative freemen. Collier settled the debt with Trumble's executors but had difficulty getting it repaid by Pelham-Hollis.

Ray A. Kelch. Author: 'Newcastle, a Duke without Money' University of California Press 1974

Henrietta (Lady Harriet) Godolphin 1701–1776. Duchess of Newcastle following marriage in 1717 to Pellham-Hollis. Granddaughter of the Duke of Marlborough, John Churchill

Sir John Vanbrugh (1664–1726) Whig. Architect (Blenheim Palace & Castle Howard), Restoration dramatist (*The Relapse* and *The Provoked Wife)*. Friend of Duke of Newcastle.

Henry Pelham. (1694-1750) Whig Prime Minster 1743-1754. Brother to Duke of Newcastle. Employed Collier as Steward to manage his estates.

Charles Lane Sayer – *1845-1927. Barrister. Great great grandson of John Collier, transcriber and editor of The Correspondence of John Collier and his Family pub. 1907*

Samuel Cant Hastings Schoolmaster and cartographer

Henry Cousins, 1843-1928 Printer, Auctioneer, Historian. Author: 'Hastings in Bygone Days and the Present', published 1912

Heather Warne – *catalogued the Collier papers for an Archive Diploma Dissertation in 1966 and wrote biographical introduction. Her classification of the papers is still used by the collection at the East Sussex Record Office.*

Richard Saville. Historian. Author of 'The Letters of John Collier of Hastings 1731-1746'

Mary Sayer, 1801-1880 Granddaughter of John Collier. Aunt to Charles Lane Sayer

John Freemantle. Senior Customs House official and friend and debtor of Collier's. Succeeded William Wood (qv) as Secretary to Commissioners of Customs in 1765. (The Secretary was a senior civil servant, directly responsible to the Commissioners for the entire customs service.)

Andrew Stone 1703–1773. Private secretary to the Duke of Newcastle. Confident of Pelham family. MP for Hastings 1741 to 1761. Government minister. Royal advisor, tutor secretary and treasurer under George II and George III.

William Cranston – Mary Collier's younger brother. John Collier's legal partner based in London. John Collier always refers to William as 'my brother' rather than brother-in-law.

Henry Simon, (d 1762) Solicitor for Bonds and Criminal Prosecutions at the Customs House in London.

William Wood, d 1765. Secretary to Commissioners of Customs from 1742. Succeeded by John Freemantle (qv).

Milward Rowe 1717-1792. Senior civil servant - Chief Clark of the Treasury and Commissioner of the Salt Duties 1771-82. Long-time correspondent and friend of Collier. Born Westham near Pevensey. Town Clerk Hastings 1737. Worked in Andrew Stone's office. Firm supporter of Newcastle. Beneficiary in Collier's will -left 20 guineas 'to buy a ring for remembrance' and, with William Cranston, all profits of the office of Usher and Crier of the court of King's Bench in trust for Collier's five daughters.

Richard Patrick. 1710(or11)- 1763. Legal clerk then, in 1747, apprentice attorney to Collier and latterly manager of his estates. Hastings Town Clerk 1741 & 1750-62. m 1746 Elizabeth Carswell, (daughter of Thomas Carswell qv). A beneficiary of Collier's will.

Chapter 19

Loose Ends

For a lawyer as experienced as John Collier it seems surprising, even amazing, that his will should have become such a battleground and have taken such an excessive time to settle. Part of the problem may have been that his brother-in-law William Cranston, one of his executors, was himself ill and died just two years after Collier. In mid 1762 Cranston was corresponding regularly with his widowed sister Mary, but was clearly unwell. By September he had left central London for Turnham Green from where he wrote to her:

> *From the first Sunday I set foot in this place to the present I have been continuously ill and a great part of the time unable to do any business. Or even to put pen to paper at all.* [7 September 1762]

Cranston subsequently journeyed back into the City in a sedan chair. A seven and a half mile journey that Mary concluded *'did him much hurt'*. On 21st November his son John, who was practising law at 3 King's Bench Walk in the Inner Temple, wrote to his Aunt:

> *Dear Madam, my poor father died this morning about 11 of the clock. As I am sensible of the great love and affection you all had for him in Hastings I have as well on my own account, as by the particular desire of my Mother dispatched a messenger with the melancholy news.*

John subsequently took over his father's practice, which included administering Collier's will. Even two years after his death this was already becoming an extremely protracted affair. One reason may have been to do with Collier's former clerk and subsequently legal partner in Hastings, Richard Patrick who had been appointed to manage his estates. Before his death, William Cranston had fairly laid into him:

> In respect to Patrick's conduct, I know not what to say to it. Indolent and idle he certainly is – he was ever backwards in accounts and yet when obtained always exact and intelligible. Whether his backwardness proceeds only from indolence or whether there is want sometimes of being able to pay the balance I really know not.

Whether it was the interregnum between the Cranstons' administration of the will, or whether Richard Patrick's 'conduct' in managing the estate was holding things up, the delay was clearly affecting finances of the Collier girls:

> Money now runs so short that I am forced to write to you again to desire you will let me have the hundred pounds (which we agreed was to be got out of the stocks) as soon as possible ... pray lose no time for a few Guineas is all my stock. [Sarah Collier to John Cranston undated but probably Summer of 1763]

> I am desired by Sally to mention the two hundred pounds which she is to have

from the stocks – poor Girle. [Mary to John Cranston 15 October 1763]

It seems likely that a Mr Frewin – possibly with the forename Thomas but almost certainly unrelated to the medical Thomas Frewin of Rye and Northiam – was working with the Cranstons on administering the will. Indeed he was probably the solicitor in Cranston's London practice who was supervising the young John Cranston before he qualified. In any event it seems little progress could be made unless Mr Frewin came down to Hastings and met with all the beneficiaries:

> *I suppose whenever Mr Frewin comes to Hastings all partys must be present, and I hope all will agree. I don't see how it can be otherwise without, they are determined not to be satisfied with whatever is lotted them which I hope will not be ye case.* [Jane Collier (Green) to Mary 6 July 1763].

All was clearly not well, and to make matters worse, Edward Milward – sarcastically dubbed our 'wise man' or our 'great man' by Mary - was interfering. As Mary told John Cranston after he had said he couldn't be at the family meeting:

> *I know Mr Frewin was very desirous of your being present, not only upon my account, but the others who have no friend to speak for them, and likewise support you father's abilities, which have been called into question for I have heard that there are several things in the will which Mr Frewin did not find*

351

*out till our wise man here let him into
the secret.* [16 August 1763]

Poor Mary Collier seems to have been the subject of this 'secret' mistake as a note in her hand, written around this time, makes clear:

Mrs Murray is desired to ask ... John Cranston if he knows what mistakes in (her) father's will was pointed out by Mr Milward to Mr Frewen, which he allowed to be right, for Mr Milward has thrown it out again and won't let me know what it is. I suppose it is something that regards my income and beg he would let me hear from him about it. She (Mrs Murray) told me yesterday I had no right ... to the quitt rent for the land was not mine; and I had my brother's authority who said it was mine for life and sent in his account of the rents which belong to me.

All this might perhaps seem unsurprising given the extent and complexity of Collier's bequests. Essentially he left Mary Old Hastings House, its stables, outhouses and gardens and grounds, including Torresfield, as well as a life interest in *'all messuages, farms and land in Hastings St Clement, All Saints, St Mary in the Castle and St Mary Magdalen, marshlands in Pevensey and Bexhill, Newhouse Farm in Peasmarsh and Beckley'.* On Mary's death this part of his estate was to be joined with the rest, divided into five parts and distributed to his five daughters. But how this was to be done was far from straightforward. William and his vicar brother James Cranston were to hold one fifth in trust for

Cordelia. This may have been a device to prevent her husband, the impecunious James Murray, from getting his hands on it. To soften the blow Murray was specifically forgiven any outstanding debts he owed to Collier.

This generosity to his Jacobite son-in-law was not exactly repaid. The hero of the siege of Quebec and now the Governor General of all Canada remained angry that his wife still refused to join him on his side of the Atlantic. In February 1763 he wrote to John Cranston in the following uncompromising and, it may be thought, somewhat vindictive terms:

> *I have no thought of visiting England. Indeed I had some time ago determined to settle in America whatever might be the consequences of the peace. I like the climate and shall certainly never leave it unless the King's service obliges me – with this view are my affairs to be managed and I must therefore entreat you who I now look upon as my agent, to consult with my trustees. I shall be glad to know what annuity left by Mr Collier to Mrs Murray & your humble servant doth amount to, that I may regulate my wife's allowance. She writes to me that she absolutely will not come to me. I consequently owe her no obligation. I however shall do what appears to me to be reasonable. In the meantime I do positively desire that my money may not be squandered by her and that she is restricted to her father's annuity.*

Four months later, on 27th June, he wrote again to Cranston, commiserating on his father's death, but demanding that monetary affairs were expedited:

> I have appointed my brothers George and Gideon Murray with my nephew Mr James Ferguson, as my trustees and I have instructed them to constitute you as my Agent. I trust Mrs Cranston and your father's other executors will speedily settle up with them, and that my money may be disposed of as I have ordered, and I flatter myself that you will be able to give them some account of my share of the dividend of Mr Collier's estate. It is now three years since he died, and I am still totally ignorant of every circumstance related to it; nor do I know that one Shilling has been received from that quarter on my account ...

Still nothing appeared to happen, and the following month Murray sacked John Cranston as his agent, telling him he was 'unalterably fixed in this American world' and that 'I shall as soon as possible convert into it every shilling of property I have on earth.'

But Murray had reckoned without the politics of Britain's latest colony and the enmity between the original largely agrarian French settlers and the English newcomers – mainly merchants and traders. The latter, given the English colonial administration, sought dominance over the French Canadians. The Governor would have none of it: 'nothing will satisfy the licentious fanatics trading here but the expulsion of the Canadians,

Lieutenant. -General James Murray
from a print around 1773

who are perhaps the bravest and best race upon the globe' he wrote home to the British government in October 1764.

It was a sentiment not best calculated to appease the increasingly powerful trader lobby who petitioned, successfully, for Murray's recall. In July 1766 he arrived back in England to face a government inquiry into his governorship – and to try to sort out the inordinate delay in settling the Collier estate.

Ultimately, in April 1767, Murray was completely vindicated by the Lords of Committee of Council – effectively the Board of Trade - who dismissed the charges against him as *'groundless, scandalous and derogatory to the Honour of the said Governor, who stood before the Committee unimpeached.'* However Murray did not resume his post as governor and remained in Britain with time on his hands. Time to grapple with the Collier family and what he seemed to regard as 'his' inheritance. Before moving on to that though, it is worth noting a couple of facets of Murray's character at this stage in his career. He was now 46 years of age, a successful career soldier and a hero of the siege of Quebec. He had also distinguished himself – in French Canadian minds anyway – with his governorship of the province. Canadian biographical accounts speak highly both of his military and civil rule. But there is one other facet of the man we should be aware of. It seems he was, albeit possibly on a small, domestic, scale a slave owner. An advertisement appeared in the *Quebec Gazette* in 1769 for a "negro woman, aged 25 years, with a mulatto male child ... formerly the property of General Murray". Family memoranda of the Sayers also question his fidelity to Cordelia while he was in the Americas though they did not connect that to his 'negro' woman and her child.

That James and Cordelia's relationship was at a pretty low ebb is clearly evidenced not only by Murray's letter to Cranston about Cordelia's money, but also by a letter from Dely to her cousin shortly before the General returned from Canada. In it she implies that there had been no communication between her and her husband for many months:

I had a very polite card from Quebec by the last packet which is the first scrap for two years, so maybe we shall all come to wrights again: at least there is some hope now... (Cordelia to John Cranston 30 October 1765)

The fact that Murray had bought an estate between Hastings and Battle seems to point to the fact he was keen for a reconciliation and was prepared settle in the Hastings area. This land later became Beauport where he built a substantial house and lived both with Cordelia and, following her death, with his second wife Anne Witham.

After Murray had returned from Canada in 1766, the simmering discontent over Collier's will erupted into a full-blown family feud. In brief it concerned the apparently trivial question of whether some real estate known as Paul's Land should be sold or reserved to form part the grounds of the Collier 'mansion' – aka Old Hastings House. Sarah's lawyer husband, Henry Sayer, argued it was so close that, if disposed of separately, it could become a 'nuisance' to the residents of the house. This view initially prevailed, and an agreement dated 1 October 1766 was signed by Edward Milward, William Green, Henry Sayer and Henrietta Collier. It was also signed by Murray. However he subsequently argued that he had been misinformed - in fact 'duped' - by Sayer and he refused to abide by the agreement. At that point Milward changed his position and supported the General. In a letter from Murray to Henry Sayer on 24 October 1766 he accuses the latter of *'misrepresentation'* of the circumstances of Collier's will, and of his making a *'capital error'* and being the *'source of mischief'*.

The sole unmarried daughter at this stage, Henrietta, sought to pour oil on troubled water and invited the General and Mrs Murray along with the Milwards to meet on the 19th November *"which I hope will end all quarrels, which to be sure are very disagreeable things."*

It didn't work. Indeed, things went from bad to worse with Henry Sayer initiating a lawsuit for the 'performance' of the original agreement, and John Cranston, as the family solicitor handling the division of the estate, unhappily caught in the middle of the affair. He sought counsel's opinion which, as he told Mr Green in a letter of 20 November 1766, was:

> *...clearly that the Court of Chancery will establish the Agreement. I shall acquaint Gen Murray of the circumstance and see if that will produce any alteration in him so as to avoid law if we can.*

It didn't budge the General from his stance. Nor did a proposal to 'cast lots for Paul's Land'. Jane's husband William Green sought to mediate and wrote to instruct John Cranston to negotiate between Murray and Sayer. In the same letter of 11 December 1766, he added:

> *Mr Murray has told me his dislike to Mr Sayer is personal, and if so, let it, in the name of god, be so in its consequences*

*and not involve the rest of the Family in
quarrels where they would chose to stand
neuter.*

Editor of the 1907 transcriptions of the Collier
correspondence, Charles Lane Sayer, suggests that
Murray's dislike of the Sayers was because he believed
they, and in particular Sarah, had sought to dissuade
Cordelia Murray from joining her husband in Canada,
though there is scant evidence of this in the letters, and it
would seem that Cordelia herself was the one who
consistently declined to make the long sea voyage.

We have probably taken up enough time and
space with this quarrel. Suffice it to say that the views of
the General and Milward did not prevail and that the
agreement was ultimately adhered to, without the matter
having to be decided by the court. However Henry Sayer
did submit a bill to the Collier estate for £55 14s 3d for
expenses over the affair. Interestingly it did not
permanently sour family relations. According to Charles
Lane Sayer, the General later stood as godparent for the
Sayer's daughter Kitty and Henry Sayer became Murray's
legal advisor in his court martial following his surrender
at Port Mahon in Minorca in 1782.

Eventually agreement was reached by all
concerned members of the family and the partition of the
Collier estate took place in 1766. Now the full extent of
his wealth became apparent. On his death he had
£15,800 invested in stocks – around £3 million in today's
money. We've noted that the real estate was worth more
than £30,000 – around £6 million today. And to give an
indication of its scope it is worth recording the part that
went to Cordelia alone:

*Manor or mansion house called Denne
House in Warnham,*
*The demesne lands called Whitelands,
30 acres called New Acre Mead, the
Corner Croft,*
*The Whitelands Garden, the Holly Mead
and Lagg,*
*The Greening Wood Field and Whiteland
Lane and all the ghylls, Rough grounds
and wastes belonging,*
*The Lagg on the west side of Denne
House and the Pond garden, and Ockley
garden adjoining the house, called Stony
Croft,*
*Lady Grove, Letts Leggs, Poundfield, the
Upper Charfield, the Little Charfield,
Denn Wood, The Twelve Acres (formerly
part of Denn Wood), the Two Acres
adjoining and the New Wood Field (90
acres),*
*All in Warnham messuage (dwelling
house and outbuildings) and Letts Farm
(60 acres) in Ockley in Surrey;*
*12 acres called the Church House Farm
in Ninfield and the Lower Lands and
Court Lands (46 acres) in Ninfield,*
*The Court Woods (24 acres) and The
Deans (20 acres) in Ninfield,*
*Messuage, barns, buildings and 60 acres
called Daws Farm in Warnham,*
*Piece of fresh marsh or brookland called
Blackwall (5 acres),*
*Piece of upland called Catheridge (9
acres),*

*Piece of marsh or brook ground (9
acres) and another piece (3½ acres)
with the way over the foreland to
Blackwall Lane and Several pieces of
marsh near Sewers Bridge (12 acres), all
in Hooe,
Two messuages and gardens in Hastings
St Clement,
The reversion on the death of Mary
Collier of a messuage, malthouse,
buildings and land (90 acres) called
Catesleys and Cheneys in Hastings St
Mary Magdalen,
Messuage with outhouses and stables
called the George Inn in Hastings;
Three parcels of land called the Boot, the
Great Brook and the Hither Stonefield
(12 acres) in Hastings St Clement and St
Mary in the Castle;
Stable or building ground formerly
belonging to the Swan Inn in Hastings
barn and four pieces of land (17 acres,
being two of the three pieces called the
Loudens, the Great Barn field and the
Mill Field) in Hastings St Mary of the
Castle.*

It is true that many of these properties were tenanted, probably producing only modest rents, but nonetheless the sheer scale of the property is extraordinary, and this comprised only about one fifth of the total that had been accrued by Collier during his lifetime.

§§§

Perhaps it was the very large sums involved that fermented such discord among Collier's beneficiaries. We saw how James Murray's intransigence caused Henry Sayer to resort to the courts to protect an earlier agreement, and there was more acrimony to come. Judging from the letters it would probably be true to say that the sisters themselves remained fairly close, but there was not much love lost between their husbands. Or between them and their mother-in-law. Mary Collier sat at the apex of this triangle of discord. Doubtless devastated by her husband's demise, and herself a lady well into her sixties, she might have been forgiven had she been closed and bitter. But in fact her letters following Collier's death show her exercising a rather greater degree of freedom and sense of humour than anything she wrote while he was alive. Some of it, though, was pretty uncompromising, particularly about her daughter's partners. Forinstance in one letter to John Cranston three years into her widowhood she fairly laid into to both Mary's husband, Edward Milward, and Sally's intended, Henry Sayer:

> *If Milward was not such a wretch I should not have troubled you about it, but I can't trust him with anything ... I say nothing of your letter so could not tell Sally. I am amazed at her choice for he is so Old, Ugly, and Poor.* [3 March 1763]

As we have seen, Mary seldom referred to Milward without the sobriquet our 'great' or our 'wise' man. And daughter Sarah clearly believed him untrustworthy:

As to Mr M(ilward) I said before I received yours he would pretend to make some excuse for settling matters and throw the blame somewhere else... [20 March 1764 Sarah Sayer to Mary Collier]

Jane's husband William Green didn't have much good to say about him either, expressing himself delighted that *"our business is at last done with Mr Milward"*, and in terms that today would be felt far from politically correct, criticised him as unprincipled and avaricious:

We are obliged for your trouble in Mr M(ilward's) affair of interest; this has been a true specimen of his character, not to do that which himself is convinced of being right , without a quibble, so much he is used to it; and so good opinion I have of him that I believe he would turn Turk for gain, but on consideration I am afraid their principles are too honest for him. [William Green to John Cranston 21 May 1764]

Both Mary and at least two of her daughters clearly regarded him as peculiar – or in the argot of the time, queer:

We were quite surprised at finding Mr Milward gone from London as he told us he was certain he would be in town when we came back - but we rather think he went on purpose the day before as Mrs Murray says he was very queer when he called upon her with the chaise at the door. [Sarah Sayer to Mary Collier 13.3.64]

Mr Milward is very quere and we think a
quarrel will be the end of it... [Cordelia Murray
to Mrs Collier 6.3.64]

However peculiar they thought Milward was, he
clearly believed in being proactive – particularly in
relation to the protracted administration of the Collier
estate. It seems that there were a number of people who
owed the estate money. But they weren't all aristocrats
like the Duke of Newcastle. Two, Mrs Meadow and Mrs
Geerys were local Hastings women who, it appeared
were down on their luck. Mary Collier and her youngest
daughter Henrietta were inclined to leniency over the
money they owed. Milward was clearly not:

> *I suppose you know poor Mrs Meadow is*
> *confined to her house ... I am very sorry*
> *for her, and the Mother is expected to*
> *die every day and should think my*
> *family very cruel if they should insist her*
> *house should be sold to pay off the debt*
> *here and it must ruin the whole family*
> *... but I hear our great man wants to*
> *place Luckman in it.* [21 January 1764 Mary
> Collier to John Cranston]

> *Mrs Geerys' debt is still remaining which*
> *I have some thoughts ...of taking on*
> *myself, but would not do it without*
> *consulting with you ... but I think by*
> *doing it will give her as she is an old*
> *woman more time than she will have at*
> *present. I have said not a word to Mr*
> *Milward nor don't intend it till I have*

your answer. [23 October 1764 Henrietta Collier to John Cranston]

I have pressed Mrs Meadows all in my power and then she waits on Mrs Collier ... so there appears to me no hopes of ever settling the Meadows and Geerys affairs friendly ... I plainly see that the least threats are displeasing to some of our family and there is nothing to be done without compulsion. [20 October 1764 Edward Milward to John Cranston]

Whether Milward was also behind the family's treatment of Collier's old friend John Freemantle is not clear. It will be recalled that Collier had loaned him £400 in 1746 on the promise that he would *"endeavour by every way in the world"* to repay it within three months. But it seems the debt remained outstanding eighteen years later, and Mr Hall, first a clerk and then probably a solicitor in John Cranston's legal practice, had been tasked with pursuing it. On 30th June 1764 he told Cranston he had called several times on Mr Freemantle but had not been able to find him at home, and that he had threatened him with proceedings if he did not pay the money he owed or part of it. Freemantle, it must be remembered, was a senior civil servant in the Customs Service and so not, one might have imagined, a person to avoid paying his debts. But avoid it he did and, by the end of July, Hall's clerk was writing to Cranston to tell him that Freemantle had been arrested. The correspondence is silent on what happened thereafter. However the following year Freemantle succeeded William Wood as Secretary to Commissioners of Customs so we can assume the debt was settled.

Fortunately the administrators of Collier's estate did not have to take such drastic measures with the Duke of Newcastle whose debt of £1000 had still not been paid. In July 1764 Sarah Sayer wrote to Mary Collier with news:

We were quite surprised to find the Duke of Newcastle has paid any of his debt poor man, I suppose he is determined to have no obligation to the family.

At the time the Whigs were out of the Government, and thus Newcastle was out of office, which presumably occasioned Sarah's sympathy for him. George III had ascended the throne in 1760, following which his ally the Earl of Bute became Foreign Secretary. Bute then engineered Newcastle's resignation as Prime Minister – a role he then himself assumed – and proceeded to move against Newcastle and his supporters in what became known as the 'Massacre of the Pelhamite Innocents'.

As so often seems to have been the case with Newcastle, alacrity in repaying his debts was not a top priority, and so it was that more than six months went by before Mary Milward was able to write to her mother Mary Collier with further news:

Dear Madam, Mr Milward desires me to let you know that Mr Mitchel has orders to pay the Duke of Newcastle's Bond for which purpose he will call on you before he leaves Hasting. This notice is so you may have the Bond in readiness... [Mary Milward to Mary Collier 13 February 1765]

366

The Duke's fall from favour – and office – had been particularly problematic for Edward Milward who had assiduously followed Collier in cultivating his patronage. On Collier's recommendation the Duke had appointed Milward to succeed him as Surveyor General for the Customs in Kent. In fact Collier had written a fulsome testimonial for his son-in-law describing him as:

a person in this town who married one of my daughters, who is an active person about 30, very capable of performing the duty in all respects, and I truly believe with honour and reputation, and has an Estate, and on which he lives in a prudent, respectable manner. He was bred to the Law, but not pursued it.

Collier seems to have shown few of the reservations about Milward that his wife Mary had. And Milward himself seemed able to take considerable liberties with his father-in-law's possessions, including the produce from his garden:

Have made free with your Garden to relieve our necessities. This day Morris (the Gardener) brought us three fine "Cowcumbers," being first we have had here. [31 May 1755. Edward Milward to John Collier recuperating in Bath]

Millward had also followed in Collier's footsteps in other ways - as Hastings Mayor – five times before the latter's death and twenty-one times afterwards; as agent to the Duke of Newcastle, following Collier's death; and as one of the town's Barons to carry the canopy at the coronation of George III in 1761. The correspondence shows him often in London, and suggests that Newcastle's fall meant he had to apply himself to the Duke's successor, Lord Bute, for advancement – something mocked by Mary Collier in her characteristically forthright manner:

> *I don't imagine Mr Milward will leave London till he gets something, tis not everyone who should dunn soe much, but importunity often succeeds. I think he must look a little odd, after such stories as he has told of some of the great folks which he pretended to be in the secret of the opposition, but money is his darling and that will carry him through all.* [Mary Collier to John Cranston 29 Feb 1763]

Jane Collier was rather more sympathetic to the Milwards' plight when her sister and brother-in-law travelled abroad:

> *I think ye Milwards must be a melancholy Party if only the two of them go to France by themselves and am sorry that affairs are in such a situation that they don't visit ye great Folks as I am sure it must be a great mortification to them both.*
> [Jane Green to Mary Collier 6 July 1763]

We could go on charting the petty squabbles of the extended family for there is no shortage of evidence in the letters. But perhaps the most serious remaining dispute was over the disposition of Collier's home, Old Hastings House. Mary lived on there until her death on 25th April 1768. Though apparently not unexpected, her demise was nevertheless a severe shock for her

368

daughters, as Henry Sayer told John Cranston: "*I need not tell you that Mrs Sayer's distress is unutterable...*". Within a few days Cranston summoned the family to a meeting:

> *As the house and land at Hasting is now come amongst you all I hope means may be found to quiet all the contentions that have been upon this head. It was agreed on at Hasting by all parties to meet at that place on Midsummer day next to determine the business respecting the house and land ... If my compliments will be acceptable to Mrs Murray, please to make them.* [John Cranston to General Murray around 12th April 1768]

The last phrase in Cranston's letter is telling. There was clearly considerable bad feeling between Cordelia and her first cousin, the family solicitor – though nothing on the scale of what was about to transpire between Cranston and the General.

Oh to have been a fly on the wall at the meeting that midsummer's day, the 24th of June! Sadly there is no relevant correspondence between the 11th of June when Murray agrees to attend the meeting, and the 11th September when he writes again to Cranston about its outcome. But I think we can imagine the gathering, probably in the elegant drawing-room on the first floor of the house with the long windows admitting the summer light and affording views out over the town nestled in the Bourne valley. Cordelia and James Murray are perhaps on one side of the room, opposite and well separated from Sarah and Henry Sayer. Although the court case between these two parties has been dropped it is unlikely to have ended their enmity. It was the General who had, ultimately, to withdraw on receipt of the adverse legal opinion obtained by Cranston. A man of Murray's character, not to mention his military background, would no doubt have hated having to retreat.

The Milwards, Mary and Edward, might have been sitting between the two factions – though their position over the lawsuit would hardly have made them popular with anyone. Milward, after initially opposing Murray, then switched sides. The Greens – Jane and William and the Colliers' remaining daughter Henrietta might have shuffled uncomfortably between the differing parties.

The issue to be decided was what was to happen to the family home. All five daughters had been brought up there and would have had strong memories of childhood adventures and tragedies that took place within those walls. The ghosts of paterfamilias, John Collier, and his stoical, ever pregnant and often lonely wife Mary would have looked down on the gathering and, doubtless, been aghast to hear of Murray's initial proposal – to turn the house into an inn! We know from a subsequent letter that Cordelia opposed her husband's plan and was supported by Harriet. I think we can also imagine the reaction of Mary, Jane and Sarah to the proposal assuming Murray articulated it at that midsummer meeting. But if that idea didn't find favour the General had a fall-back position. He wanted to buy the house himself and then sell off the stables and the 'little low garden adjoining' for £1,200. As he wrote after the meeting:

> *I am offered a thousand for them and as the purchasers are a set of gentlemen who have entered into a subscription to make Hastings (a) bathing place, and think the stables necessary for an*

assembly room, &c, I have little doubt of getting the sum I ask. [James Murray to John Cranston 11 September 1768]

The problem for Murray it seemed was that he didn't have sufficient money to buy the house and stables as well as to do work on Beauport, his house between Ore and Battle, so he proposed a complicated financial scheme. He requested that part of Cordelia's share of Collier's estate should be advanced to him as a mortgage on Beauport together with the house and grounds at Hastings. In the 11th of September letter he continued:

I hope I shall not be refused this requisition. I wish to live in a mutual course of friendship and good offices with all my wife's relations. I settled among them expecting to live in harmony with them.

We cannot know what was the reaction of the rest of the family on that summer's day to this scheme. But one might hazard some doubt about whether the plan was enthusiastically received. Several years down the line the Milwards ended up owing and living in the house themselves so it's a fair bet that Edward – the John Collier manqué - would have wanted to acquire it back then. Henry Sayer along with the other daughters and their partners would also likely have been suspicious of almost any Murray proposal.

What we do know is that some sort of formal agreement was reached, and we know that Murray immediately pursued his plan to buy the Collier house and poor John Cranston was expected to expedite it post haste. He replied to Murray around the 12th September:

James Murray's home, Beauport House,

I entirely agree with you in your opinion of settling this business with all convenient speed, but at the same time must observe that it is very seldom Business of this sort is settled precisely on the day limited.

Cranston's letter also dealt with the General's scheme to release Cordelia's trust money for his mortgage. The problem was that it had to have the approval of the trustees, the last remaining one of whom was Cranston's uncle James, who had been the rector of Stowing, and was now in his late 70s.

This matter stands in the same predicament as it always did ... my uncle Cranston ... must be acquainted with the particular circumstances of this business so that till the affair is represented to him and I have his answer, I cannot consistently promise the performance of your request.

This wasn't the answer Murray wanted, and he continued to press Cranston to little or no avail. The matter finally came to a head in the middle of October when Murray wrote an excoriating letter to the family's solicitor, kinsman and friend:

Sir, I came to London to finish everything on my part relative to the house &c., at Hasting. I called at Johnsons Court when I was told that neither you nor Mr Hall were expected in town until a fortnight hence. This has been a disappointment to me and has put me to some unnecessary expense, I must wish that all matters betwixt us were finally settled, that I may no longer be subject to the will and pleasure of other men. I return to the country on Tuesday; I shall not take a second journey to London but shall be ready to fulfil my part of the Agreement in the country the moment it is prepared for me, but still I must insist on copies of the agreement of the 24th June, of the conveyance to me in consequence of it and to the title deeds of the premises ... The contempt and silence you have been pleased to show in this business is a greater reflexion on you than me. I know good Manners & that it is perhaps very unreasonable to expect them from every Body. [Murray to John Cranston 15 October 1768]

This letter is consistent with Murray's bombastic - some might say downright rude - approach to business affairs with either Henry Sayer or John Cranston. What clearly annoyed Murray was that Cranston refused to commend the mortgage scheme to his uncle despite Murray's - and Cordelia's - entreaties. It seems clear enough that Cranston was trying to protect Dely's trust fund from Murray's grasp, hence his procrastination and insistence that his uncle, the sole remaining trustee of Collier's bequest, should approve it. It seems he was right to do so because, ultimately, he obtained counsel's opinion on the scheme which suggested it would be unlawful. In consequence Murray had, again, to back down.

The result of all this was that the Murrays did get the Collier House but in Cordelia's name not the General's – and they did not consequently sell the stables. It is uncertain as to whether they lived there or at Beauport, but it seems that none of Cordelia's trust money was spent on improving her husband's property.

Murray's military career had been partially on hold since his return from Canada but in 1774 he was appointed Lieutenant-Governor of the Island of Minorca, a British possession of some strategic importance in the Mediterranean. Cordelia's relations with her husband had clearly improved sine he'd been in Britain, and she seemed determined to join him in his new posting. However it proved a fatal decision. The hot climate and insanitary conditions disagreed with her and she became so ill she was forced to return to England in 1779. She managed to reach Beauport just a few hours before she died.

It is clear that Old Hastings House had remained in Cordelia's ownership because, following her death, it reverted to the four remaining sisters. As we noted earlier, the Milwards bought out the others' shares and Edward, the 'great' man, finally acquired the last remaining piece of John Collier's mantle. Ilis tenure of both the house and the mayoralty of the town must be a subject for another time, as must Murray's heroic - and ultimately failed - defence of Fort St Phillips at Port Mahon on Minorca. After his exoneration at the subsequent court martial he retired to Beauport, becoming involved in civic affairs and continuing to clash occasionally with Edward Milward.

James and Cordelia had no children, nor did Jane and William Green nor Henrietta and her husband Henry Jackson whom she married in 1771. So the Collier line lived on only through two of his daughters, Mary and Sarah.

Mary and Edward Milward had four daughters and a son, Edward junior. Sarah and Henry Sayer had a son and two daughters. This son, the Rev Edward Lane Sayer, in turn had four sons, the third of whom was Charles Lane Sayer. It was he who rescued the Collier correspondence from various depositories but largely, he says, from the family home of John Cranston at East Grinstead. His belief was that the letters had been acquired by Cranston's father William in his capacity as Collier's executor. There's a chilling note from the former's widow Anne Cranston in 1763, writing to Mary Collier, thanking her for sending ...

> the letters of dear Mr Cranston, but (I) can't tell whether I had best destroy or keep them but suppose they have been seen by the family about you, so if they should be found among my papers when I am gone it will not signify much.

In not destroying them, we have much to thank Anne Cranston for. Likewise Charles Layne Sayer for bringing them all into the public domain and transcribing so many for posterity.

§§§

Who's Who in Chapter 19 – Loose Ends

William Cranston – Mary Collier's younger brother. John Collier's legal partner based in London. Executor and administrator of Collier's estate but died just two years after him

John Cranston. William's son – thus Mary Collier's nephew, and cousin to the Collier children. John seems to have taken over his father's legal practice in London after William's death in 1762 but moved to East Grinstead around 1764. He was an administrator and executor of Collier's will.

Anne Cranston. William Cranston's widow. Inherited (and preserved) Cranston's correspondence with Collier.

Rev James Cranston 1692-1771 William Cranston's brother. Rector of Stowing. Executor of Collier's will and trustee of Cordelia's trust fund from the will

Richard Patrick. 1710(or11) - 1763. Legal clerk then, in 1747, apprentice attorney to Collier. Hastings Town Clerk 1741 & 1750-62. M. 1746 Elizabeth Carswell, (daughter of Thomas Carswell qv). A beneficiary of Collier's will. Manager of Collier's estates before and after his death in 1760.

Mary Collier 1676-1768 (nee Cranston) John Collier's widow, mother of the five Collier girls. Aunt to John Cranston

Sarah Collier/Sayer. (Sally) b1740. Fourth daughter of John and Mary. Married lawyer Henry Sayer qv. 1763.

Henry Sayer – 1744-1784. Solicitor. Husband of Sarah Collier (m 1763)

Kitty Sayer 1771-1845 - their daughter

Jane Collier/Green (Jenny) b 1727. Third daughter of John and Mary. Rejected advances of Milward Snr, eloped and married William Green in 1761.

William Green – c1735-1820 Engineer. Husband of Jane Collier

Henrietta Collier/Jackson (Harriet) b 1741. Fifth daughter John and Mary. Married Lawyer Henry Jackson

Mary Collier/Milward - (Molly) 1725-1783. Second daughter of John and Mary. Married Edward Milward Snr qv.

Edward Milward (2 - snr) 1723 –1811 Collier's son-in-law via marriage to his daughter Mary in 1754. 26 times Mayor of Hastings (1750 and every alternate year from 1753 to 1801). Succeeded Collier in 1756 as Surveyor-General of Customs Riding Officers for Kent. Hastings political agent for Duke of Newcastle. Became a man of considerable property and influence in Hastings, though he was not universally liked.

Cordelia Collier/Murray (Dely) - eldest daughter 1722-1779. Married (General) James Murray qv.

James Murray 1721-1794. John Collier's son-in-law having married Cordelia Collier in 1748. Born into family of aristocratic Scottish Catholic Jacobites. Successful army career, Captain 1742, Major 1745, Lt Col 1751, Major General 1762. Served with General Wolfe in Canada. Governor Quebec 1760-68, Deputy Governor Minorca 1774-84. Owner Beauport Park Hastings.

George Murray 6th Lord Elibank 1706-1785. James Murray's brother. Captain in Royal Navy. Sailed with commodore Anson's squadron on round the world voyage in 1740 but became separated and his ship the

Pearl returned straight to London. Accused of deliberately deserting his squadron on active service. Robustly defended by his descendant Col Arthur C Murray.

Gideon Murray (1710-1776) James Murray's brother. Rev. Dr. Gideon Murray became chaplain-general to the army and a cannon At Durham Cathedral. Was present with George II at the Battle of Dettingen in 1743. Chaplain of 43rd (afterwards 42nd) Highlanders.

James Fergusson nephew to James Murray

Anne Witham Second Wife to James Murray

Thomas Frewin - Solicitor in Cranston's London Legal Practice. Probably John's supervising solicitor during his apprenticeship. Seems to have been in charge of administering Collier's will after William Cranston's death before John took over.

Mr Hall, a clerk then solicitor in Cranston's London practice

Charles Lane Sayer – 1845-1927. Barrister. Great great grandson of John Collier, transcriber and editor of The Correspondence of John Collier and his Family published 1907. His notes, relying on historical research as well as family memories, are an important source.

Mrs Meadow. Hastings resident who owned money to the Collier estate

Mrs Geery. Hastings resident who owned money to the Collier estate

John Freemantle. Senior Customs House official and friend and debtor of Collier's. Succeeded William Wood (qv) as Secretary to Commissioners of Customs in 1765. (The Secretary was a senior civil servant, directly responsible to the Commissioners for the entire customs service.) Part or all of the £400 debt remained unpaid at

Collier's death. His executors pursued it and Freemantle was arrested in 1764.

Duke of Newcastle – Thomas Pelham-Holles. 1693-1768. Whig statesman, party manager and fixer. Sussex Land owner. Elder brother of Henry Pelham. Secretary of State for 30 years . Prime Minister 1754-1756 & 1757-1762. Benefactor of John Collier and, initially, Edward Milward.

Earl of Bute, 1713-1792. Scottish nobleman, appointed tutor to prince of Wales, later King George III. This connection enabled Bute to move against William Pitt and the Duke of Newcastle forcing both their resignations from office. He became Prime Minister in 1763. He had earlier eloped with Mary Wortley Montagu (qv) whom he married in 1736.

George III. b 1738. King of Britain 1760-1820. Perhaps best known for the loss of the American colonies in 1783 and the defeat of Napoleon in 1815. Edward Milward was a canopy bearer at his coronation.

Chapter 20

The Closing View

Come with me up Croft road, past St Clements's Church where Collier lies buried, and we'll climb the steep path to the West Hill. From here you have probably the best view in Hastings. Certainly it's one of the best views *of* Hastings. Look to your left and you see the old town shoehorned tightly into the Bourne valley. It hardly seems to have changed at all in the two and a half centuries since Collier himself stood here. It's nice, if curious, that this hill is the only place to afford him any public recognition – and that only by naming a short street after him. Curious because in his correspondence he gave us more historical information about Hastings in the first half of the 18th century than any other source. And curious because he probably did more for Hastings than almost any other citizen in its history and yet he remains virtually unrecognised.

Let's sit for a while and admire the view. The fishing boats are pulled up securely on the shingle at the Stade – just as they would have been in the 1700s, or the 1600s ... or the 1500s come to that. It's curious to think that, although the port may have moved from the Priory Stream a short distance to the West, little had otherwise changed little since the arrival of the Conqueror and quite possibly since the coming of the Romans. It's the sea that made Hastings ... gave it its reason to exist ... elevated it into the exclusive and influential club of the Cinque Ports. And provided a livelihood, both legitimate and less so, to its mariners and people.

On a clear day you can see France from up on this hill. Throughout almost all of Collier's life Britain was at war with her neighbour. The townspeople fervently hoped the ships patrolling the channel out there belonged to the Royal Navy and not the French. It wasn't so many centuries since Hastings had been burned to the ground by Gallic marauders at the start of the Hundred Years War.

So, at the beginning of the 1700s, Hastings remained a sleepy backwater with fewer than 2000 inhabitants, almost all of whom were involved in maritime businesses, manual labour or trade of some sort. The Colliers – the embodiment of the Middling Sort - were an exception. So much so that their children had almost invariably to go to Battle or beyond to find any type of genteel companionship.

But by the end of Collier's century Hastings was a very different place – poised on the cusp of recognition and expansion. In that one hundred years the population had almost doubled to more than 3000. Less than a century on from Collier's death it would stand at more than 17,000. And it was all down to the sea. The fashion for sea bathing that was to become something of a mania began during Collier's life. He himself had been asked as early as 1740 by William Battine - Surveyor-general of the customs for Sussex - about accommodation for visitors wishing to take advantage of sea water cures:

> *Some ladies that are related to Mr Commissioner Hill are advised to wash in the sea for the recovery of their health and he has commanded me to enquire of you whether they can have private lodgings and accommodation at your town for that purpose.*

Collier replied, offering his own house as really the only suitable place anyone could stay:

'I wish I could say more to the advantage of this town as to accommodation than it will afford, but you know its situation in all respects'.

He was probably not being immodest. The Swan Inn, for all its hosting of civic functions, was at that time likely to be little more than a simple coaching establishment which would have offered straw mattresses, strangers sharing a bed and mutton chops served in the bar. Nevertheless an article in the Universal Magazine of 1760 - just 20 years later - says that there was a pretty good choice of lodgings and claimed that there were 'advantages' offered by the Swan for people visiting Hastings as a *'health and pleasure resort'*.

So things were changing, and sea bathing was fast becoming de rigueur among the gentility. In the summer of 1763 Mrs Green - Sarah Collier - wrote to her mother Mary from Brighton that:

It's ye fashion in this place to call everything Nervous, and Bathing in ye sea cures all ills, and I talk of beginning next week for it will not only be good for ye toothache but take down a little of my fat which will not be amiss.

We saw that in 1768 James Murray was contemplating selling the stables to a set of *"gentlemen who have entered into a subscription to make Hastings a bathing place"* Although, ultimately, they didn't use the buildings, they clearly did have some success in improving the accommodation for visitors. The first

Hastings guidebook was published in 1797, less than 30 years after Murray's plans, and it was extolling the local facilities

> The lodgings here are numerous and good, several new houses having within three or four years been built for the purpose of letting.
>
> Here is a fine beach and the purest water for bathing of any along the coast for which purpose great numbers of the gentry have of late years resorted from London and the neighbouring country during the summer season
>
> No watering place can excel Hasting in the convenience of bathing, few can equal it. The sea here is at all times free from weeds or dirt which is so common at many other parts of the coast and the water perfectly clear and pure.

It should be noted that the unnamed author of the guide did admit to being an 'inhabitant' of Hastings and so may not be thought to be completely impartial. But there is no doubt at all that the town was about to change out of all recognition. As the new century got underway, houses were going up on Marine Parade and the Albion Hotel was being contemplated. By 1825 Pelham Crescent, Pelham Place and Pelham Arcade were under construction and James Burton was planning his elegant new town in St Leonards.

We have tracked many of the other changes that had been either instigated or supported by John Collier, including a supply of clean water, street lighting, new roads and pavements and a fire engine. Many of these were aided or financed by the town's MPs. That they had been elected there, and that Hastings had remained a Whig stronghold for nearly four decades, was also very largely down to Collier.

If we can chart his civic achievements and his wealth from his correspondence, we also see a picture slowly unfolding of the man himself. We know he was a staunch Anglican and a regular churchgoer. His evident love of money and desire to accumulate wealth is somewhat offset by his compassion for the poor and unfortunate – for instance his wish to help the children of the deceased Sussex coffee shop proprietor, and his evident discomfort at the whipping of Dame Arthur. He regularly gave money to the poor of the Parish and in his will wrote:

> I recommend to my wife and children a continuance of the weekly charity or dole I have for many years given on a Sunday after morning service to the poor inhabitants of the said town of Hasting.

Collier's social conscience was not just confined to those in the town. When, in 1757, corn prices across the country reached unusually high levels, he wrote a long screed to Colonel Pelham:

> ...the behaviour of the farmers, millers and mealsellers is a very great grievance to the people and greatly oppressive to the poor in general, and loudly calls for redress...and some coercive strict law be made to put an end to it for its plain there is no bowels of compassion to the distressed poor...

Collier's view of 18th Century Hastings from the West Hill

Collier seems from his letters to have been a man of modest habits. He appears to have liked a pinch of snuff but was not, apparently, a great consumer of alcohol, telling Mary in one letter from London how he had been avoiding going out drinking. He was evidently quite a moral man. He disliked bawdy talk in the Swan; was disparaging about prostitutes at the pleasure gardens; and was quite censorious about Edwin Wardroper's long-running affair with Mrs Holt of Peasmarsh which must be 'condemned by all'.

So there are clues there in the letters but the mists of time still obscure the man himself. If only we could meet face to face and engage in even a short conversation. Even if we can't physically bridge the gap of two hundred and seventy years, we can perhaps imagine the encounter.

Before his health deteriorated Collier would undoubtedly have come up here to the West Hill both to check his rabbits were safe from poachers, but also, doubtless, to admire the view and look out over the town. By now 1750, he owned large parts of Hastings, including this very hill itself.

As we're musing thus, a man comes and sits down next to us. He's wearing a frock coat and sporting a powdered wig. But, as we've observed before, elaborate costume is hardly remarkable in Hastings. Our companion is in his mid-sixties, his face is lined and careworn, his teeth poor. He glances at the copies of the letters we're holding and, rather to our surprise, begins to cross-examine us:

"So sir, you've been reading my letters and studying my life, have you? And what, pray, do you fancy you have discovered?"

"Oh, I think we've found you to be a man of your time, firmly placed in what becomes known as the early Georgian era. A period of artistic expression and delicacy of design, sumptuous architecture, literature, music, and style. It was the era that made the modern world we know today. You were lucky to be in London during such a time of expansion and burgeoning culture, and perhaps unlucky to have been in Hastings before it became more fashionable and attracted more intellectual company."

"Hmm, interesting. And in your study of my life what have you found that perhaps you didn't like so much about me or my character?"

"Golly, that's a tough one! I suppose to our modern way of thinking increasing your wealth through government sinecures is pretty unacceptable, and fixing elections by bribing or cajoling or even threatening the electorate would be both illegal and ethically reprehensible. As far as you personally are concerned, though, you seem a man of moral rectitude – though today it might be considered that your concern for the poor was a bit tokenistic. You were an extremely rich man, however you didn't spread that wealth very widely. As I say you were a product of your age, and doubtless more compassionate than many of your peers. But we want to hear from you. How would *you* sum up your life's work and achievements?"

"Well I think I can truthfully say I was unafraid of hard work. I put in very long hours writing what

others might consider lengthy and perhaps dry legal arguments. And although you may not approve of how much money I earned, or how exactly I came by it, it did require some little skill in keeping that number of jobs going or, as a circus juggler might say, that many balls in the air ...."

"What about your family? Any regrets there."

"Oh yes. Without doubt. It's hard to get over the death of any child, but for me, losing my two sons once they were out of infancy was a vast blow from which I don't think I ever fully recovered. Of course, life goes on and you can't spend your whole existence grieving, but I always wondered how things would have been different if I hadn't sent them up to Westminster, and hadn't left them in London that Christmas of 1732. Those decision led directly to Jackie's death and I believe indirectly to Jemmy's. I'll never know if it might have been different, but it does torment me

"And Mary? She had thirteen of her children die before her – and eleven only babies..."

"Hmm. I suspect you might not like me putting it this way, but it was her role to bear children. That's what women – what wives – did. And children do die young. But you are right, it did have a profound effect on her. She had a somewhat nervous disposition and found it hard to cope at the best of times. I needed someone to run my house and ensure that all my domestic affairs were properly regulated and that was Mary's role. But I was aware she was occasionally unhappy in

Hasting, especially as the girls grew and went away from home, visiting friends and staying with them in London or Battle. I suppose it must have been lonely for Mary. The trouble was that I loved Hasting. I had to be in London or on tour of the Customs, but all I really wanted to do was to be back in my house with my books... and with Mary who I did really love. I think I did provide well for her, allowing her a good standing in the community and a good standard of living."

"Did you *really* like Hastings? You made quite a lot of enemies there, particularly over the water scheme and eligibility to become a freeman? Didn't you find many of the people rather dull and petty."

"Why of course. I loved Hasting. What a question. Hasting was my town. It was very good to me and I worked hard for it. I had a real position and a real role there. I even loved the local politics, the small politics of the corporation, and I tolerated the petty jealousies of those who sought to oppose me. By and large they were good people. I'm proud of what I achieved here. Just look out over the valley from this hill. Is there anywhere more beautiful? Is there any town more admirable? If you want an epitaph for me, let it be simply:

*John Collier, **Mister** Hasting."*

§§§

Appendices

i. John Collier – a Chronology

For those who like their history in chronological order, and also for ease of reference, here is a synthesis of the Colliers' lives and achievements.

1685

John Collier is born on 1st November the second son of Peter Collier (1653-1717) and Sarah, née Cheapman (1663-1734), both of Eastbourne. Peter Collier kept the Lamb Inn 36 High St, Old Town, Eastbourne. His father, Richard Collier, (1614-1690) had been a thatcher in the town. John had a brother Peter (1786-1760) and and two sisters, Sarah (1693-1725) who married Samuel Cruttenden, and Mary (1691-1751) who married Thomas Smith.

1686 - 1706

No records have been found of John's upbringing, education or legal training. It is possible or even likely that he attended the local Parish school in Eastbourne attached to the church. There he would almost certainly have learned Latin and would probably have left school at around 14 to take up a five-year apprenticeship in the law as a solicitor or attorney. But we don't know where or with whom. Before the Attorneys and Solicitors Act of 1728 there were no records kept of legal apprenticeships. John Collier's training would have been expensive, costing up to £20 a year. It remains a mystery as to how he or his family afforded it.

1706 - 1714

In 1706, aged 20, Collier was appointed Town Clerk to the Hastings Corporation at an annual salary of £10. It is assumed he moved to Hastings to take up the post, though he might possibly already have been a resident of the town. Certainly in May that year he married Elizabeth, daughter of Edmund Elphick of Willingdon near Eastbourne. In November Collier bought, for £300, Old Hastings House, also known as the Mansion House or the Collier House, at the northern end of the High Street – then called Market Street. His work for the corporation involved acting as clerk for the Hastings courts – the Quarter Sessions, the Court of Record, the Hundred Court and the Assembly of Freemen. He would also have been a Justice of the Peace, deputy coroner, clerk to the Hastings Militia as well as Commissioner for Land Tax for Sussex. In 1707 he was registered by the Church of St Margaret's in Westminster as the attorney responsible for collecting their rents in Pett, Guestling and Fairlight.

In 1708 he was appointed by the Commissioners of Sewers to be clerk and sole collector of Hooe, Barnhorne, Cowding and East Levels, at an annual salary of £12. In 1714 he was appointed joint solicitor of the Cinque Ports.

Collier was also establishing his own legal practice in Hastings and, in 1712, he took on his first recorded apprentice – John Thompson of Winchelsea. Richard Saville wonders whether he "may have been acting together with another local attorney, or with several attorneys, sharing part of the late Jonas Chambers' caseload?" Chambers had been Town Clerk immediately before Collier assumed the role.

Between 1706 and 1714 the Colliers had six children; Elizabeth, who was baptized on 14 March 1706 (ten weeks before the Colliers marriage on 28th May). She later Married George Worge, a Battle solicitor. Mary was born 1709 and another Mary born 1710 who died the same year. It is presumed that the first Mary had also died before her sister was born. Their next daughter Sarah arrived in 1711, later marrying Roger Mortimer. Another daughter whose name is unknown was born in 1713 and a son, John, was born in 1714 but died the same year. 1714 was the year that their mother, Elizabeth, also died leaving John Collier a widower at the age of 29. It is not clear whether her death was connected with that of the baby John.

1715

Collier meets the Duke of Newcastle at a civic function at the Swan Inn.

1716

The first letter in the Correspondence of *John Collier (Deceased) and his Family 1716-1780* is recorded on 3rd May 1716. He writes a love letter to Miss Mary Cranston who is staying in London. Mary is daughter of the Rev James Cranston, vicar of both All Saints and St Clements churches Hastings. She had been born in July 1696. Her elder brother James became vicar of Stowing, her younger brother William Cranston (1706-1762) trained as a solicitor and became Collier's London law partner.

1717

The marriage of John Collier, now aged 32, and Mary Cranston took place on 13th August 1717 at 'the lower church' St. Clement's in Hastings. Mary who was 21, moved into the Collier home, Old Hastings House, just across the road from the All Saints vicarage where she'd been brought up, and was immediately step-mother to John's 'girles' from his first marriage – Elizabeth, then aged 10 and Sarah who was 6. It is possible that the unnamed daughter born in 1713 was also alive and resident with them, though it seems more likely that she was already deceased. In the same year John's father Peter died and he inherited 'all his properties in Eastbourne and elsewhere' – though his mother Sarah lived on for another 17 years and must have had provision made for her.

1718

In 1718 Collier, aged 32, was selected as a Jurat of Hastings – this is a Cinque Port title roughly equivalent to an alderman today's local government hierarchy.

1719

John Collier was elected as Mayor for the first time, aged 33.

1720

Birth of John, nicknamed Jackie, Collier's favourite son and heir. (He was to die of smallpox in London in 1732).

1721

James Collier (Jemmy), second son, was born on 21st May. Like his brother he attended Westminster School. He then went up to Clare College, Cambridge, studied law and entered the Middle Temple in 1742. In 1745 James Collier became mayor of Hastings, but his career was terminated by his death in the summer of 1747 at the age of 26. He had written some of the most interesting and politically informative letters in the collection.

1722

John Collier, aged 37, is elected as Mayor for the second time.

1726

Collier's brother-in-law William Cranston completes his apprenticeship as an attorney and becomes Collier's de-facto or actual legal partner. From then on the bulk of the Collier correspondence is between the two men. It is uncertain when Collier established his legal practice in London as opposed to Hastings. He is certainly to be found visiting London regularly for the law terms from 1716, and writing home to Mary from there. He had lodgings off Fleet Street and maintained, during law terms, chambers at Johnson's court. From 1726 Johnson's court seems to have been his and Cranston's main or only full-time office as well, subsequently, as the Cranston's family home.

1727

Elizabeth, Collier's daughter by his first marriage, weds George Worge a solicitor of Battle in 1727. They are mentioned regularly in the correspondence and are clearly close friends to Collier's second family. Collier's granddaughter Mary Sayer questioned whether Collier was actually Elizabeth's father. The evidence for Mary Sayer's assertion that her mother, Elizabeth Elphick, had engaged in 'misconduct' seems to be that records show the daughter's birth occurred before the Collier's marriage.

Collier – as a Cinq Port Baron - is chosen to be a Canopy bearer at the coronation of George II, one of the proudest moments of his life. Subsequently he has the silver stave melted down to form a silver Punchbowl which he presents to the Hastings Corporation.

His income from his law practices reaches as much at £500 in some months (the equivalent of around £100,000 today).

1729

There is a Smallpox epidemic in Hastings in which 97 died, 608 survived. 206 were said to have escaped infection.

1730

Collier's third term as Mayor aged 44.

1731

Collier becomes Newcastle's election agent in Hastings and agent for his Sussex estate. The Duke's patronage marks a turning point in his fortunes.

1732

Collier becomes Cryer and Usher of the King's Bench. It is not certain whether he purchased this sinecure or was given it by the Duke of Newcastle. The Duke had told Collier he should have the *'little place dropped in the law that I would gladly accept'*. It was worth somewhere around £100 a year and appeared to require little or no work from Collier himself.

In August Collier's sons John and James start at Westminster and stay with their Uncle William Cranston over Christmas period. Jacky (John) contracts Smallpox and dies. He was buried in Westminster Abbey.

1733

In February Collier commissions work to start on his plan to lay pipes for fresh water for Hastings.

In September 1733 The Duke of Newcastle is told by his brother Henry Pelham that if Prime Minister Sir Robert Walpole had a mind to have two Whigs chosen at Hastings, Newcastle *'must provide handsomely for Collier'*

In November that year John Collier obtains through the Duke of Newcastle the post of Surveyor-General of the Riding Officers of the Customs for the County of Kent. It came with a salary of between £200 - £400 a year. From then on, for the next decade, Collier conducted an annual tour or inspection of Customs houses in Kent.

In the same year Collier became agent for all the Pelham family estates in the county of Sussex as well as Newcastle's election agent in Hastings

Collier starts to campaign for Whig candidates in Hastings and Sussex for the forthcoming 1734 elections.

1734

Collier's mother Sarah died on February 11th, at Hollington near Hastings, and was buried at St Clement's church on 20th February. Collier was in London and unable to attend.

Collier acts as political agent to the Duke of Newcastle in the General Election on 29th April. Whigs Sir William Ashburton and Thomas Pelham were elected in Hastings. In the subsequent County election Henry Pelham and James Butler were returned, beating John Fuller and Sir Cecil Bishop.

Whistler Webster had been an unsuccessful Tory candidate for Hastings. Later, his father Sir Thomas Webster – owner of Battle Abbey – supported (an ultimately successful) lawsuit by John Sargent and Henry Moore to become Freeman of Hastings - a right that they had been denied by Collier and the Corporation on the grounds that sons of Freemen were not entitled to inherit the privilege.

Newcastle agreed to underwrite the cost of defending the lawsuit but failed to pay and Collier was left to reimburse Hastings lawyer Anthony Trumble for his costs to the sum of £1000.

Collier became the Duke of Newcastle's Deputy Vice-Admiral for Sussex.

On 16th September Collier embarks on his first tour of the Customs houses of Kent in his role as Surveyor.

Collier is a defendant in legal actions over his water pipe scheme

1736

Collier and the Corporation of Hastings lose the court case over entitlement to the Freedom of the town.

1737

This year sees Collier's fourth term as Hastings Mayor aged 46. He ensured he was absent when Henry Moore was admitted as Freeman so Moor had to kiss the cheek of the deputy mayor instead.

1738

James Collier is admitted as a fellow commoner to Clare College Cambridge having left Westminster school that summer.

1739

Collier tries unsuccessfully to get Newcastle to pay the £1000 he is owed over Trumble's fees and expenses. It remains unpaid at Collier's death in 1760.

1740

Thomas Carswell, Riding Officer and fellow Mayoral colleague of Collier, is killed by smugglers near Robertsbridge.

1741

Collier is Hastings's Mayor for the fifth and final time.

1742

James Collier enters Middle Temple to study law. An argument with his father over the cost of his accommodation and allowances is mediated by William Cranston.

Collier acts as banker for the Hastings Corporation, holding £300 of its money and paying 3% interest.

1744

John Collier decides to stop prosecuting smugglers *"I gave my utmost assistance to Mr Coppard, the Collector in the affair, and conducted it as well as I could, but in the present situation, and the menaces and insults I have receiv'd, I shall decline acting as Solicitor in any proceedings against the Smugglers."*

Admiral Edward Vernon in his pamphlet 'Some Seasonable Advice from an Honest Sailor' accuses Collier of protecting a 'traitor', Zebelton Morphett.

Collier observes the ceremony to mark the declaration of war with France, comments on the problems with billeting troops in Hastings and provides intelligence on the success of Sir John Norris against the French Fleet in Romney bay.

1745

The year of the Jacobite rebellion led by Bonnie Prince Charlie. Collier is asked to provide lookouts for the

French fleet along the coast. He is involved with the capture and detention of possible Jacobite spies James Bishopp and Abraham Ibbotson

James Collier is elected mayor of Hastings.

1746

Collier receives praise from the King for his role in apprehending alleged Jacobite traitors. The Young Pretender, Bonnie Prince Charlie, is defeated at Culloden.

Samuel Cant draws his first map of Hastings.

In May Collier notes he is recovering from a 'Paralitick Disorder' the previous winter which affected his memory and made business 'very irksom'.

1747

James Collier dies at his Chambers in the Temple on May 30th, aged 27, and was buried in the north Cloister of Westminster Abbey.

1748

In December Cordelia (Dely) marries Capt. James Murray, the youngest son of Scottish Jacobite Lord Elibank. The marriage was opposed on both sides; by Collier because of Murray's religion, politics and lack of money, and by the Elibanks because of Cordelia's lower social standing. Collier ended up advancing considerable sums of money to Murray who eventually rose to be a Major General as well as Governor General of Canada following his military success at the siege of Quebec in which General Wolfe was killed.

In September Collier suffers *'a sort of Appoplectick fit'* which was probably a stroke, as he says it *'deprived me of use of my left side'*.

1749

Collier gives up his role as Hastings' Town Clerk after 43 years service, broken only by his terms as Mayor.

From Bath, Collier instructs Richard Patrick to seize the best anchor and cable belonging to the wrecked Dutch East Indiaman, the Amsterdam.

Collier commissions Samuel Cant to draw a map of his estate.

1750

Collier helps obtain the first fire-engine in Hastings.

Has his four unmarried daughters inoculated against Smallpox by Dr Thomas Frewin in Northiam.

1753

Helps with the establishment of Hastings' first workhouse in George Street.

1754

Mary Collier, the second surviving daughter of John Collier, is married in May at the age of 28 to Edward Milward, Mayor of Hastings in 1750 and then every alternate year between 1753 and 1801. Milward had earlier unsuccessfully wooed Mary's younger sister, Jane.

The Prime Minister Henry Pelham died on 4th March, aged 60. He had represented the County of Sussex in Parliament since 1722 and Collier was agent for his estates. His relative, Thomas Pelham, of Stanmer (later the Earl of Chichester), was elected the member for Sussex in his place.

1756

Due to ill health Collier resigns as Surveyor General of Riding Officers of the Customs for county of Kent and is succeeded in the post by his son-in law Edward Milward.

1757

James Murray sails for Canada but Cordelia stays at home, unable or unwilling to make the long sea voyage.

1758

By this year Collier has virtually retired from public life due to his ill-health. However in this same year he becomes owner of the Swan Inn.

1759

He suffers another severe attack of illness after which Cranston says "*I gave Mr Collier intirely over for gone*".

There are no surviving letters in Collier's hand after May in this year.

1760

December 9th John Collier dies aged 75.

1761

Jane Collier elopes with William Green whom she later marries.

1762

William Cranston dies on November 21st after an illness lasting several months. William, with his brother, the reverend James was an executor of Collier's will so his death considerably delayed administration of the estate and led to constant rows within the family.

Duke of Newcastle is replaced as Prime Minister by Lord Bute.

1763

Sarah Collier marries Henry Sayer a lawyer of Lincoln's Inn. They live in Red Lion Square in London. They were grandparents to Charles Lane Sayer who published the first transcriptions of the Collier Correspondence in 1907

Richard Patrick, Collier's former clerk, latterly manager of his estates, dies.

1766

General James Murray arrives back in England to face a government inquiry into his governorship of Canada which ultimately exonerates him.

The Deed of partition of Colliers estate is completed and reveals that he owned land in Sussex, Surrey and Kent to the value of £30,866 – about £6 million in today's figures.

Henry Sayer initiates a case in Chancery against James Murray over an agreement regarding the disposition of land at Old Hastings House. Murray ultimately backed down.

1768

Mary Collier dies on 25th April. A family meeting on midsummer's day, 24 June, seeks to determines that the Murrays will have the Collier Home, Old Hastings House. Murray's plans to turn it into an inn or sell off the stables came to nothing.

1771

Collier's youngest daughter, Henrietta, marries Henry Jackson of the Middle Temple, eldest son of Thomas Jackson of Ifield

Rev James Cranston, Mary's brother, dies.

1774

Murray appointed as appointed Lieutenant-Governor of the Island of Minorca in the Mediterranean.

1779

Cordelia returns to England from Minorca where she had become ill and dies having just reached Beauport.

ii.   Who's Who

Historians, writers or persons who are not contemporaries of John Collier are in italics. Some dates of births, marriages and deaths are from genealogy websites whose results are not always consistent.

A.

Earl (1st) of Asburnham - John Ashburnham 1687 - 1737. Hastings MP 1710. Resigned seat same year after inheriting brother's Baronetcy. Collier was steward to his estates in Sussex and was on dining terms with him. Became a courtier, Lord of Bedchamber 1728-31. Created Earl of Ashburnham 1730.

2nd Earl of Ashburnham, John. 1724-1812. Inherited father's title and estates. Was a friend and intimate of James Collier

Sir William Ashburnham 1678-1755 (2nd Baronet of Broomham). Hastings MP 1710-1713 and 1722-1734. Fellow coronation canopy bearer with Collier 1727

Queen Anne 1665-1714. Daughter of James II but raised a protestant and succeeded to throne following death of King William III in 1702. Most notable for creating United Kingdom following Act of Union with Scotland in 1707. Married to Prince George of Denmark

B.

*J Manwaring Baines. Hastings Historian. Author of
Historic Hastings a Tapestry of Life.*

Doctor Barrowby – London Physician

James Bossom, 1688-1764. Boat owner and carrier
between Hastings and London. Freeman and Jurat of
Hastings. Sometime friend of Collier's and with him co-
owner of a boat, the Charming Molly.

Nicholas Bossom. His ne'er-do-well brother also co-
owner of the boat with Collier.

James Boswell 1740–1795, Scottish biographer and
diarist. Best known for the biography of his friend and
contemporary Samuel Johnson.

James Bishopp. Apprehended in Hooe 1745 and
questioned by Collier (and later Newcastle) as alleged
Jacobite traitor. He was younger brother of Sir Cecil
Bishopp - 6th Baronet of Parham in Sussex and an MP.

Earl of Bute, 1713-1792. Scottish nobleman, appointed
tutor to Prince of Wales, later King George III. This
connection enabled Bute to move against William Pitt
and the Duke of Newcastle forcing both their
resignations from office. He became Prime Minister in
1763. He had earlier eloped with Mary Wortley
Montagu (qv) whom he married in 1736.

C.

Dr Archibald Cameron. Prominent leader in the Jacobite rising of 1745. He was a co-conspirator in the 1752 Elibank Plot along with Alexander Murray. He was the last Jacobite to be executed for high treason in 1753.

Samuel Cant Hastings Schoolmaster and cartographer.

Rev George Carleton Schoolmaster at Westminster.

Dr Henry Carleton. The Collier's friend and physician in Hastings. A former Mayor and deputy Mayor.

Queen Caroline 1683–1737. Wife of George II. Formerly Caroline of Brandenburg-Ansbach. Supporter of Robert Walpole's Whig faction. Popular queen widely mourned following death in 1737.

Thomas Carswell 1690-1740. Hastings Freeman and Jurat. Mayor 1734. Riding Officer, killed by smugglers of the Hawkhurst gang at Silver Hill near Hurst Green on 26th December 1740.

William Coppard, Hastings Mayor 1727, 1735, 1742, 1746, 1751.

John Coppinger, resident of Hampstead, family friend and probably fellow lawyer.

Henry Cousins, 1843-1928 Printer, Auctioneer, Historian. Author: 'Hastings in Bygone Days and the Present', published 1912.

Rev James Cranston. 1650-1726. John Collier's father-in-law. Hastings vicar. Married Cordelia Delves (1665-1711). Father to James, Mary (later Collier) and William.

Rev James Cranston (jnr) 1691-1770. Mary's and William's elder brother. Rector of Stowing. Executor of Collier's will and trustee of Cordelia's trust fund from the will.

Mary Cranston (qv under Collier) 1696-1768, second wife to John Collier. Elder sister of William Cranston, Collier's London partner.

William Cranston 1706-1762. Mary Collier's younger brother. John Collier's legal partner based in London. John Collier always refers to William as 'my brother' rather than brother-in-law. Executor and administrator of Collier's estate but died just two years after him.

Mary Cranston, nee Swaysland, 1703-1747 (aprox). First wife (m 1731) to William Cranston. Mother of James and John Cranston. Died aged 44.

Anne Cranston nee White, second wife (m 1747) to William. Mother of William (jnr).

John Cranston. 1736-1781 (Jackie). William's son with his first wife – thus John and Mary Collier's nephew, and cousin to the Collier children. John Cranston became a solicitor and seems to have taken over his father's legal practice in London after William's death in 1762, He was an administrator and executor of Collier's will. He moved to East Grinstead around 1764.

Catherine Cranston (nee Green) 1742-1823. Wife of John Cranston. (m 1759)

Oliver Cromwell 1599–1658. English Civil War military and political leader. Head of state and of government as Lord Protector of the Commonwealth 1653 until his death. Signatory of King Charles I's death warrant 1649.

Nathaniel Cruttenden. Hastings Mayor 1733, 1738, 1744, 1749. Brickmaker, land owner, Commissioner for Sussex Land Tax, Commissioner Hastings' Land and Window taxes.

Duke of Cumberland Prince William Augustus. 1721 - 1765.   Third and youngest son of King George II and Caroline of Ansbach. Commanded British army at defeat of battle of Battle of Fontenoy 1745. Led loyalist British forces against Jacobite rebellion in 1745. Defeated Young Pretender Charles Stuart at Battle of Culloden 1746. Dubbed the 'butcher' for his ruthless pursuit of Jacobite forces.

The Colliers

Richard Collier 1614-1690, John Collier's Grandfather. A thatcher of Eastbourne.

Peter Collier 1653-1717, John Collier's Father. An innkeeper of Eastbourne.

Sarah Cheapman 1663-1734, John Collier's mother.

Peter Collier 1786-1760, John's elder brother.

John Collier 1685-1760

Sarah Cruttenden (nee Collier) 1693-1725 John's younger sister. Married Samuel Cruttenden. They later lived in a cottage in the grounds of Collier's house in Hastings.

Mary Smith 1691-1551– nee Collier. John's youngest sister. Married Thomas Smith.

Elizabeth Collier – nee Elphick (c1681-1714) John Collier's first wife, m. 28 May 1706 Eastbourne. Daughter of Edmund Elphick of Willington.

Collier's Children with Elizabeth to survive to adulthood:

Elizabeth Worge (nee Collier). 1706-1766. Eldest daughter - indeed born before the marriage of John Collier and Elizabeth Elphick. Married George Worge solicitor of Battle qv 1727. A close friend of the second Collier family and constant host to the children when they visited Battle. Received £2000 in Collier's will

Mary Collier. b 1709. Second daughter of John Collier and Elizabeth Elphick.

Sarah Mortimer (nee Collier) third daughter of John Collier and Elizabeth Elphick.

Mary Collier (nee Cranston) 1676-1768. Daughter of Rev James Cranston, rector of St Clements and All Saints in Hastings. Second wife of John Collier and bore him 18 children, 11 of whom died as infants. A large proportion of Collier's letters are to her.

Collier's Children with Mary to survive beyond the age of 10:

John Collier (Jacky) 1720-1732 first son of John Collier and Mary Cranston to survive infancy but died aged 12. His memorial in Westminster Abbey reads:

John Collier, eldest son of John Collier, gentleman of Hastings in the county of Sussex: died 31st day of December 1732 in the 13th year of his age: a youth dear to his parents, his friends and his teachers, because of the blamelessness of his manners, the sweetness of his character and his surpassing zeal for learning. So short-lived was this darling of his family, lest their loss should ever become insupportable

James Collier. (Jemmy) John and Mary's second son. 1721-1747. Died aged 26. Attended Westminster and Cambridge. Lawyer. Hastings Mayor 1745.

Cordelia Collier (Dcly) 1722-1779, eldest surviving daughter. Married (General) James Murray qv.

Mary Collier - (Molly) 1725-1783. Second daughter of John and Mary. Married Edward Milward Snr qv.

Jane Collier (Jenny) 1727-c1802. Third daughter of John and Mary. Rejected advances of Milward Snr, eloped and married William Green qv. in 1762.

Sarah Collier. (Sally) 1739-1822. Fourth daughter of John and Mary. Married lawyer Henry Sayer qv. 1763.

Henrietta Collier (Harriet) b 1741. Fifth daughter John and Mary. Married Lawyer Henry Jackson.

D.

Edward Dyne. Hastings Jurat 1708. Mayor 1720,1724,1726,1728. Fellow coronation canopy bearer with Collier 1727. Died 1732.

E.

Elizabeth Elphick. Collier's first wife. Died 1714. (See above under The Colliers).

Edmund Elphick of Willingdon. d 1707, her father.

Sir Charles Eversfield 1682-1749. MP Horsham 1705-10 & 1713-16 & 1721-41 MP Stenying 1741-47 MP Sussex 1710-13. Sussex landowner (Part of the Eversfield Estate was bought by James Burton and became St Leonards new town in 1820s).

Sir Thomas Eversfield Royalist MP for Hastings from 1640-44

F.

Henry Fox, 1st Baron Holland, 1705 –1774. Orator, politician and minister in Duke of Newcastle's government 1755. Known for scandalous elopement with Lady Caroline Lennox – daughter of Duke of Richmond, 18 years his junior. Father of politician Charles James Fox.

John Freemantle. Senior Customs House official and friend and debtor of Collier. Succeeded William Wood (qv) as Secretary to Commissioners of Customs in 1765. (The Secretary was a senior civil servant, directly responsible to the Commissioners for the entire customs service.) Part or all of the £400 debt remained unpaid at Collier's death. His executors pursued it and Freemantle was arrested.

Dr Thomas Frewen 1704-1791. Rye doctor and friend of the Colliers. Pioneer of Smallpox inoculation in Sussex. Author of The Theory and Practice of Inoculation (1749). Successfully treated four Collier daughters in 1750.

Mr Thomas Frewen. Mentioned frequently in relation to the administration of Collier's will. It seems likely that he was a solicitor in William Cranston's London practice and may have been supervising John Cranston before he qualified as a solicitor. Curiously there exist at least four receipts dated between 11th September 1746 and 3rs March 1769 for payments made by John Collier and then his executors of a legacy to Thomas Frewin and then to his heirs, Collier presumably being a trustee of the legacies.

John Fuller 1680-1745. Brightling Ironmaster. Unsuccessful Tory Candidate for Sussex in 1734 election. Fuller's children are mentioned – though seldom by first name - in various Collier letters. Among them may be elder daughter Elizabeth, sons John b 1706, Rose b 1708, Henry b 1713 and Stephen b 1716. (Henry married a cousin, Frances Fuller, and their son, 'mad' Jack, became a famous eccentric and MP later in the century.)

G.

Thomas Gage, (1st Viscount Gage) of Firle Place Sussex. MP for 33 years between 1717 and 1753. Roman Catholic whose inherited Baronetcy had originally been purchased from James I.

David Garrick 1717–1779. Popular actor, playwright, theatre manager and producer, immensely influential on 18th Century theatre. A pupil and friend of Dr Samuel Johnson.

Prince George of Denmark 1653-1708. Husband to Queen Anne of England.

King George I of England 1660-1727. Born Hanover. Great grandson James I. Succeeded Queen Anne in 1714.

King George II (George Augustus) 1683-1760. Prince of Wales, later King George II, succeeding George I in 1727. Father of Prince George William. He was Duke of Brunswick-Lüneburg (Hanover) and a prince-elector of the Holy Roman Empire. Married 1705 Caroline of Ansbach. Collier was her canopy bearer at his coronation.

Prince George William (1717-1718) Second son of George Augustus (see above) and Caroline of Brandenburg-Ansbach, later Queen Caroline. Prince George was the subject of a family feud after King George I overruled his son's choice of name and godparents for his grandson. Prince George died aged 3 months 4 days from a polyp on the heart.

George III. 1738-1820 King of Britain from1760. Perhaps best known for the loss of the American colonies (1783) and the defeat of Napoleon (1815). Edward Milward was a canopy bearer at his coronation.

Thomas Godley - Apprentice to John Collier 1717. Town Clerk 1719 & 1722. Jurat, Mayor 1732. Supporter of the waterworks project 1733. Manager and postmaster Hastings Post Office 1742. m Elizabeth Wicking 1744.

H.

Henrietta (Lady Harriet) Godolphin 1701–1776. Duchess of Newcastle following marriage in 1717 to Pelham-Hollis. Granddaughter of the Duke of Marlborough, John Churchill.

G.

John Geery Hastings Postmaster until 1733.

Mr Green(e) Senior and Junior. A Mr Green is mentioned frequently in the letters, particularly in those from Cranston and James Collier. But it's not always clear which Green is being referred to. Thomas or Tommy seems to have been 'the young Mr Green' who it seems was a contemporary of James Collier and clearly a close family friend as he regularly accompanies them on outings. Mr Green senior, his father, was a friend of John Collier who, in November 1734 invited Green, his wife and his son to dinner at Johnson's court. Green seems to have had land in Norfolk, and it looks as if Collier was an executor of his will and loaned his estate a considerable sum of money.

William Green – c1735-1820, Engineer. Eloped with and then married 1761, Jane Collier.

John Greening Steward to Duke of Newcastle initially in charge of the grounds, gardens and trees at Duke's Palladian residence, Claremont, built in 1708 by Sir John Vanbrugh near Esher in Surrey.

H.

Mr Hall a clerk then solicitor in Cranston's London practice.

Mr Halsted - employee of Hastings Post Office applied to succeed John Geery.

Judge Lord Hardwicke - Philip Yorke, 1690 –1764. Barrister1715. MP for Lewes (Whig) 1719. Solicitor-General and knighthood 1720. Lord Chief Justice of the King's Bench 1733 with title Lord Hardwicke. Lord Chancellor in Walpole's cabinet 1737. Friend and Confidant of Duke of Newcastle.

General Henry Hawley 1685 –1759 British army officer, served at Battles of Dettington and Fontenoy. Military commander in Scotland during Jacobite uprising. Defeated at Falkirk but commanded cavalry under Cumberland at Culloden 1746.

J.

Dr Samuel Johnson 1709–1784 poet, playwright, essayist, moralist, literary critic, biographer, editor and lexicographer made famous by James Boswell qv.

L.

James Lamb 1693–1756. 20 times Mayor of Rye. Builder of the Lamb House where he entertained King Gorge 1 in 1726. The house was later a residence of writers Henry James and EF Benson

M.

Peter Marsden, Marine Archaeologist, Museum of London. Head of first excavation of Amsterdam 1969-70. Author: The Wreck of the Amsterdam 1985.

Benjamin Meadow 1671-1745. Freeman. Sued John Collier and Dr Henry Carleton over their piped water scheme in the 1730s

Edward Milward (1) 1682-1749. Hastings Freeman, Jurat and Mayor 1721. His son, also Edward, married Collier's Daughter Mary in 1754. His grandson, also Edward (1765–1833), was 20 times Mayor of Hastings.

Edward Milward (2) snr. 1723 –1811. Collier's son-in-law via marriage to his daughter Mary 1754. 26 times Mayor of Hastings (1750 and every alternate year from 1753 to 1801). Succeeded Collier in 1756 as Surveyor-General of Customs Riding Officers for Kent. Hastings political agent for Duke of Newcastle. Became a man of considerable property and influence in Hastings, though he was not universally liked.

Edward Milward (3) jnr 1765 –1833. Grandson to john Collier. 20 times Mayor of Hastings.

William George Moss. Historian. Author: The History and Antiquities of the Town and Port of Hastings 1824.

Lady Mary Wortley Montague 1689–1762 introduced smallpox inoculation to England. Eloped with and then married the Earl of Bute (qv)

Henry Moore claimed Freedom of Hastings on grounds that his father had been a freeman and successfully took Hastings Corporation to court in a lawsuit financed by Sir Thomas Webster.

Thomas Moore, Captain, ship owner, freeman. Opposed corporation's position over eligibility for freedom of town

James Murray 1721-1794. John Collier's son-in-law having married Cordelia Collier (qv) in 1748. Fifth son of 4th Lord Elibank, a family of Scottish Roman Catholic Jacobites. Successful army career: Captain 1742, Major 1745, Lt Col 1751, Major General 1762. Served with General Wolfe in Canada. Governor Qubec 1760-68, Deputy Govenor Minorca 1774-84. Owner Beauport Park Hastings. Married Anne Witham following Cordelia's death.

Elizabeth 'Bare Betty' Murray nee Stirling. James' mother. Daughter of George Stirling. Born around 1683. Married Alexander Murray (4th Lord Elibank) February 1698. Mother of James Murray (thus Cordelia Murray/Collier's mother-in-law) and four other sons and 5 five daughters. Died November 1756.

Patrick Murray 5th Lord Elibank 1703-1778. James Murray's eldest brother. Jacobite. Army colonel. Wit and member of Edinburgh literary circle.

George Murray 6th Lord Elibank 1706-1785. Brother to Patrick and James. Captain in Royal Navy. Sailed with commodore Anson's squadron on round the world voyage in 1740 but became separated and his ship the Pearl returned straight to London. Accused of deliberately deserting his squadron on active service. Robustly defended by his descendant Col Arthur C Murray.

Gideon Murray (1710-1776) Brother to James. Rev. Dr. Gideon Murray became chaplain-general to the army and a cannon at Durham Cathedral. Was present with George II at the Battle of Dettingen in 1743. Chaplain of 43rd (afterwards 42nd) Highlanders.

Alexander Murray 1712-1778 Brother to James. Soldier then politician. Nicknamed the Jacobite Earl of Westminster. Jailed for refusing to kneel at the Bar to the House of Commons following allegations of defamation during 1750 Westminster Election. Fled to Paris, joined entourage of (Bonnie Prince) Charles Edward Stuart. Co-conspirator in 'Elibank Plot' to overthrow George II.

Arthur C Murray. 20th century army colonel. Biographer. Author of The Murrays of Elibank and The Five sons of 'Bare' Betty (1936).

N.

Duke of Newcastle – Thomas Pelham-Holles. 1693-1768. Whig statesman, party manager and fixer. Sussex Landowner. Elder brother of Henry Pelham. Secretary of State for 30 years. Prime Minister 1754-1756 & 1757-1762. Benefactor of John Collier.

Sir John Norris 1670 -1749 – Admiral of the Fleet. Served during Nine Years War, War of Spanish Succession, Great Northern War, and War of Jenkins' Ear. Commander of the Channel Fleet in war with France and Jacobite rebellion 1744-1746.

O.

Samuel Oates Rector of All Saints 1660 to 1674 father of Titus.

Titus Oates, 1649–1705. Perjurer, curate of All Saints, Hastings, falsely accused William Parker of sodomy and, later, fabricated a conspiracy asserting a Papist plot to kill Charles II.

P.

William Parker Rector of All Saints in the early 17th Century and believed founder of the Hastings Grammar School.

William Parker (2) great nephew - Schoolmaster Hastings Grammar, falsely accused by Titus Oates of sodomy with a pupil.

Richard Patrick. 1710 (or11)-1763. Legal clerk then, in 1747, apprentice attorney to Collier. Hastings Town Clerk 1741 & 1750-62. M. 1746 Elizabeth Carswell, (daughter of Thomas Carswell qv). A beneficiary of Collier's will. Manager of Collier's estates shortly before and following his death in 1760.

Henry Pelham.1694-1750. Whig Prime Minster 1743-1754. Brother to Duke of Newcastle. Employed Collier as Steward to manage his estates.

Henry Pelham of Stanmer 1694-1725 1st Cousin to Newcastle and Prime Minister Pelham. Hastings MP 1715–1722. MP Lewes 1722-1725

Thomas Pelham ('Turk') of Stanmer. Younger Brother of Henry. Whig. MP Lewes 1741-43. Coronation canopy bearer with Collier 1727.

Thomas Pelham of Lewes (1705-1743). Son of Thomas Pelham of Stanmer. MP Hastings 1728-1741.

Colonel James Pelham (Jemmy) of Crowhurst. Cousin to D. of Newcastle. Hastings MP 1741-61. Coronation canopy bearer with Collier 1727.

William Pitt, 1st Earl of Chatham 1708 –1778. (Pitt the Elder) Politician and leader of "Patriot Whigs" who opposed Walpole and Newcastle's Whig faction. A Brilliant orator nicknamed the 'Great Commoner' being usually opposed to the governing grouping. A leading minster 1756 to 1761. Prime Minister 1766-1768. Known as key supporter the Seven Years' War and for single-minded devotion to victory over France. Forced out of office by Lord Bute (qv).

Walter Plumer MP. 1682-1746. Whig politician later member of the opposition or 'Patriot' Whigs. Campaigned in parliament against the Salt Duty,

John Pulteney Whig. Hastings MP 1695-1710. Unsuccessful candidate 1722

R.

Duke of Richmond, Charles Lennox, 1701–1750 MP for Chichester 1722 before inheriting title in 1723. Courtier. Served as army General against 1745 Jacobite uprising. Led campaign to prosecute Hawkhurst Gang smugglers. Owned Goodwood estate in Sussex. Notable for correspondence with Duke of Newcastle. Early patron of Cricket.

Milward Rowe 1717-1792. Senior civil servant - Chief Clark of the Treasury and   Commissioner of the Salt Duties 1771-82. Long-time correspondent and friend of Collier. Born Westham near Pevensey. Town Clerk Hastings 1737. Worked in Andrew Stone's office. Loyal supporter of Newcastle. Beneficiary in Collier's will - left 20 guineas 'to buy a ring for remembrance' and, with William Cranston, all profits of the office of Usher and Crier of the court of King's Bench in trust for Collier's five daughters'. Companion of James Collier at Cricket Match between Kent and All England, Bromley Common July 1745. Sarah Sayer described his wife Sukey (Susanna nee Henley) whom she met in London as 'the finest lady I visit' but 'so conceited and affected that I shall give myself no further trouble about her'. However CL Sayer believes she was later godmother to Sarah Sayer's daughter Mary.

Elizabeth Russell – Proprietor of private boarding school in Church Row Hampstead, attended by the Collier daughters. She was a mourner at the funeral of John (Jackie) Collier in 1732.

Dr Richard Russell 1687-1759. Physician of Lewes consulted by John Collier over the health of daughters Mary and Cordelia.

S.

John Sargent claimed Freedom of Hastings on grounds that his father had been a freeman and successfully took Hastings Corporation to court in a lawsuit financed by Sir Thomas Webster. Member of extended Hastings family.

Henry Sargent – Hastings brewer, possibly brother or cousin to John – successfully sued Collier for trespass for taking water from the Bourne.

James Saunders, founder of second Hastings School 1708.

Richard Saville. Historian. Editor of 'The Letters of John Collier of Hastings 1731-1746'. His introductory biography and notes are an invaluable source.

Henry Sayer – 1744-1784. Solicitor. Husband of Sarah Collier (m 1763).

Kitty Sayer 1771-1845 – daughter of Henry Sayer and Sarah Collier.

Charles Lane Sayer – 1845-1927. Barrister. Great-great grandson of John Collier, transcriber and editor of 'The Correspondence of John Collier and his Family' published in two volumes in 1907. His notes, relying on historical research as well as family memories, are an important source.

Mary Sayer, 1801-1880 Granddaughter of John Collier. Aunt to Charles Lane Sayer.

Henry Simon, Solicitor for Bonds and Criminal Prosecutions at the Customs House in London.

James Stanford alias Trip or Tripp. Wealthy smuggler. Member of Hawkhurst Gang. Reputedly involved in the murder of Thomas Carswell

Elizabeth 'Bare Betty' Stirling. Daughter of George Stirling born around 1683. Married Alexander Murray (4th Lord Elibank) February 1698. Mother of James Murray - thus Cordelia Murray nee Collier's mother-in-law - and of 4 other sons and 5 daughters. Died November 1756.

Andrew Stone 1703–1773. Private secretary to the Duke of Newcastle. Confidant of Pelham family. MP for Hastings 1741 to 1761. Government minister. Royal advisor, tutor secretary and treasurer under George II and George III.

Charles Stuart – King Charles II 1660-1685. A Protestant.

James Stuart – King James II 1685–1689. A Catholic.

James Francis Edward Stuart. 1688 -1766, The 'Old Pretender'. Catholic. Son of James Stuart. Half-brother of Mary Stuart.

Charles Edward Stuart 1720 –1788 'The Young Pretender. Aka Bonnie Prince Charlie. Catholic great grandson of King James II. Jacobite claimant to the throne. Led the 1745 uprisings. Defeated at Culloden April 1746. Escaped from Scotland and lived rest of his life on the continent.

Mary Stuart 1662-1694 – Protestant, daughter of James II. Queen (with husband William) from 1689 until her death in 1694.

Thomas Smith, Collier's brother-in-law having married:

Mary Smith – nee Collier, John's youngest sister. They were house sitting while John was in Bath in 1749 and sent him the first news of the wreck of the Amsterdam.

T.

William Thorpe Hastings Mayor 1736, 1743, 1748, 1752.

Mrs Thorpe (not related to Mayor William) Proprietor of school in Battle attended by Collier children. Companion to Mary Collier. Friend of the family.

Doctor Tilden – London Physician.

'Mr' Tilden, Hastings coroner in 1749

Gabriel Tomkins. Convicted Smuggler. Reputed leader of the Mayfield Gang around 1717. 1733 Testified before Sir John Cope's inquiry into the Customs service, 1734 and joined the Revenue Service as riding officer in Kent, keeper of the Dartford Customs House and Bailiff to Sheriff of Sussex, supervised by Collier. 1750 executed Bedford Jail for highway robbery.

Hon Thomas Townsend. 1701– 1780. Elected MP Hastings 1727 but chose to represent Cambridge. Nephew to Duke of Newcastle

Lord Trentham (Granville Leveson Gower) 1721-1803 Brother-in-law of Duke of Bedford. Spent £4,400 to become MP for Westminster in 1747. Appointed Lord of Admiralty and had to seek re-election in 1750. Opposed by Sir George Vandeput, wealthy Huguenot. Bedford, supported by governing faction, rigged the election. A petition from (among others) Alexander Murray accused the High Bailiff of electoral fraud but in turn Murray found himself charged with 'menaces and seditious behaviour'.

Anthony Trumble. Sussex lawyer and coroner. Agent and steward to Duke of Newcastle. Died 1733 owed £1000 by the Duke for work and expenses defending the lawsuit of Henry Moore and other putative freemen. Collier settled the debt with Trumble's executors but had difficulty getting it repaid by Pelham-Hollis.

V.

Sir John Vanbrugh 1664–1726 Whig. Architect (Blenheim Palace & Castle Howard), Restoration dramatist (The Relapse and The Provoked Wife). Friend of Duke of Newcastle.

Sir George Vandeput, second baronet of Twickenham. Descendant of Henry Vandeput of Antwerp who fled religious persecution with other Protestants in 1568. Contested Westminster Parliamentary seat in 1750 and was beaten in rigged election by Lord Trentham. Supported by Lord Elibank and Alexander Murray (qv).

Admiral Edward Vernon 1684 –1757. MP. Distinguished naval officer particularly in War of Jenkins' Ear where he captured Porto Bello but failed to take Cartagena de Indias, despite a long siege. Subsequently author of two pamphlets critical of Admiralty: "A Specimen of Naked Truth from a British Sailor" and "Some Seasonal Advice from an Honest Sailor", leading to his dismissal from the Navy in 1746. The latter publication accused Collier of treachery.

W.

James Waller, agent to Duke of Newcastle

Heather Warne – catalogued the Collier papers for an Archive Diploma Dissertation in 1966 and wrote valuable biographical introduction. Her classification of the papers is still used by the collection at the East Sussex Record Office.

William of Orange 1650-1702. William III, King of England 1689 -1702, following overthrow of James II in the 'Glorious Revolution His mother was daughter of Charles I. William ruled jointly with wife Mary until her death in 1694. He was dubbed King 'Billy'. His death following a riding accident in which his horse tripped over a molehill gave rise to the Jacobite toast to the 'gentleman in the black velvet waistcoat' i.e. the mole.

William Wood, d 1765. Secretary to Commissioners of Customs from 1742. Succeeded by John Freemantle (qv) (The Secretary was a senior civil servant, directly responsible to the Commissioners for the entire customs service.)

George Worge.1705-1765. Collier's son-in-law (as husband to Elizabeth Collier – his daughter from his first marriage). Solicitor in Battle. Confidant and friend.

Robert Walpole. Leader of Whig administration 1727–1740. Considered first British 'Prime Minister'.
Edwin Wardroper town clerk and later mayor of Winchelsea, dubbed a 'Rye Beau,' by Cranston and was, by all accounts, a bit of a rake. Supported by Newcastle he opposed James Lamb's mayoral hold on Rye and, despite his morals, was a friend and colleague of Collier's. He held office in the Customs as Collier's deputy, acting as sub agent for the eastern part of Sussex. He died in Boulogne in 1771.
Sir Thomas Webster, 1679-1751 clothing manufacturer elected MP Colchester 1705 and 1711. Subsequently expelled from Parliament on both occasions. Financed legal action against Hastings Corporation. Owner Battle Abbey and, later Bodiam Castle.

Sir Whistler Webster, 1699-1779 son of Sir Thomas. Unsuccessful Tory candidate for Hastings in 1734 election.

Miss Webster - probably daughter to Sir Thomas and sister to Whistler. Friend of Cordelia Collier.

Elizabeth Wicking – Widow of Stephen Wicking, Hastings Schoolmaster. Married 1744 Thomas Godley, Postmaster and former Mayor.

Lord Wilmington – Spencer Compton – 1673-1743. Whig statesman, Speaker of House of Commons, and minister under Wapole but fell out with him. Created Baron 1728, associated with Patriot Whigs. Prime Minister 1742-3. Owner East Borne estate Sussex (later Compton Place).

Anne Witham. Second wife to James Murray

General James Woolf. 1727-1759. British Army officer, served in War of Austrian Succession, Jacobite Rebellion and Seven Years War. Second-in-command of expedition to capture the Fortress of Louisbourg. Commander of British forces (including James Murray qv) which sailed up the Saint Lawrence River to capture Quebec City. After a long siege Wolfe was killed at the height of the Battle of the Plains of Abraham.

ii. Genealogy

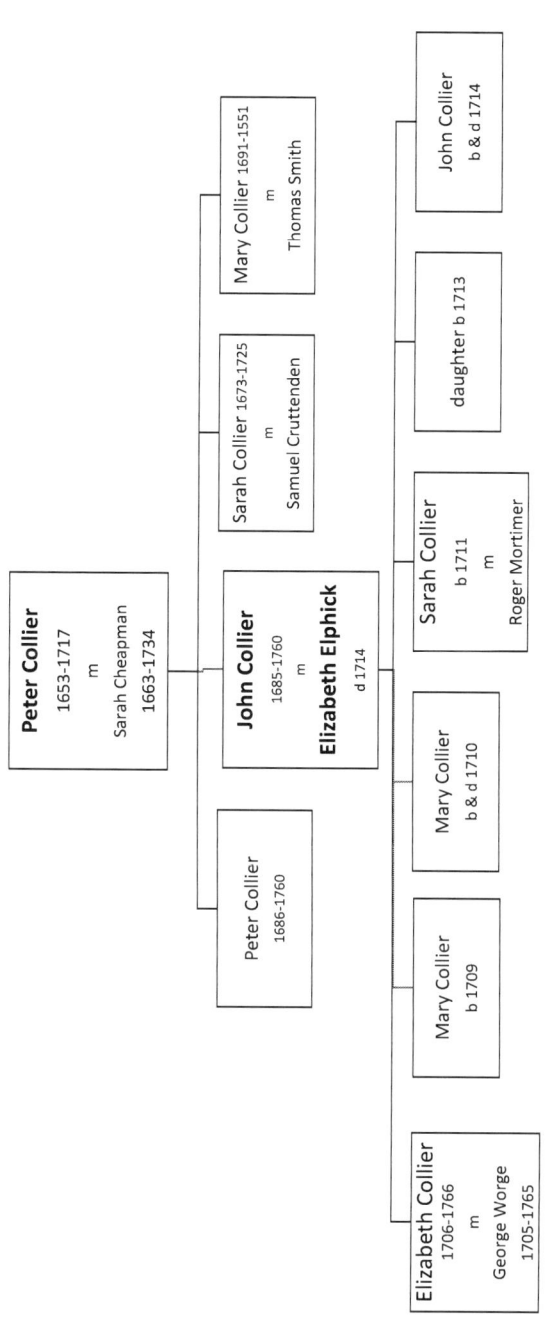

Peter Collier
1653-1717
m
Sarah Cheapman
1663-1734

Peter Collier
1686-1760

John Collier
1685-1760
m
Elizabeth Elphick
d 1714

Sarah Collier 1673-1725
m
Samuel Cruttenden

Mary Collier 1691-1551
m
Thomas Smith

Elizabeth Collier
1706-1766
m
George Worge
1705-1765

Mary Collier
b 1709

Mary Collier
b & d 1710

Sarah Collier
b 1711
m
Roger Mortimer

daughter b 1713

John Collier
b & d 1714

Children of **Peter Collier**
and of his son **John Collier** with his first wife **Elizabeth Elphick**

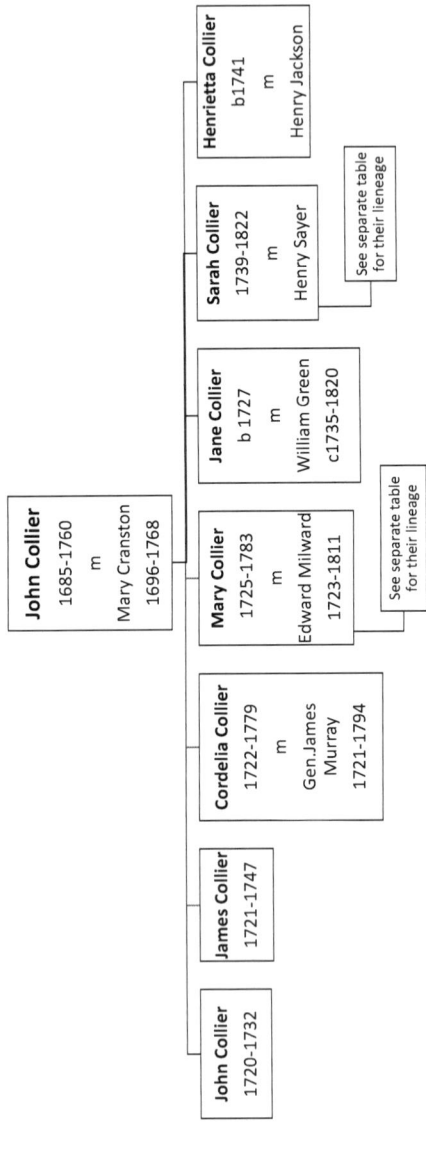

Children of John Collier and his second wife Mary Cranston to survive to their teens

– 11 others died in infancy

John Collier
1685-1760
m
Mary Cranston
1696-1768

John Collier
1720-1732

James Collier
1721-1747

Cordelia Collier
1722-1779
m
Gen.James
Murray
1721-1794

Mary Collier
1725-1783
m
Edward Milward
1723-1811

See separate table
for their lineage

Jane Collier
b 1727
m
William Green
c1735-1820

See separate table
for their lieneage

Sarah Collier
1739-1822
m
Henry Sayer

Henrietta Collier
b1741
m
Henry Jackson

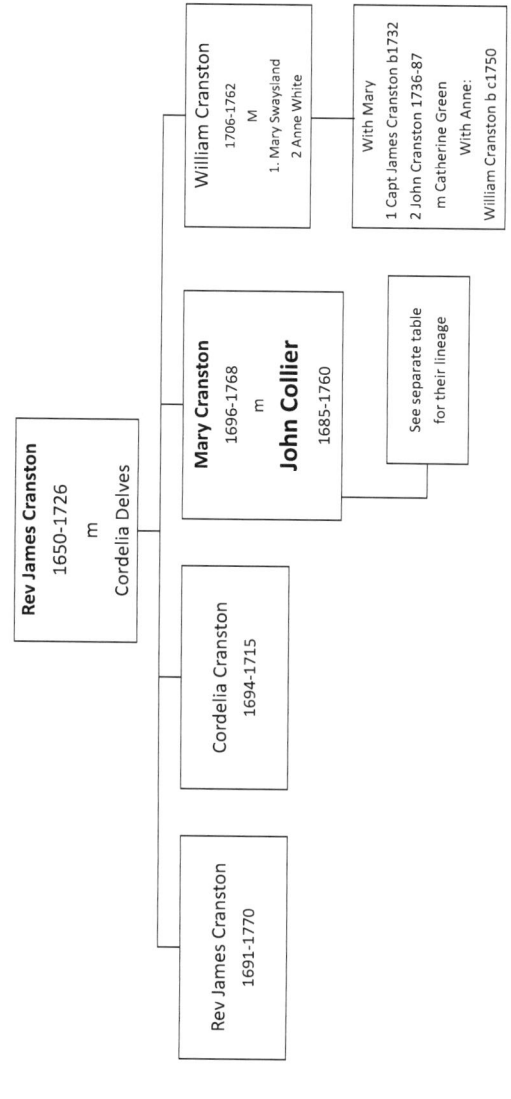

The Cranston Family

Showing children who survived childhood

Rev James Cranston
1650-1726
m
Cordelia Delves

Rev James Cranston
1691-1770

Cordelia Cranston
1694-1715

Mary Cranston
1696-1768
m
John Collier
1685-1760

See separate table
for their lineage

William Cranston
1706-1762
M
1. Mary Swaysland
2 Anne White

With Mary
1 Capt James Cranston b1732
2 John Cranston 1736-87
m Catherine Green
With Anne:
William Cranston b c1750

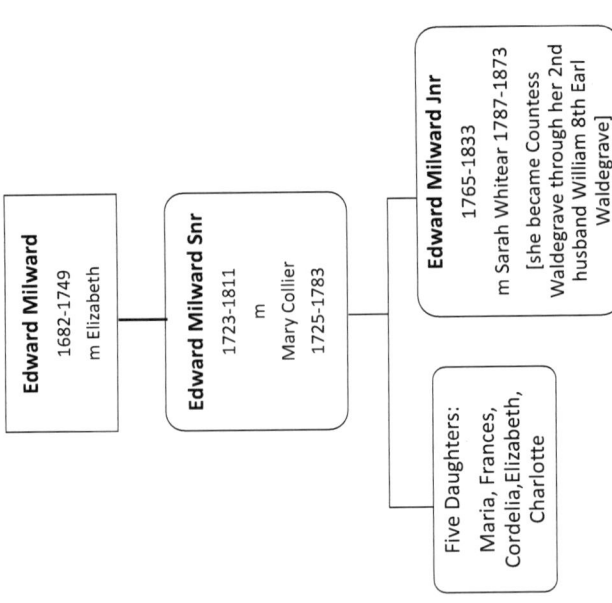

Edward Milward
1682-1749
m Elizabeth

Edward Milward Snr
1723-1811
m
Mary Collier
1725-1783

Edward Milward Jnr
1765-1833
m Sarah Whitear 1787-1873
[she became Countess
Waldegrave through her 2nd
husband William 8th Earl
Waldegrave]

Five Daughters:
Maria, Frances,
Cordelia,Elizabeth,
Charlotte

The Millward Family

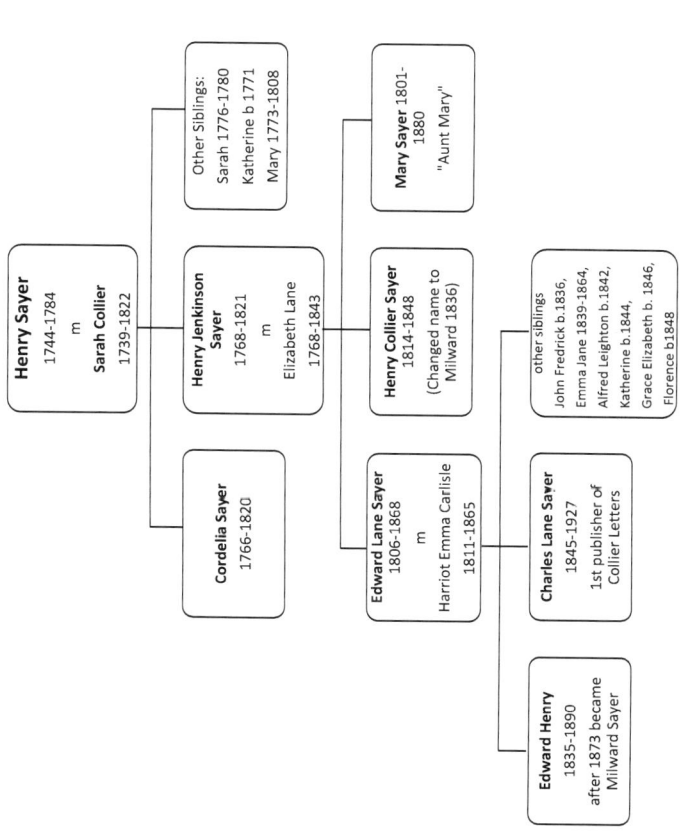

Henry Sayer
1744-1784
m
Sarah Collier
1739-1822

Other Siblings:
Sarah 1776-1780
Katherine b 1771
Mary 1773-1808

Henry Jenkinson Sayer
1768-1821
m
Elizbeth Lane
1768-1843

Cordelia Sayer
1766-1820

Mary Sayer 1801-1880
"Aunt Mary"

Henry Collier Sayer
1814-1848
(Changed name to Milward 1836)

Edward Lane Sayer
1806-1868
m
Harriot Emma Carlisle
1811-1865

other siblings
John Fredrick b.1836,
Emma Jane 1839-1864,
Alfred Leighton b.1842,
Katherine b.1844,
Grace Elizabeth b. 1846,
Florence b1848

Charles Lane Sayer
1845-1927
1st publisher of
Collier Letters

Edward Henry
1835-1890
after 1873 became
Milward Sayer

The Sayers

iv. Sources and Bibliography

The Letters of John Collier of Hastings 1731-1746 edited by Richard Saville, published by the Sussex Record Society 2014.

This is an extraordinary work of scholarship. Only crediting RS as the editor really doesn't do him justice. To start with he transcribed fully 622 letters or documents from the originals in the National Archives – a tremendous and intensely time-consuming labour. Then he wrote a comprehensive and thoroughly researched introduction and which he supplemented with notes throughout that are eclectic and erudite.

Correspondence of Mr John Collier (Deceased) and his Family 1716-1780, edited by Charles Lane Sayer. Published in two volumes in 1907, printed by CF Hodgson & Son.

Charles Lane Sayer was John Collier's great, great grandson, and it was his transcription of perhaps half of the original letters that has fostered the interest in Collier as a contemporary social commentator and important historical source. Sayer's notes, which also draw on family memories, are fascinating. Not in any way to disparage the enormity of his task and achievement, it is perhaps a pity that he was somewhat selective in what he transcribed, quite often paraphrasing or synopsizing the full letters. This limitation was overcome for the years 1731-1746 by Richard Saville who transcribed every letter in full

The Collier Papers an Archive Diploma Dissertation by Heather Warne. She catalogued and re-organised the Collier papers for her dissertation in 1966 and wrote a valuable biographical introduction. Again this was a monumental piece of work. Her classification of the papers is still used by the collection in the National Archives at the East Sussex Record Office and has been absolutely invaluable to researchers ever since.

The Correspondence of John Collier, Five Times Mayor of Hastings and His Connection with the Pelham Family. A monograph by William Vandeleur Crake published in volume 45 of the Sussex Archaeological Collections in 1902. Crake was loaned a selection of the Collier letters by Charles Lane Sayer, so while his analysis of them is new, the content is almost invariably contained in Sayer's work. Nonetheless, a valuable source of information.

The Pioneer of Modern Hastings. A chapter From **Hastings of Bygone Days and the Present** by Henry Cousins published around 1902. Again taking transcriptions from CL Sayer, Cousins provides a fresh analysis of the correspondence. The book itself is a useful history of Hastings.

Historic Hastings J Manwaring Baines. 1986 Cinque Port Press. Baines is generally recognized as Hastings' most important historian using extraordinarily detailed primary sources from the records of the Hastings Corporation. However, this doesn't necessarily make his narrative easy to read.

Hastings and St Leonards Chronicle. An excellent on-line database and history of Hastings curated and largely written by Steve Peak.

Other useful guides and potted histories of Hastings include:

The Hastings Guide – a description of that Ancient Town and Port. By 'An Inhabitant' 1797

The History and Antiquities of the Town and Port of Hastings by William George Moss 1824

Diplock's Hand-Book for Hastings and St Leonards 1846

Hastings by L.F. Salzman (part of his series - The Story of English Towns) 1921

Hastings a Survey of Times Past and Present by Anthony Belt 1937

The Cinque Ports RF & FW Jessop 1952

Duke of Newcastle and the 1734 election. A monograph by Basil Williams. Published in the English Historical Review 1897.

Other Histories and historical sources:

The Murder of Mr Grebell – Madness and Civility in an English Town, by Paul Kleber Monod. Published Yale University 2003. This is a consummately researched and written history of 18th Century Rye concentrating on the aftermath of the murder of Alan Grebell, former Mayor and Brother-in-law of then current mayor James Lamb. Written by an American academic, its analysis of local politics is astute.

A New History of Rye by Leopold Amon Vidler. The 'standard' work on the town with editions reprinted from 1934 until after 1970. However Monod is extremely disparaging about Vidler's lack of rigor in his research of the Grebell murder, and the rest of the New History of Rye has to be read in that light.

The Swan, Hastings 1523-1943 by David Russell. Published 2013 by HastingsPubHistory.Com,

The Wreck of the Amsterdam, by Peter Marsden. Hutchinson 1985

The Five Sons of Bare Betty, by Arthur C Murray, Published by John Murray 1938. A terrific account of one generation of Elibank boys, including James Murray.

The Pleasures of London by Felix Barker and Peter Jackson, London Topographical Society 2008.

Bygone Pleasures of London, by W.S. Scott. Published by Marsland 1948.

London, 2000 years of a City and its People. By Felix Barker and Peter Jackson, Cassell 1974

Johnson's England. Ed A.S. Turberville Clarenden Press 1933

Newcastle, A duke without Money, Ray A Kelch. University of California Press 1974

The Middling Sort, by Margaret R. Hunt. University of California Press 1996

Fuller of Sussex - a Georgian Squire, by Geoff Hutchinson 1997

Defying the Demon – Smallpox in Sussex. By Diane Crook Dale House Press 2006

The Smuggling Life of Gabriel Tomkins, by Kent Barker. KBP, 2011. There are many other much more comprehensive histories of 18th century smuggling in Sussex and Kent, but this pseudo-autobiography, based on solid historical research, imagines the career of Tomkins, and charts his life and the progress of the Hawkhurst gang as seen through his eyes.

v. Index

Acknowledgements and notes

A huge number of people have been exceedingly generous of their time in helping with this work. Foremost among them is Richard Saville who has guided and aided throughout and generously provided additional material which he was not able to include in his 'Letters of John Collier'.

By and large this book is based on a single primary source – Collier's correspondence. However this has obviously been supplemented by a good deal of other research and information, and I have endeavoured to make it clear - and give credit - when I am quoting from secondary sources or using facts which are not immediately verifiable. My aim was to make Collier's life and times as accessible as possible to as wide an audience as possible without compromising accuracy.

I am grateful to all who have helped with this project, including especially Heather Warne and Jannie and Annie Sayer; the staff at The East Sussex Record Office at The Keep and the staff and volunteers at the Hastings Museum. Thanks to Lorraine Sencicle for allowing me to reproduce images from her excellent website The Dover Historian. Thank you to the Magdalen and Lasher Charity which runs the care home at Old Hastings House for letting me look round Collier's home, and to Hastings Borough Council for showing me the silver punch bowl which Collier presented to the Corporation after the coronation of King George II. I am particularly grateful to Heather Hookey for her eagle-eyed proof-reading, and to Jeremy Brook for his lovely cover design.

Above all I am grateful to John Collier, his family and his descendants who wrote and then preserved the correspondence down the ages for our edification and enjoyment today.

Hastings Local History Group
Publications in Print

Hastings Bygones 1	£5-00
Hastings Bygones 2	£6-50
Hastings Bygones 3	£6-50
Hastings Bygones 4	£6-50
Hastings Bygones 5	£6-50
Hastings Bygones 6	£6-50
Hastings Bygones 7	£6-50
Hastings Bygones 8	£7-00
Hastings Bygones 9	£7-00
Priory Meadow & Town Centre	£4-50
Hollington	£4-50
Ore	£4-50
A History of Clive Vale	£6-50
A History of Silverhill	£12-00
Hastings During World War I	£7-00
Hastings Voices	£6-00
Hastings Tramways	£8-50
The Hastings Omnibus	£12.00
Chubb's Walk & Hessey's History	£3-50
The Albert Memorial	£4-50
Bygone Weather	£5-50
Hastings Hikes: Cream Tea Path	£2-50
HH: Pilgrimage to Hastings Castle	£3-50
Edith's Last Embrace	£7-50
Hastings A to Z	£12-50
Answering the Bell (fire brigade)	£5-50
The Moneyers Tale	£2-50
The Albert Memorial	£4-50
Bygone Weather	£5-50
Hastings Hikes: Cream Tea Path	£2-50
HH: Pilgrimage to Hastings Castle	£3-50
Edith's Last Embrace	£7-50
Hastings A to Z	£12-50
Answering the Bell (fire brigade)	£5 -00

Available at local Hastings bookshops and from: The Secretary, HLHG, 64, Tower Rd West, St. Leonards-on-Sea, E. SussexTN38 0RL. Email: heather.grief@talktalk.net   Tel: 01424 - 444277

Cover Illustrations.

Front/Back Cover:
    Hastings From the Sea. JWM Turner
Inside Front Cover:
    John Collier by Arthur Devis
Inside back cover:
    Collier's Daughters by or attrib. Arthur Devis

    Clockwise from top left:
    Cordelia, Mary, Sarah, Jane.

Portrait of Mary courtesy Magdalen and Lasher Charity
Other portraits courtesy of Sayer family